Idaho's Salmo

Reflections of a River Guide

Volume 1

By: Gary Lane

Fourth Edition – May 2018

Copyright ©2018 by Gary Lane

All rights reserved. No part of this publication may be reproduced or transmitted in any form, or by any means, without the express written consent of the author, except in the case of brief quotations embodied in reviews.

ISBN: 978-1980440895

Independently published

To Jay,

Always seek the river within and becoming an earth friendly wake.

Gary Lane

July 2018

"August Float"

TABLE OF CONTENTS

ACKNOWLEDGEMENTS

FORWARD

PREFACE ~ EVOLUTION OF A BOATMAN

Chapter 1. A Boatman's Worst Nightmare ------- 1

Chapter 2. Bigfoot on the River ------- 9

Chapter 3. Devoured by Salmon River ------- 18

Chapter 4. Negotiating the Middle ------- 24

Chapter 5. Sports and Nature ------- 27

Chapter 6. Shoup Soup ------- 40

Chapter 7. Shattered Dreams and Unusual Meeting Place ------- 51

Chapter 8. Nomadic Spirits Are Precipitated Souls ------- 56

Chapter 9. The Green Room ------- 65

Chapter 10. From Bigfoot to Bambi ------- 67

Chapter 11. Salmon Falls Folly ------- 69

Chapter 12. Dancing with the Devil on Fool's Rock ------- 72

Chapter 13. Old-timers That Painted the Canyon with Their Character ------- 79

Chapter 14. Kayak Magic ------- 83

Chapter 15. Rollercoaster, Skookumchuck, and Space Aliens ------- 86

Chapter 16. Wildman Rick ------- 89

Chapter 17. Doctor Death --------- 91

Chapter 18. Flower Power --------- 93

Chapter 19. Following My Shadow --------- 98

Chapter 20. The Riggins River Rush --------- 103

Chapter 21. Purple Heart at Eye of the Needle --------- 118

Chapter 22. Salmon River Triple Digit Club --------- 129

Chapter 23. When All Hell Broke Loose --------- 136

Chapter 24. The Killer Pillars --------- 145

Chapter 25. Sermons on the Salmon --------- 150

Chapter 26. Eastern Oregon Dismantlers and Pullman Pounders --------- 152

Chapter 27. Birth of Big Water Blowout --------- 155

Chapter 28. Estrogen Express --------- 158

Chapter 29. One Breath Away from Death --------- 167

Chapter 30. Following Natures Lead --------- 171

Chapter 31. Romance on the River --------- 177

Chapter 32. Hypnotism and the River of No Turtles --------- 185

Chapter 33. An Unbridled World and Natural Selection --------- 189

Chapter 34. Social Conquest, Evolution, and Salmon River Sacrifice Zones --------- 200

Chapter 35. Chief Joseph Saga and Lower Salmon River Crossings --------- 205

Chapter 36. Sgt Ordway, Wapshilla Ranch, and Jackson Sundown Story --------- 209

Chapter 37. Blue Canyon and Deerhead Rapid --------- 214

Chapter 38. The Wapiti Moment --- 221

Chapter 39. Tumbleweed Sweed -- 228

Chapter 40. Survival of the Fittest --- 235

Chapter 41. Swallowed Whole by Salmon River Ilt-swi-tsichs --------------------- 239

Chapter 42. A Man and His Boat --- 242

Chapter 43. River Medicine -- 247

BIBLIOGRAPHY --- 251

APPENDIX -- 253

ABOUT THE AUTHOR -- 260

ACKNOWLEDGMENTS

For All My Relatives and the Great Mystery that flows through all life-enhancing relationships in nature.

Rivers are the veins and water is the lifeblood of Mother Earth.

"You should write a book," I heard repeatedly after telling tall tales of previous adventures and escapades around many riverside campfires. Until one day it suddenly sank in and I did. In truth, it was mostly serious encouragement from others that launched me down the river of words.

Sincere gratitude goes to my wife Barb, who poked me with a stick when recurring writer's doubt tripped me up and convinced me not to abandon the run. My sister Renee' Sjostrom also offered much encouragement and reviewed some original manuscripts. Aside from my biased wife and sister, Tamara Fulwylar, is a previous river guest who gets credit for pushing me out from shore into the main literary current, for a more objective jump-start with much inspiration, great ideas, and some early editing help.

For me, the writing was like running a class V rapid with no oars. But, thanks to them, I grabbed my laptop and began my run through many class V transcripts, one keystroke at a time. Most, fortunately, I was aided by another previous river guest and retired newspaper editor, Larry Lowe. He negotiated a treacherous path to keep my wordsmithing afloat right-side up. So, like having a good high-sider in my boat, he knew just where to throw his weight in my writing craft. Through thick and thin, on and off rivers and manuscripts, we became good friends, too.

Once my manuscript was complete, Diana Wesley designed the cover and helped detail digital production work, as well as offering additional inspiration.

The photographer for the cover photo is Frank Mignerey. Following is a list of people whom I am grateful to for various levels of helping me along the way. It is impossible to remember everyone, so my humble apologies to anyone slipping through the cracks of my memory bank:

Roy Aiken, Kirk Barnum, Dave Bicandi, Chuck Boyd, Patty Clayton, Juanette Cremin, Doug Dennis, Jo Deurbrouck, Barry Dow, Holly Endersby, Gilbert Escandon, John Fisher, Kristin Frish, Olin Gardner, Tess Gordon, LuVerne Grussing; Rick Hamilton, Mark Hollon, Rich Howard, Ron Howell, Steve Howland, Craig Johnson, Jack Kappas, Mike & Connie Kennedy, Norm Klobetanz, Jerry Kooyers, Matt Laine, Linwood Laughy, Frank Mignerey, Joe O'Neill, Jeff Peavey, Craig Price, Swede Peterson, Charlie Ray, Tim Schomberg, Bill Sedivy, Steve Shultz, David Sisson, Greg Stahl, Scott Stouder, Ryan Turner, Morris Uebelacker, Vince Welch.

FORWARD

Does Idaho's Salmon River attract unusual characters to the canyon or does it create them? Providing evidence for both are the experiences recounted by modern day river man Gary Lane, who shares tales of adventure, mishaps, and humor from his more than 40 years of guiding people from a wide variety of backgrounds on trips down the Salmon River.

After working as a guide for five years with Martin Litton's famed Grand Canyon Dories, Gary branched off to form his own company, Eclipse Expeditions, which evolved into the present Wapiti River Guides based in Riggins, Idaho. With his unique style, Gary specializes in leading small groups on wild country river trips in Idaho and Oregon, as well as guiding hunters and fishermen. While trips usually run smoothly, he has found that the most memorable ones often include some bumps in the road caused by unforeseen circumstances. It is these situations that evoke many of the fascinating stories he tells here.

Gary's pre-guiding academic training and work as a wildlife biologist and naturalist give him a unique perspective from which to also offer insights blending scientific truth with native earth wisdom. His expertise helps guests and readers alike leave behind a high-tech world to reconnect with their foundational bonds to nature.

PREFACE

EVOLUTION OF A BOATMAN

For those who do not know me, I am often referred to, by those who think they do, as the "guy in the loin cloth." They may also use a few less than flattering adjectives such as "odd," "weird," "strange," and so on. Such is the unfortunate fate of one who chooses to live outside society's definition of the norm. It comes with the territory that I have chosen to inhabit. It simply reflects the human inclination to pre-judge "others."

It is better, therefore, that I tell this personal story rather than someone whose perspective might be shaded by fables, half-truths, or the fictions of creative imaginations. People define their own realities, and the following story is mine, as seen through my eyes. And many a wild, free-flowing river has been a big part of it.

Rivers are the soul of the land. And for those who are in harmony with rivers, the flowing water seeps inward to saturate the amniotic fabric of one's life. As easy as it is for me to see that now, reaching that conclusion came at the price of a zillion oar strokes and years of scrutinizing nature. Like many people, I came to the river to ride its flow but found there a deeper, more profound confluence of nature and inner spirituality.

While realizing that I am possessed by rivers and somewhat possessive of them, I appreciate that no river belongs to me or one else. Like raindrops that merge in the flowing river, all people, despite their differences ultimately form a human tide that carries us onward together. Chief Seattle is quoted as having said, "We are part of the earth and it is part of us." Although I later discovered the quote was actually originated by Ted Perry to give a Native American slant on ecology and the environmental movement in the early 1970s, I still appreciate the wisdom it expresses. Little did I know at the time what a major influence that wisdom would have in shaping my life story, in conjunction with my engagement with primal nature and the fundamental essence of water.

My brain seems to have a "raindrop mindfulness," like a dry sponge ever yearning for water. My evolution has been spurred on by an innate curiosity about the world and a lust for unraveling mysteries. Solved or not, one mystery has led to another and expanded my quest to learn. Ever seeking truth, my skeptically questioning of the unknown soon became my life's way.

Simple craning my neck and looking upward jump-started my seeking long ago. The night sky has fascinated me from my first gaze toward the heavens. Looking at the stars in the far beyond made me wonder where do humans come from, why we are here, and what it all means. It always seemed to me that if I looked long and hard enough into the right place at the right time, answers lay hidden in the deep dimensions of space. Peering into the cosmos, one can't help but wonder, where do all the answers to anything really reside?

I began exploring the wondrous and became an eager truth seeker at an early age, but it was not until I began running rivers that I experienced more powerful revelations. It was as if the river had a language and began talking to me through its flow. I started seriously journaling to record my exploratory adventures, and misadventures, not only for historic sake, but also to keep track of my feelings and thoughts so I

could reflect back on them in the future. Many trips were solo, while others were with friends or anyone else whom I could convince that there was a grand experience just waiting to be bagged. Most just thought I was crazy for always wanting to do things that in their eyes were dangerous. Not in my mind of course. When it came to life-and-death consequences, a haphazard manner was never my modus operandi.

Most of my early trips occurred before helpful guidebooks were available, or before I was aware of them. I did not appreciate at the time that the Lewis and Clark Journals could have served as a reference, but my feelings of kinship with those pioneering explorers addicted me to adventure. It didn't matter to me whether I was the very first person to float some obscure river, like their Corps of Discovery had done. What ultimately mattered was that it was *my* first time.

There were, of course, inherent dangers in exploring what was unknown to me, even if others had such knowledge. But I was never blind to the fact that injury, and even death, are consequences of not paying proper attention to, and lacking respect for, the natural world. I like pushing into the realm of the unknown, despite the risks involved, because confronting fear minimizes its power and can help convert the unknown that once seemed like a stranger into a great new friend.

In my river journals, I recorded things like difficult rapids, hazards, portages, camping spots, side hikes, wildlife sightings, weirdness in the night skies, and any unusual events. While practical information would be useful for future reference and return trips, I also wanted an accurate record of what I had seen, felt, and experienced. My truth-seeker side demanded objectivity in my reporting, and embellishment was avoided.

Early on, I realized that memories are captured far more vividly and accurately when you write experiences down soon after they happen. So I did, and thus my journaling was born as a way to combat the tendency of time to warp all things left entirely to the brain. Many of the following stories are based on extensive notes and journals compiled since about 1975. The only missing references are a few diaries agonizingly lost in a house fire in 1982 and digital disasters in 1995. Additional information, including childhood experiences, is based on the best of my recollections and those of other people who have known me.

Chapter 1

A BOATMAN'S WORST NIGHTMARE

No! No! This must be a dream, I thought, sure that I soon would awaken from the nightmare and prove that my pernicious premonition with the great horned owl was all wrong. Earlier in the day, I had come face to face with that feathered foe of beak and talons under shade of a most beautiful alder cathedral. It was a place to which I often led hikes for guests on trips I guided on the Lower Salmon River in west-central Idaho. It was a side canyon with a small wading creek full of fresh-water mussels, tadpoles and water skippers. It was also near a very significant ancient Nez Perce campsite.

Such sites invariably evoke guests' questions about the life ways of the indigenous people who lived there long ago. Imagining oneself in their place arouses curiosity about how those ancients evolved in a harsh environment. While archeological discoveries offer some clues, much remains unknown, especially concerning superstitions and mythologies that shaped the early people's lives. For example, in many native cultures, various animals were considered messengers carrying omens for one's future. Though science likes to discount such beliefs, perhaps they are not so easily dismissed, as I was to learn. When I saw the cathedral owl, I knew that many Indian folks view it as a bad omen. Although that made me wonder whether I should expect something negative to visit me soon, I shoved that idea to the far recesses of my mind.

The site of our hike is a place of powerful historical significance. Evidence has been found nearby proving that people were living in the area as long as 13,000 years ago. Wow! Here we were with our boats, fancy equipment, and supermarket-supplied food on a five-day excursion in the wilds, where ancient people were far more in tune with their world than we are with ours. To survive, they had to rely on themselves and each other for subsistence. We, on the other hand, often have no clue where our food was grown, what chemicals are in it, or what effects pesticides have on the areas where it originated. Out-of-sight, out-of-mind is not a good formula for perpetuation of a healthy environment.

Our troop on this trip included two married couples, who were guests and one extra guide, whom I called She-Bear. Like her, and the native people whose names were inspired by animal spirits and a relationship to nature, I have accumulated a few names of my own, including Chief One Feather, Chief Chevron, Happy Hopi, Wood Elf, Driftboat Face, Buckstone, Coyote, Laner, or just plain Chief.

She-Bear rowed a raft while I rowed a dory, and together we escorted our fun-loving group gently down the river, just like in the song we get tired of hearing people inevitably wanting to sing as we float merrily along.

My Weimaraner pup, Ruby, was also under my wing on this trip. Her name is taken from a rapid farther upriver that has flipped a lot of boats over the years. I hoped her namesake would not attach itself to the owl's potential omen.

I've always found naming in the Indian world fascinating. In native traditions, animals carry certain characteristics and special powers that they may share with humans who treat them with proper respect. Attention and intention are fundamental in acquiring a name. First, you must spend time observing an animal to gain a better understanding of its gift. Then, what intentions you have toward using the gifts the animal might share with you largely determine what it will choose to share.

In the indigenous worldview, all things in nature have spirit. During a vision quest seeking a name and potential guidance, the appearance of an animal, bird, insect, or natural element, and the manner in which they are experienced, are interpreted with the help of elders, mentors, or medicine people. Rendering of a name is the final result.

Some native worldviews hold that, like the gifts that animals might share, dreams can also bring messages, both good and bad. They may take the form of a wonderful dream or a horrible nightmare. In the case of nightmares, they may be imagined in the dream state or they may be a terrifying real-life experience.

The latter turned out to be my dilemma when, late the second night of our trip, I awoke on my boat with torrents of adrenaline suddenly surging through my veins as if ready for battle. It felt like the devil was running a pitchfork down my spine. Being nude and mummified by a goose down bag is not the ideal warrior regalia for a crisis in the middle of the night. And an 8-month-old Weimaraner pup hopping wildly around the boat in panic mode is not the best battle comrade.

Usually, people awake from nocturnal terrors, not to them. I was engulfed by a wave of fear as the truth of the situation hit me square in the face. I was adrift. With no moon. No life jacket. No oars in the locks. To use an old boatman's cliché, "No shit, there I was."

My dory, the Eclipse, is a 17-foot-long wooden row boat. It is an offshoot design from the old-style Grand Banks fishing dories, which have identical high bows on each end. This design causes the sides to flare dramatically between each end and is a great combination to punch through beach surf and ride out rolling ocean waves.

However, most modern river-running dories have a tombstone-shaped stern with a squared-off bottom rather than a sharp point like the bow. This stern design can accommodate a motor, but it also has a subtle and important function in whitewater. It can prevent backward slippage when climbing a steep wave as the blunt edge digs in and plows water, helping push the boat over the top.

Ferrying a blunt-ended stern also promotes better lateral stability when skirting big holes in serious water. The extreme curvature of true double-enders makes it difficult to move across current when one oar is in the air as the boat waddles from side to side.

For me, a dory ride is so exhilarating that rowing anything else becomes mostly secondary. That is under normal conditions, in the light of day, and when trying to execute planned runs. Never mind that a tombstone is following me everywhere I run.

Little did I know that day, after our hike up the side stream to the cathedral of overhanging alders that the makings of a nightmare were conspiring to unfold that night.

We made camp above a rapid that we would run the next morning. It was a tiny, yet quite magical, campsite with a difficult beach to reach, and once there, boat parking was limited. Stretching our stern tie-down lines across a small beach to reach the boulders farther ashore would have created trip-traps endangering everyone. So, to avoid potential face-plant fiascos, I had stuck a small shovel into the sand close to shore and tied my boat to it.

My critical error was neglecting to check this anchoring system after also tethering my pup Ruby to it. Puppy play loosened the line, and as we retired to the deck of my boat that night, Ruby and I drifted off to more than just sleep.

Precious seconds fled by as I struggled to awaken fully. Still groggy, I thought it must be an illusion. I fully expected the intimidating whitecaps ahead to disappear at any second. They didn't.

Running class V whitewater demands seriousness and heightened awareness, straddling the line between thrill and terror. Such rapids are a tempting lure in the daytime, but things are different at night. The rapid looming ahead was called Lorna's Lulu. It is a class III by daylight, considered only of moderate difficulty. Class IV is more challenging, but the consequences for error are still relatively benign, usually resulting in a capsized boat and/or arduous swim. However, in the black of night, Lulu would become a class V, which is much more serious. This level of difficulty contains risk of death should things go south. In this case, it was like being caught in an episode of "The Twilight Zone." My mind flashed back to the image of the owl. Maybe it had been a bad omen after all.

I had no idea how my dory could still be right side up. In my sleep, I had somehow managed to get through the huge entry wave at the head of the rapids. Normally, one must use both oars to slide down the tongue and negotiate passage through this mega-wall of water.

Time was of the essence. I was on course toward a huge boulder waiting resolutely downstream. I was also still in my sleeping bag, and there was no time to get out of it. I wildly grabbed an oar lying on the deck by my side and jammed it into the left lock. The other oar, tangled by safety lines to the spare oar, was worthless with such limited time to act.

Though my thoughts raced, time seemed to be moving in slow motion. "What do I do now?" I thought. "Do I hit the boulder with my bow, head-on, or take one oar stroke to turn and hit it broadside?" Deciding on a compromise between the two, I turned the boat to a slight upstream angle with one precise stroke of the oar.

I hoped that the main current would catch the stern as I collided with the rock, sweeping me left and away. I knew I needed to avoid going to the right, where the current would take me into a swirling eddy dubbed the Room of Doom because of its violent boils, whirlpools, and a treacherous eddy fence. The vortex and throbbing hydraulics were a dangerous mix, even with a lifejacket, which I lacked.

Kerrrunch! The mahogany bow-stem of my dory crashed into the boulder. The crash was ferocious, but my angle tactic worked. The current pulled me left into the diminishing tail waves and to salvation. I was filled with elation - I was still alive!

Under less stress and with calmer water, I managed to free my other oar and row to shore. There was a huge sandbar at the foot of the rapid where a party of about 30 people was camped. I rowed as quietly as possible, hoping the sleeping strangers would not hear my boat crash into rocks along the shore and wake as I reached land. Luckily, snoring was all I heard as I peacefully docked and rolled my sleeping bag out on the sand. I recognized the group as one that had stopped by our camp, now upriver about a mile, earlier in the day seeking information. I had given them advice on available campsites. When I recommended this one, little did I imagine I would soon be sharing it with them?

The night was spent mostly on mental reruns of my terrorizing ride. I slept little and awoke at the crack of dawn, but adrenaline still haunted my veins and kept me from feeling tired.

My mind was working overtime trying to formulate a plan to get back upstream. After all, I was a professional guide. What would my guests think of this predicament?

A grinning trip leader was the first one up from the large group camped on the sandbar. He was overly eager to hear my story. "Coffee on?" I asked. I hoped to borrow an inflatable kayak and eddy-hop (a boatman's term for catching upstream current caused by obstacles and geology) back upriver. Feeling sheepish, I wanted to gulp down some caffeine and leave before facing curious interrogation from too many other early risers.

Soon I was carrying a kayak up the sandbar through a sea of sleeping people, careful not to step on any bodies or let my pup lick their faces.

Above the rapid, Ruby and I launched to begin our upstream expedition. Crossing the river back and forth to catch the upstream eddy current and portaging rapids too hard to paddle against was an arduous process.

As the caffeine wore off, Ruby and I made it back to our original camp. Everything was in disarray as the group had hastily packed up to look for us. At first, they had thought my absence was a practical joke - a frequent occurrence in most of our camps. Soon, however, they had pieced together the true picture.

She-Bear told me of a strange dream she had had in which I drifted off in my boat in the middle of the night. She was freaked out to awake and find the dream had been frightfully true.

I thought back to the owl I had seen the previous day. Had my feelings been a premonition or simply a coincidence?

Reunited with my party, I helped break camp, and we headed downriver toward Lorna's. When we reached the rapid, scene of my midnight brush with Lulu, a new idea flashed through my mind. Why not try surfing this giant wave, the same one I had narrowly escaped in the dark? It was a perfect opportunity to test the limits of the inflatable kayak I had borrowed.

As I slid backward down the face of the wave in the kayak, I was now in view of the sandbar camp where I had spent the night, and all 60 eyes in the group below were watching. They probably thought this undertaking to be a brainless idiot's folly, but I saw myself as a bold surfer-warrior. The surf was up, and I could not deny my spontaneous spirit of adventure. The wave slapped me down and spit me out, and my thirst for adventure was quenched by a long swim. The agony of defeat is just as real as the glory of success, and extremely humbling.

Saving the kayak, the paddle, and myself without overshooting the sandbar camp would be a hard trick, even with a lifejacket on. At only 5'4" and 150 pounds, I'm not a big person, but I was in good physical shape from school athletics and a vigorous outdoor lifestyle. Even so, this swim was difficult enough in the daytime to make me appreciate my narrow escape the night before.

I returned the kayak to the waiting group's leader and shared a few more details of the incident. Then, after surviving some good-natured ribbing, my troops rallied and we headed downriver, faking a departure more suitable for noble knights riding off into the sunset.

Poetic Justice

A year later, my wife and niece were with me on a training trip for another lower gorge trip. We put in at Hammer Creek and had only gone about 3 miles when a guy on the left shore began hollering my name and waving me toward his camp. He was too far away to recognize, but I headed toward him all the same, as he looked quite distressed.

He told us that after he and his buddies had gone to bed the night before, an ember had rolled out of their firepan and had burned the stern line that tethered their only raft to shore. It was gone when they awoke, so the three of them put their lifejackets on and swam with their Paco sleeping pads downriver in search of their raft. Lucky, it had eddied out on the far side of the river in Green Canyon just above Little Son of Bitch Rapid. While two guys remained with the raft, the third swam back across the river and then walked upriver to their camp, hoping to flag down the next rafting party floating down river.

Well, that was us, in my dory boat, and as it turned out, the guy we stopped to help was the very same person who had helped me out when I made my midnight run the previous season. With the large number of other outfitters and private parties on the river at any given time, the odds of that happening were extremely slim. Indeed, it seemed poetic justice was at work, which, along with all the other weird coincidences in this story, deepens the heebie-jeebie mystery of it all.

Chapter 2

BIGFOOT ON THE RIVER

How can you tell when a boatman is lying to you? "His lips are moving" is the standard guide's answer. You be the judge after reading the following extraordinary tale told around a campfire on a dreadfully dark night in Hells Canyon. It all happened to me many years ago, believe it or not.

The footprint was compressed nearly 2 inches into the semi-rigid mud and was bigger than any human track I had ever seen. It measured 17 inches long by about 6 inches wide. I know because I measured it and took a plaster cast of the five-toed print. More intriguing, none of the toes showed any claw marks. Remember, only cats can retract their claws.

But the most telling aspect was the placement of the big toe. It was to the inside of the foot, just like a human's. Bears are just the opposite. The big toe of their hind foot is located to the outside. They also have a forepaw that is only about half the size of the back foot. No such forepaw prints were found in a series of tracks that raised the hair on the back of my neck as I stared at them in disbelief. These clearly had been made by a bipedal animal.

Even with my plaster-cast evidence, the excitement of finding that print wasn't nearly as thrilling as were all the other things that happened to me on that college-age adventure in 1970. It was all part of a semi-dare and self-prescribed expedition to find Bigfoot.

Yeti, Sasquatch, and Abominable Snowman are among the dozens of other names various cultures have conjured up to describe a mysterious overgrown, ape-like, hairy, foul-smelling, humanoid creature. Numerous sightings have been reported, but little actual evidence has been gathered to support the existence of these fantasy-fringed shaggy giants. Though some extravagant hoaxes have been debunked, other claims remain unexplained. Even plaster casts like mine are not good enough proof for the skeptics.

My real-life adventure was started by a heated discussion with a biology professor in Mammals 101 class. I was a young wildlife student at Oregon State University in Corvallis. Someone (OK, it was me) asked the professor the likelihood that Bigfoot does exist.

The poor kid (me again) practically got laughed out of class and was denigrated for not being more skeptical. After all, scientists are supposed to be unwaveringly critical and use only measurable evidence to analyze findings. Silly me to seriously consider whether such a beast might be real.

Though I was learning all about the science of wildlife management, it angered me to encounter such closed mindedness from an esteemed academic. So I hatched a plan with my roommate, another wildlife student. It was nearing spring break, and we were looking for something fun to do anyway. Why not head out to Bigfoot country and practice some skills that budding wildlife biologists should be learning?

Having done a good bit of research and being loaded for bear, or Bigfoot in this case, we were excited to go. With cold-weather camping gear, semi-professional scientific instruments, tracking equipment, and a titanic amount of enthusiasm, we set out for the High Cascades in southern Washington State. This was the nearest place where Bigfoot sightings had been reported.

Our destination was the back side of Mount St. Helens, which would become famous when it blew its top in 1980. Who knows, maybe that volcanic eruption was the mountain's protest against all the wannabe Bigfoot hunters like us who came searching for a first specimen. The land did seem to be in cahoots with the hairy ones, conspiring against humans to hide clues to their mystery. When she finally blew her stack, the mountain's upheaval would obliterate pieces of the puzzle with acres of rearranged earth and a blackened, skeletal forest.

But, before telling the rest of this tale, fast forward to 1975 and the depths of Hells Canyon and the Snake River. It was there, in the bowels of the deepest canyon of North America on an inky black night that I began my story.

What a perfect setting for my first Hells Canyon trip with Martin Litton's Grand Canyon Dories. Upon leaving Boatland with my new river guide friends, I became the new rookie/apprentice tag-along baggage boatman, being tested to see if I had the right stuff to become a guide. Although I had several years of rafting and kayaking under my belt, this trip was my first encounter with dory boats. Little did I know it would soon blossom into my lifelong love affair with dories and wild rivers.

As our campfire crackled sparks toward the stars, everyone squeezed closer together. Flickering shadows cast by the flames, along with synchronistic calls of nearby coyotes, added a hair-raising eeriness to my story. Shivers raced down my spine, too, even though I was the one who knew what would be coming next.

My story to this circle of guests and fellow guides, who were still scrutinizing my character and sizing me up, was a reminder of an experience during with my junior year at OSU. I was taking a final exam for a required speech class, something I would not have signed up for of my own free will. For me, talking in front of people is about as scary as the Bigfoot encounter. My fellow students were shaking in their boots, too, but it was a toss-up as to whether it was the story I told or their fear of speaking next that scared them the most.

Talking in front of people around a campfire is much easier, so I continued on. My friend and I left school driving an old four-wheel-drive jeep with chains, winch, come-along, and extra jacks, all to negotiate mud, snow, steep pitch, or any other obstacle we might encounter. Our goal was "Ape Canyon," a large U-shaped gorge flanked by lava-born cliffs with vertical columns of basalt.

Rather than hiking up from the bottom, we wanted to save time by heading to the rocky rim at the head of the canyon. Most previous Bigfoot sightings had been reported in the area immediately below the towering cliffs that guarded the drainage. However, this plan entailed several hardships, like getting stuck far too many times, chaining-up all four wheels, and winching through slippery snow-laden bogs. Oh, and did I mention the 100-foot rappel down the sheer face of a terrifying cliff?

It was a vertical drop over the rimmed abyss, something almost as frightening as the thought of our bivouac in the possible vicinity of a large unknown hominoid. Unfortunately, this route was the only way in from our top-down approach to Ape Canyon, and part of our steep admission price.

Fighting back apprehension, we made the descent and set up a base camp as ground zero for our search. To assuage our fears, I had brought a 30.06 rifle for backup, and my buddy, John, had a .357 Magnum pistol. Of course, that questionable caliber was probably of more use on himself than a charging Bigfoot. Turning the gun on oneself might be better than being torn limb by limb by a vengeful monster.

We had intended to bring an animal-capture gun as well, but the high-powered sedative Etorphine (M99), which is the choice of real professionals, requires a narcotics license that we couldn't get. Instead we took a 35 mm Nikon with a long lens, a super 8 movie camera, and a simple tape recorder. This was before the age of digital video and the GoPros that so many people now have atop their heads when on such an expedition.

For two days we searched, using a grid system, but found little more than neat views of wild country and some interesting birds. Snow was about a foot deep, and most big game animals were on winter range far below. Then, on our third night, a shroud of weirdness fell over our camp. A chain of strange things began to happen. As we were sitting around the fire discussing our next day's plan, an eerie sound whistled from a patch of brush about 50 yards away. Neither one of us recognized it. Even though we knew the calls of most owls and other nocturnal sounds, or so we thought, this one had us bewildered, and a bit jumpy. It stirred the primal juices of fear and conjured up bad images in our fantasies of the unknown.

We slept with one eye open and a finger on the trigger. Well, almost anyway, such was our level of intimidation. Light finally saved us from the boogeyman of the dark, and we put on some coffee to help relieve our morning tension. As we sipped the strong brew, that same eerie whistle began again. Only this time we could pinpoint its location much better.

What now? Were we as brave as our earlier campus barroom planning made us out to be? Before we could decide, a strong odor hit our nostrils like a brick in the face. The stench almost made us vomit. Wow, what was this thing?

With a healthy dose of self-preservation, I got up from the fire to grab my rifle. We then heard something tear off through the brush going away from us. Whew! Better than heading in our direction. The breaking of heavy branches sounded more like a bear running through the brush. Could it be? We thought bears would still be hibernating.

It took several minutes for us to gather enough courage to go in pursuit. Having loaded guns greatly helped. The fleeing creature had left a trail of huge prints with an astoundingly long stride.

Tracks were easy to follow in the snow but harder in the melted-out areas. However, the sticky mud in the meadow was a good substrate for the track casting I made later. That plaster replica sits on my bookshelf at home to this day.

When we came to a huge boulder at the bottom of a steep side slope, we heard the sudden snap of a twig. With our ears fined-tuned by fear, we looked up just in time to see a large creature racing up the hill. It appeared to have something on its back, but it was too far away for us to see what that might be. We could see that this was not a bear. It climbed the hill like a human but moved faster. When it reached the ridge top, it stopped and looked back over its shoulder in our direction.

I raised my rifle to look at it through the scope. I couldn't believe my eyes. It had reddish hair about 6 inches long from head to foot, except for the face. The long distance, maybe 300 yards, did not allow me a sharp image, but it appeared to be apelike. There was no visible muzzle like that on a bear. It seemed more like a human, and it sent shivers down my spine again. There was no way I could ever shoot something as humanoid as that.

Through my scope, I could also see that it was holding something over its shoulder, like a bag or basket. What the hell was it? I wondered. Then I fired my rifle over its head, just to scare it in the hope that it might drop whatever it was holding. Instead, it whirled around, bolted over the top, and disappeared down the other side.

It took several more minutes to marshal our bravery again and about another hour to reach the spot where we had last seen the Bigfoot, or whatever the hell it was. From a high vantage point we could see its tracks on the open slope leading into a forested stream bottom just beyond a small meadow. Then I spied an object just to the side of its trail, which indicated it had been running with long strides. It was about 50 yards beyond where we stood. I almost didn't see it because it blended into the surroundings so well.

Feeling a safe distance from Bigfoot, we climbed down to see what it had dropped in the snow. To our surprise, it was a coarse basket woven together with meadow sedges. Apparently, these creatures are quite intelligent. Unlike grasses, which have round stems, sedges are triangular in shape. This difference makes the sedge a much stronger material for weaving.

But our biggest shock was what we found in the basket.

As has happened many times when I have told this story, someone in the party quickly asked, "What was it?" My reply: "Baloney, just like I'm feeding you." A loud chorus of long ooow-like sighs erupted, as they always do. It was a more dangerous time to me, than the story itself. Who knows when a disgruntled river guest might go off the deep end, coaxed over the top by such outrageous storytelling?

Some people always laugh, some claim they didn't believe it all along, and some are disappointed that it wasn't true. Nearly all admit that they were entertained, as was the teacher in my college speech class who gave me an "A" when I told the same story for my final exam.

This radical embellishment was actually inspired by a real experience I had as a kid with my cousin Phil.
So, for those disappointed people, here is the story that really happened.

Only the title should be changed to "Little Foot on Little Creek" to better represent what we saw and where.

I was in seventh grade, and my cousin Phil was in fifth. We were both fishing Little Creek near the town of Union in northeastern Oregon. This is not typical Bigfoot habitat, if there is such a thing, as it is in the foothills of the Wallowa Mountains and meadowlands of the Grande Ronde Valley. It's not the dense rainforest Westside setting where most sightings have been reported.

Phil and I were about 10 feet apart, fishing the same hole. Having to pee, I turned around, dropped my fishing rod, and relieved myself. When I turned back and stepped into the shoreline water to fish again, movement across the creek caught my attention. At first I thought it was just a cow, as we were in the middle of farm country and vast ranch lands.

I soon could tell it wasn't a cow, so my next conjecture was a dog on its hind legs. It stood about our same height, maybe 5 feet tall, and was only about 25 feet away from us. Then, because of its human-like face and reddish hair flowing about 6 inches down each side of the head, I thought it was a girl spying on us.

That embarrassed me, and I'm sure I turned as red as her hair, thinking she had just seen me pee. But then the hairs on every part of my body bristled like a porcupine. Fear paralyzed me for the moment as I realized this thing was more ape-like, with a face typical of a gorilla. It had a flat nose, short facial hair, and an upper body all covered with reddish hair about 6 inches long. The rest of the body was hidden by a bush, but I could see it was not huge. Rather, it was more like a "Little Foot."
After the initial shock, survival mode kicked in. It's weird how the mind works at times of high stress. I pretended that I didn't see it, even though we were locked in an embracing eye-to-eye stare-down for at least 30 seconds. I looked over at Phil as he looked back at me with about the same level of fear in his eyes. "Let's get out of here," I whispered.

Both of us pretended not to be afraid as we turned around and walked a few yards to a barbed wire fence, crawled under, hit the road, and then ran like hell as far as we could. When we got far enough to feel safe, a few hundred yards closer to home, I asked Phil what he had seen. I was checking my own sanity, thinking it was just me seeing things. However, he confirmed having seen the same thing I had.

We then trotted the rest of the way home to excitedly tell my parents. But they only laughed and shrugged it off; convinced someone was just trying to scare the hell out of us. It worked, as we never again went back there to fish.

To this day, I don't believe it was a person in a monkey suit trying to frighten us. We were not trouble makers, didn't cut fences, tip over outhouses, or do anything malicious to any person or property. Fishing was our total focus.

We never did hear of anyone, before or after, who reported a similar sighting. An escaped orangutan is my best guess at an explanation, though it seems an extreme stretch of the imagination. Why were we the only ones to see it?

If I could roll back time, I would return to look for hair and footprints. Gathering evidence, as any scientist would do, is impossible now, but I can assure you there was no basket with baloney in it.

The biggest impact this story had to my life was earning me high esteem in the eyes of my fellow guides on that dark night in Hells Canyon. It was a huge factor in landing me a job that would end up changing my life's direction forever. Such is the power of a good story, and I have many more to share.

Chapter 3

DEVOURED BY THE SALMON RIVER

It ate me fast. As I inched out across the eddyline, it flipped me quicker than the blink of a crocodile's eye and abruptly munched me as if chomping me with its jaws. Without the skill to roll and right myself in an upside-down kayak, swimming was my only option. The river taught me a few lessons that first day in a kayak on the Salmon River. Those long-lasting lessons were earned the hard way and easily remembered because they slapped me hard in the face in such an intimately personal way.

"To be or not to be" meant nothing to me when forced to read Shakespeare during my school days, but it suddenly became relevant as I was engaged so rudely by the river.

My first lesson was to learn how one's destiny could be changed in a mere heartbeat by natural forces much more powerful than I naively expected. After my initiation by the river and having survived its savageness, I gained a profound respect for it. Knowing that one's life can be at stake when engaging raw nature builds astute awareness, like a rabbit's eye ever attuned to the peripheral for potential hawk's wings. "Expect the unexpected" quickly became my motto for survival as I discovered how important it is to pay acute attention to detail and the subtle nuances of river hydrology.

Lesson two was that being timid doesn't work when crossing strong eddylines in a kayak. Charging hard and anticipating what the differential between upstream and downstream current would do to my kayak helped tremendously. A hard lean into an eddy turn also makes a big difference between being upside-down or right-side-up. It took many pancakes to learn that lesson. I was also extremely intimidated when I edged up to the main current and saw all that power of water rushing by, seeming so arrogant and higher and mightier than me. I meant nothing to it, and its indifference reminded me of my pitiful human frailty. Humility grows when omnipotent nature has one underfoot. It seemed a bit ironic that aggression was a good strategy against a force that dwarfed me like an elephant stepping on an ant.

With lots of practice and tons of swims, I became adept at rolling, as it was much faster than swimming to avoid the jaws of death that seemed to loom hungrily below the surface.

This kayak experience near the small community of Shoup, Idaho, was my very first direct encounter with the Salmon River, which is famed as the "River of No Return." About 25 miles upriver of there, where the jarring rattle-trap river road meets the pavement of Highway 93 between Darby, Montana, and Salmon, Idaho, is the small community of North Fork. It takes its name from the North Fork of the Salmon River that enters the main river there. More notably, it is where Lewis and Clark turned back in 1805 when local Indians warned them that if they went down the river, they would "no return." Unlike them, I was lured to fuller engagement with this enchanting river. For me, "no return" meant not wanting to go back to where I came from. I wanted to remain on the Salmon River for as long as I could.

Why not? The Salmon River is one of the longest free-flowing rivers within one state, outside of Alaska, stretching more than 425 miles. Even Texans can't brag about having a bigger canyon or river. Only Alaskans can claim greater riverscapes and such vastness.

Shoup is about midway along the 50-mile pot-holed, washboard-like road that starts in North Fork and ends at Corn Creek. At that isolated terminus is a campground and ramp used by boaters launching trips into the remote wilds of the Frank Church River of No Return Wilderness. We, and future generations, can thank Senator Frank Church for his hard-fought battles to establish the necessary protections for this area of Idaho's central mountains. Legislation in 1980 designated the wilderness status, but it included "grandfathered" approval for jetboat access to private in-holdings and public lands, even though motorized boating is banned in most other such places.

Before diving deeper into the depths of the Salmon River, this would be a good place to explain how my relationship with this special waterway became instrumental in my evolution as a human being. It seems a long time ago as I look back to my port of earthly entry in Eugene, Oregon, where I was born in 1949.

From my perspective now, I see it as an amazing period in history, before most of the dams on the Columbia River were put into place. The dams were crucial to how the region's history unfolded and were integral to the extreme environmental facelift that resulted.

There were only three dams on the entire Columbia watershed before I was born. Now there are 14. The Dalles Dam, completed in 1960, was a Caucasian blunder that still serves as a concrete testimonial to the arrogance of the dominant culture to which I belong. With a row of spillway chutes that look like the serrated jaws of a giant predator, it is a perfect symbol of the difference between two worldviews about what nature is and what it is for.

While all dams are serious impediments to the salmon that run up their namesake river in Idaho where I live, The Dalles Dam has a more significant environmental and cultural impact than any other in the Pacific Northwest. It is located on the northernmost part of the Cascade Mountain Range within Oregon, where the Columbia River divides it from Washington.

There, about 200 miles upriver of the Pacific Ocean, was a great natural cascade named Celilo Falls. With flows about tenfold greater than the famous Niagara River, it was a major geological wonder of great magnitude and a serious impediment to upriver fish migration. Before the arrival of white influence, it also served as a vital fishing hub and nexus for trade and commerce for First Nations peoples. The Dalles Dam changed all that.

Damming up rivers is like trying to contain their currents in a bucket, where the water stagnates and death follows. But more than proving disastrous to all the salmonids, The Dalles Dam also drowned out a way of life that had prospered there for generations. Short-sighted Europeans were too industrious and too filled with ego-driven avarice to pay much heed to primal peoples or their philosophical perspectives.

After all, how could "ignorant savages," who were often treated as less than animals, have any valuable knowledge? God had higher plans for the chosen people, having made them in his image and given them complete dominion over nature, according to Christian doctrine. Sadly, the stealing of indigenous homelands led to an egocentric stewardship of natural resources that became mostly about exploitation at any cost.

The resulting ecological and cultural loss significantly impacted the region, setting off a ripple effect that disenfranchised native peoples and depleted the natural economy in ways that are still felt today. The scars of Manifest Destiny run deep and long. Like bloodied boxers sparring in a championship fight, the social battle between rugged individualism and community spirit has been long and costly. The stakes are higher now than ever in the competition between those seeking to control nature and those living more in tune and cooperatively with it. Which side will win and at what peril? When it comes to ultimate salvation, the Earth cannot accommodate both worldviews any more than you can run a wild river with a foot in each of two boats at the same time.

Too many rivers have succumbed to the constant assault of human technology that mostly aims to impede their unbridled natural currents. An out-of-control industrial world has the capacity to brown out that blue dot that is Earth as seen from space. Whatever future footprints we might put down on other planets will be determined by the ones we make on our own.

Self-awareness and personal intention determine the size and meaning of whatever tracks we leave behind. Where we step and what kind of footprints we make matter, because stepping blindly on a rattlesnake invites a venomous outcome. Knowing how our tracks will oppose or complement nature is important to our survival. We are all raindrops, and the architecture of our actions will determine whether the resulting water is pure or dirty.

I remember before I was 10 watching Indians on their platforms along the edge of Celilo Falls as they fished for leaping salmon trying to negotiate the difficult passage. Aside from these imprinted images of dip-netters and spear fishermen, Indians had little meaning to me as a kid. My first personal contact with an Indian was in third grade, when I became best friends with a Navajo named Tim. Although, he had been adopted by white parents and I doubt that he knew much about his original cultural heritage at the time, he was still my Indian friend. Both of us were racially color blind in our bond of friendship and quite oblivious to the Anglo acculturation process that operated far above the conscious level of our youthful innocence. In our high school history class, the slanted stories of how the West was won often left out significant facts, including what really happened to native people.

What still most sticks in my mind from that boring class are the horrible images from old photographs and films of the atrocious barbarity during the German/Jewish Holocaust. At that time, I didn't appreciate my own country's revisionist history and the fact that most victors of war write sanitized versions of the truth. Being deprived of the truth kept my ignorance in line and the reality of the ruthless concept of Manifest Destiny and the American Holocaust off my radar.

Promoting flag worship and the Pledge of Allegiance to God and country in grade school was an effective aid to shape nationalism and help sculpt kids into a voluntary flock of followers. Preachers worked along the same lines, even though it was always taught in class that our Founding Fathers established a federal government that separated church and state. As I grew older, questioning authority, exploring science, and researching native perspectives all contributed to a paradigm shift in my thinking. It led me to look at history and religion through a different lens, which turned me into a hard-core skeptic, and it continues to shape my perception of the big picture of everything in today's world.

While my parents did send my sister and me to Sunday school a few times during early childhood, the teachings never stuck, and church going never was a family affair. My own curiosity later took me inside various congregations to see what they were being taught, but the rampant hypocrisy demonstrated by people who said one thing in church and acted differently in the real world made me sick. While many people go to church to get answers, I found it only generated new questions.

It was just as easy for me to believe in Santa Claus, tooth fairies, and wood elves as it was to absorb many of the religious teachings that could only be accepted on faith. I needed measurable evidence. The awe of mystery replaced my "fear of God."

Ironically, it was my own culture's fascination with sophisticated technologies that led to my learning about native cultures. My family got our first television in 1954 when I was in kindergarten, and it came at a time when black-and-white westerns about cowboys and Indians were quite popular.

I sided with the Indians whenever they had battles. The bow and arrow, feathered headdresses, and various buckskin wardrobes were probably the big draws for me, as it all reeked of a certain purity of nature. What greatly impressed me was the primal mindset of a people who incorporated the many beautiful aspects of the flora and fauna into their hand-to-mouth way of life. It fascinated me and made far more sense than a culture that was always striving to control nature.

Chapter 4

NEGOTIATING THE MIDDLE

Growing up in middle class America, I was lucky enough to start out with loving parents, Max and Wy, though with a view somewhat sheltered from the world's darker side. I was the first born, almost two years older than my only sister, Renee'. We grew up having typical sibling rivalries and kid wars during early childhood, but that only lasted until we got to high school.

Despite our occasional screaming and hair-pulling tirades, we shared common character-building experiences through many outdoor camping vacations. Early on, our physical labor on the family's cherry orchard imbued us with a strong work ethic. As soon as we could carry a tin can, we learned how to pick cherries, and what "elbow grease" was all about. Of course, at that age, we ate about as many cherries as we put in the can. A few cherry wars also erupted as we slung fruit at one another, staining our less than stellar behavior, as well as our clothes.

The cherry farm was in the small northeastern Oregon town of Cove. It was a very small farming and ranching community with fewer than 400 residents. It was 18 miles across the Grande Ronde Valley from the college town of LaGrande, which had a population of about 11,000.

Our cherry orchard came from my dad's side of the family. He had grown up with parents who were migrant fruit pickers. The entire family, including Dad and his brother Jack who was 8 years younger, followed the fruit circuit to make a living.

Eventually they bought their own cherry orchard, changing status from migrant workers to land owners. Although they became less nomadic, the work didn't get much easier, just slightly more profitable. It was a relatively stable way of life, but, as any orchardist, rancher, or farmer can warn you, their lifestyles are not for anyone who wants much certainty in life. Weather and many other factors can be fickle, affecting crops and bottom line.

Dad married while in college and later purchased another cherry farm of about 20 acres across a gravely dirt road from my grandparents' place. The properties were named Warm Creek Orchards. Separate branches of Warm Creek ran down the middle of each orchard, and I spent countless hours as a child honing my fishing prowess using a simple stick and line to catch native rainbow trout.

With only about 20 acres of cherries, my mom, dad, sister, grandparents, and I worked the entire orchard. Only occasionally, when crops were exceptional, did we need extra help at harvest time. This was back before Mexican crews began to show up for work. Instead, the fruit pickers were mostly lower-income to poverty-level white folks who made the seasonal migrant rounds.

Many of them came from Oklahoma and were known colloquially as Okie Drifters. They were a product of the Dust Bowl and Depression days that had driven them from their homes in search of a livelihood. They came west to California, Washington, and Oregon, following in the footsteps of the pioneers who had come a century earlier on the Oregon Trail. This time, "The Nation's Longest Graveyard," as the Oregon Trail was referred to in the early days, was less treacherous to travel. Back then, one in 10 who traveled it died, mostly due to disease or accident and not by the hands of Indians, as many erroneously believed. These days, there are not many white people willing to do the hard labor of harvesting. Rather, it is now mostly Mexican crews that are willing to hit the fields to keep fruits and vegetables on American tables.

After Dad graduated from the University of Oregon in Eugene, he became a math teacher and athletic coach. A series of job openings around Oregon landed us in Monmouth; Alsea; Baker, where I went to kindergarten and first grade; Pilot Rock, where I went to second grade; and finally Portland, where I made it from third grade through high school. My sister and I eventually graduated from David Douglas High School, which was in the Metro League of Southeast Portland.

As a teacher, Dad had summers off, so we spent most of our time in Cove when not in school and away from Portland. Our mother also had grown up in Cove, as part of the "Puckett Clan," as we liked to call them. It was a big family, and Mom was the oldest of nine kids, including four boys and five girls. They were raised on a farm with cows, horses, chickens, gardens, and it was not an easy way of life. When my sister and I escaped the city and returned to Cove each summer, we had great times with our cousins Pam and Phil, full-time country kids who were our best friends.

Chapter 5

SPORTS AND NATURE

Growing up with a healthy dose of outdoor activities, along with having a dad who coached football, basketball, and track, there was little doubt that I would be drawn to sports. The only limitation was my size. Although I played a lot of football until my freshman year in high school, I did not grow into a big, burly body, nor did I have the Neanderthal need to bang heads with other gridiron beasts. And though I liked basketball and played first string on my eighth-grade team, I wasn't tall enough in high school to be more than a bench warmer in that sport.

Faced with these realizations, and drawing inspiration from my pre-high school days, I decided to try out for the track team. I remembered when my folks took me to track meets at the University of Oregon to watch my famous uncle, Jim Puckett, run the 100 yard dash.

In high school he was known as the "Cove Comet," and he established the Oregon state record for the 100 yard dash at 9.6 seconds that still stands. Of course, that is partly because the event was changed to 100 meters in 1966, so it is no longer possible to break the record for the shorter distance.

I recall Uncle Jim taking me into the Oregon Duck's locker room, where I got to meet two iconic figures I will never forget. The first was Bill Bowerman, the famous coach of well-known distance runner Steve

Prefontaine. He was also co-founder of the Nike running shoes company. My dad told me that when he was coaching at Marshall High School, Phil Knight, the other co-founder of Nike, came to the field to show him some prototype track shoes out of his car trunk. Little did Dad know at the time how far reaching and famous Nike would eventually become! My second hero-worship figure I was thrilled to meet and shake hands with was the Ducks' sub 4-minute miler and Olympian Dyrol Burleson. Today, Eugene is known as Tracktown USA, and their track venue, Hayward Field, is a Mecca for aspiring track athletes.

Uncle Jim gave me my first green and yellow "Duck" track shoes, which made me want to become a sprinter. Unfortunately, no matter how hard I tried, I just did not have much natural speed. All the training in the world can't make a fast runner if it isn't in his genes. Denial doesn't last as long when you are a kid, so I quickly accepted I was not going to be a speedster on the track.

Luckily, my dad coached track as well as football and basketball. Though I went to a different high school than where he taught and coached, he was still my best source for good advice and direct access to sports accessories when I was in grade school. He brought home a metal vaulting pole and slider box when I was in seventh grade. He helped me make a pit and a runway so I could practice at home in the backyard. I soon fell in love with vaulting and practiced endlessly after school and on weekends.

By eighth grade, I was the best vaulter at my junior high school, clearing the bar at about 8 feet. As a freshman in high school, I went out for the cross country running team to stay in shape for vaulting. Discovering that I was pretty good at long-distance running, I decided to compete in both vaulting and the mile run.

But as my freshman year progressed, I seemed to hit a ceiling of 10 feet vaulting. This was with a metal pole, and though fiberglass poles were just beginning to catch on, I did not like the added flex and new catapulting technique. Also, the extreme requirements of both vaulting and running distance were a bad combination. Being better at running, I opted to give up the fun of sailing over a bar in favor of gut-grueling workouts racing repetitiously around the oval cindered track.

Thus, I ended up following more in the footsteps of my other uncle Ray, who was the youngest of the Puckett kids and only a couple of years behind Jim. He was the distance runner among the family's athletes because he, too, didn't have that fast-twitch muscle fiber or those thick thighs that most sprinters have.

So the mile run became my race. But even in the mile my lack of speed became a problem because I lacked a strong kick at the end of the race. I changed over to run two miles, which better suited my sloth-like pace. I could hold a good, steady pace over time and even came within three-tenths of a second of breaking our school record of 9:45.3.

Because the long winter months separated the fall cross country and spring track seasons, I decided to go out for wrestling to help stay in shape for running. I discovered I was pretty fair at that too. All three sports kept me healthy most of the time, and little did I know just how much that would help me for the rest of my life. Lessons learned and always being very active are a good recipe for a healthy future.

All three were endurance sports and conducive to competition with oneself as much as with others. I ended up lettering three years in track and four in wrestling and cross country. I barely weighed 90 pounds my freshman year, which made it easier to letter as a freshman on the varsity wresting team.

Doing well in all three sports was a significant character builder for me. My high school, which had more than 2,000 students, was the largest in Oregon. The competition was very tough, so making teams and excelling in sports boosted my self-esteem. However, it also meant sometimes getting whipped by teammates better than me, so my ego never got too big.

Fortunately, my dad always told me that if I practiced with athletes much better than me, it would make me better, too. He was right, but as good as I sometimes believed myself to be, and though I placed first or second in our league all four years in wrestling, there were sobering lessons along the way. I went to state tournaments one time in both wrestling and cross country, but I choked each time, which was highly disappointing. So perhaps my biggest life lesson from it all was learning how to deal with failure.

My dad was also very good at consoling me whenever I failed, and he always told me it is more important to get up when you fall down and to always finish the race. There will always be someone better, and bettering oneself is the real name of the game, he said. Always doing your best is what counts, and being a good sport and accepting defeat graciously when losing reveals a person's true character.

Little did I know that this lesson would so aptly apply to many situations throughout my life, even when it came to running rivers and keeping boats right side up. Win some, lose some, seems the norm for the average person.

As I engaged my adolescent growing pains, having parents who came to most of my meets or matches to watch my performance, good or bad, always provided much encouragement. In fact, at wrestling matches people enjoyed watching my mom as much, or more, than my performances. Her moves in the stands matched mine on the mat, as if she was helping me in every takedown or reversal I attempted. Her antics were quite the crowd pleaser.

When not going to school, studying, or training for sports, I was either hiking, camping, or fishing. But fishing came first, as my dad began taking me along on fishing adventures not long after I learned to walk. Mostly streams, but sometimes lakes were our destination, though moving water held my interest more. Action was at the heart of each adventure and was what drew me into being a participator in everything rather than a passive observer.

Probably the biggest impact to my early childhood was the family's first horse packing trip into the high Wallowas, on the southern flank of the

Eagle Cap Wilderness Area. Besides our family, there were favorite cousins Pam and Phil, who were Aunt Con and Uncle Will's kids, and Aunt Cecil and Uncle Boggs, my mother's brother and the oldest of the four Puckett sons. Dad drove an old stock truck with all the horse gear and supplies, along with us kids singing at the top of our lungs, in the back. We met Uncle Boggs, who trailed horses over trails and dirt roads from Cove to a place called Rock Springs. This was on a rim road overlooking the western breaks of a Y-shaped canyon where the Little and Big Minam Rivers converged.

After the grown-ups prepped and packed horses, we rode them nine miles down the steep slopes and rocky trail that descended through the Minam River breaks to an old log cabin known as The Land Ranch. Uncle Boggs had a lease from Boise Cascade, which owned it, and the Puckett family had had use of it for many years.

We kids could barely contain our excitement, and when we got to the bottom, it felt like heaven, even though to a kid's mind, we had to go through hell on horseback to get there. The horses that had been released in the meadow after our ride looked almost wild, leaving an indelible image on impressionable young minds of how the old West used to be, before it was tamed.

Speaking of an atmosphere akin to the Last Frontier, where else could a boy go in modern times to fish pristine waters with solitude as a sister, and sensuous beauty like a coveted lover?

Like a first kiss, catching my first salmon on that trip was something never to be forgotten. It was like going through some special rite of passage, where dreams are manifested, and turning fantasy into reality.

My dad was fishing a hole far below me when a big wild salmon took the flashing spoon I had hurled its way. It was a fight that I was ready for, having lots of relative experience on the many shorter trips on which my dad had taken me closer to civilization. So I did a good job of playing it enough to drag the spent fish onto the shore. We did not have a net in those days and used the old ways.

I carefully dragged it, with as much finesse as a hunter with buck fever, onto the rocky shoreline maybe 10 feet from the water's edge. But the fish came off the hook and began flopping powerfully all about. It would have been simple for me to run over and wrap my arms around it to keep if from making its way back to the river, but Dad's warning that salmon could bite you kept swimming around in my head. He had only been kidding, but I thought he was serious. Not wanting to get near those toothy jaws and in fear of getting rabies, or whatever a salmon bite could give a kid with a big imagination, I watched it flip its way back to safety in the river.

I quickly ran down to tell my dad about the experience, and he couldn't believe I had taken his joke so seriously and had lost out on catching my first salmon. When he admitted it was all just good humor and not the way of the mighty Chinook salmon, I ran back upriver to continue fishing. Later I decided to try some fly fishing for trout with a bumblebee fly and float setup.

After a couple of rainbows gave me good aerial fights, I glanced over to a large tongue of smooth water and saw two very large fish with large black spots on their backs traveling side by side upriver. Male and female Chinooks no doubt, and in an instant my fly was in front of them. They were barely below the surface of the water, and one of them rose out of the water with an open mouth wider than mine. But over enthusiasm muddied a kid's dream, and I yanked the fly right out of his mouth before he could clamp down on that black and yellow artificial bumblebee.

As the line whipped by my head with an abrupt retrieval, the hook found purchase in the high branches of an alder tree directly behind me. By the time I could climb up and free the fake bee, the fish were gone.

Losing these battles only whetted my appetite, and I kept at it until I finally did catch a salmon. Instantly and forever, I became more hooked by them than they by me. This was back in the day when fish were wild and not diluted by the gene pool of hatchery fish now in the river. Perhaps there is some sort of twisted moral irony in fishing for wild fish with fake flies now that the only thing left for fishermen to legally take are artificially raised fish, even if taken on real bait.

Almost every summer when we were kids and after cherry harvest was over, we would return with my parents on horseback into the Minam. We were fortunate to have access to this awesome country via relatives with close ties to the land and historic times. Not only The Land Ranch but also two other places were part of the broad family heritage. One was a hideout of long-ago horse rustlers called Red's Horse Ranch, which was five miles upriver from where the Little Minam River joined the Big Minam.

My great-grandfather Clarence Richards had owned Red's Horse Ranch from 1929 to 1931. He was a savvy outdoorsman but also a heavy drinker and gambler. Unfortunately, his luck ran out in a wild night of card playing, and he lost the ranch on a poor bet.

The other place, near the upper end of a long green meadow above the Horse Ranch, was called Richard's Resort. My great-grandfather's brother owned another historic cabin in the trees shortly beyond this grassy horse pasture, which also served as an airstrip for bush planes. As kids, we didn't care which place we went to as long as we got to go somewhere "into the Minam." We used the phrase as a mantra begging our parents to take us.

Shortly after graduation from high school, I teamed up with two of my distance-running buddies, brothers Tim and Dave Schomberg, to celebrate surviving academia by spending a week backpacking in the Eagle Cap Wilderness Area in the upper headwaters of the Minam River country. We were all in great shape from rigorous workouts, so though we started out from a horse and hiking trailhead near Lapover, we often left the main trails to climb over ridges and go cross country to reach scattered lakes in the high basins. All that athletic training paid off.

The experience had a big impact on all of us, and the three things I remembered most after the trip are unrelated but demonstrative of nature's inherent power. When light began to fade in the evenings out in

the wilds, I had the urge to turn on an electric light by flicking a switch on a wall that wasn't there. Sacrificing places like Celilo Falls so I could have that option to use such lights was not even a blip on my radar screen at the time. Nor did I know how much impact it would have on all the salmon we saw struggling up the wilderness rivers along which we hiked.

Second, the other thing about fish that I soon discovered on that trip was how much easier it was to eat small fish than big ones. Little fish could be eaten without cleaning, just like sardines. As kids we always tried to catch the biggest fish we could, but when it came to eating them, the big ones didn't exactly equate to better tasting.

Third, there was an experience I had when we were standing in the water of Steamboat Lake fishing in the last light of a long day of hiking. The sunset was so spectacularly beautiful that I wanted to take a picture of it. Photography had not been an interest before, but at that moment I wanted to share such beauty with the whole world, so I promised myself I would get a camera when I got back to civilization.

All my outdoor-oriented upbringing, along with sports and parental encouragement to get a college education, spurred my decision to pursue a career in the fisheries and wildlife field. With money being limited, the offer of a track scholarship led me to start my freshman year at Mt. Hood Community College. It also helped that my Uncle Jim was coaching there at the time.

This was the first year the college, located on the forested edge and in the long shadow of Mount Hood, had opened. Many of the classrooms, as well as all athletic dressing rooms, were in converted trailer houses. The cross country team, which started fall workouts on day one, didn't run through manicured campus landscapes for workouts. Our paths offered a challenging variety of backwoods hills, mountain forests, and swollen creeks to jump across. We distance guys loved it far more than the asphalt jungles of the city.

By living at home and commuting five miles to college, I was able to save money before transferring to Oregon State University for my

sophomore year. Picking cherries helped me earn enough money to get my own apartment and books when I moved to Corvallis and the big college. Since there was no financial future in track and I was only an average student, concentrating on academics seemed the best course of action.

Getting away from home and living on my own was exciting, scary, and good for building confidence. I moved into a small apartment with an old friend for a couple of terms, and then moved into one of the dorms for another two terms, mostly to save money.

But the dorm was too rowdy for me, so I moved into another apartment that I shared with a new friend I had met in a wildlife class. This was during my junior year, when peace marches and anti-Vietnam War demonstrations were ramping up big time.

As the war escalated, the military draft was changed to a lottery system, and my student deferment was no longer viable. Luck would determine the direction my life would take. I was very worried, because I wasn't sure what I would do if I got a low number. I didn't believe in the war for moral and political reasons. I felt as though people on the battlefield were like pawns on a giant chess board. All the pieces were being manipulated by the elites on either side. I knew if I ended up with a gun in my hand and an enemy about to shoot me, it would be kill or be killed. However, I knew that if I killed an enemy, the effects wouldn't just be to him but would also ripple beyond to all his relatives.

Watching friends getting killed would enrage me, and it would be hard not to wish to retaliate and kill in return. When would it ever stop, the inevitable circle of evil that only painted the world in black? Canada became a possible option, but I like America and didn't want to leave. I felt that if I moved to another country, I would have to live out my entire life there, as it would not be fair to return, even if given amnesty later. What to do?

It was a huge question that I didn't have a solid answer for and would never know until my number came up. Luckily, I ended up having been born on a good day, as Feb 3 fell somewhere in the 200s of the draft lottery. That number was high enough that I never got called and didn't have to make what would have been the hardest choice of my life. Something in the stars seemed to have aligned, and looking to the heavens, I gave thanks to whatever may have influenced my destiny, if there was anything that did such things.

But it also reminded me how whacky the world is and that our life's journey is impacted by more than the choices we make. Chance? Coincidence? Divine intervention? Science says one thing, religion another. Some say they are compatible, but I suspect mutually exclusive to be the better bet.

The summer before my senior year of college, I married my high school sweetheart. She was a close friend of my sister, and that is how we met. Coincidently, my sister met her future husband at my wedding. He was one of my college friends who shared my field of study. So when they got married, the Lane family tree ended up with two wildlife biologists.

Graduating from Oregon State in 1971 with BS degrees in wildlife science, we both faced fierce competition for the few permanent jobs in this field. The ratio of about five positions for 200 job seekers in the entire West was the norm, which was very depressing.

Sending out résumés, attending interviews, and knocking on doors became a routine exercise in my experiencing rejection. Because I had been only an average student and had no contacts with anyone remotely associated with the fisheries and wildlife field, my chances for employment were quite small. Considering that my competitors included those with high GPAs, master's degrees, and PhDs, as well as professionals already employed but seeking new positions, my chances seemed slim.

Since I was married, the pressure was huge, and the agony of defeat was, well, quite agonizing. Rejection letters were depressing. If I couldn't find work in the field for which I had spent four years preparing, what was plan B?

It should be something that gave me an opportunity to be outside and around fish and wildlife as much as possible. Considering potential avenues to outdoor employment, my thinking turned to the travel industry, including outfitting and guiding. I fired off letters to several outfitters that offered guided river trips. Why rivers? The short answer: television.

As a kid one of my favorite television programs was "I Search for Adventure." It was all about the exciting experiences of those who challenge the unknown and more dangerous pursuits in life. It sparked something inside me: a thirst for seeking far horizons and dancing upon their edge. This attitude also had been shaped by a defining moment during my freshman year in college.

I met a guy who was an expert rock climber, and he talked me into climbing Rooster Rock in the Columbia Gorge. It was an isolated spire of a rock rising vertically above the ground maybe 300 feet straight up. It had contorted angles and drastic overhangs that required technical hardware like pitons and carabineers and rope belays for extra safety. He had all the hardware and coached me the entire way. During one very treacherous maneuver that I had to make, an epiphany hit me over the head like a hammer, helping to shape my life forever.

It seemed strange, but knowing I was closer to the edge between life and death than I had ever been before made me appreciate life to a far greater degree. It was both scary and addicting, but I loved the way it made me feel: alive! The old saying that not doing something dangerous because of the fear of dying is not really living became crystal clear.

Images from several episodes of "I Search for Adventure" in which people were rafting wild rivers kept replaying in my mind. Then my thoughts digressed back to my senior year of high school, when I saved up enough money to buy a $200 "world famous" (brand) rubber raft and some paddles. This left me needing only moving water and some foolish friends willing to jump head first into an adventure.

Two such wild-spirited schoolmates, Dave Vollans and Ron Clare, agreed to try out a whitewater run on the Sandy River with me.

I had fished this river often with my dad in a section called Dodge Park. It had a great steelhead hole below a rapid called "Pipeline." That seemed like an ideal launch site because it was also a place where the raft could easily be carried back upriver. My idea was not to just run blindly down through who knows what but to tackle a big rapid over and over to gain enough experience for a longer journey later.

My only rafting "experience" was what I had seen on the TV adventure shows, and my friends hadn't even seen those, so we qualified as true novices. At first everything went according to plan as we began our loop by putting in, paddling through the rapid, then carrying back up and repeating the process.

We had so much fun we figured we should film our final run to show our friends. Ron remained on shore to film while Dave and I tackled the "mighty Colorado" of the Sandy River. But in our false sense of mastership and the ignorance of youth, we took our lifejackets off for this run. It would make for better photos, and help color our skin like bronze gods, which we hoped would attract some pretty women.

Sure enough, out in the middle of whitewater chaos, we were upside down before we even knew what had hit us. Luckily, no pretty women saw our stupid behavior, and we both managed to keep hold of the raft.

However, Ron couldn't see me because I was on the far side away from his view, and he thought I had drowned. Panicking, he quit filming and missed our recovery. The agony of our defeat was scary, most humbling, and left us with incomplete footage of our blunder. But I really liked the surge of adrenaline I had felt and never lost the thirst for it.

So with these water-logged memories bubbling back to the surface, I fired off letters to several river adventure outfitters. If I couldn't land a job to manage critters, maybe I could have some active fun and at least live close to them in their world.

However, I had zero experience guiding, so who would hire me for that? Most outfitters didn't even take the time to send me a rejection letter. Only one guy responded and was desperate enough to take a chance on hiring me despite my lack of experience. His name was Dave Giles, and he was a big-game outfitter who operated in what would be designated later, in 1980, as the Frank Church Wilderness Area.

He needed someone to take care of horses through the summer and then guide for deer and elk hunters come fall. But I noticed that he also had a Salmon River rafting permit and hired whitewater guides for that, too. So, seeing this as an opportunity to get my foot in the door, I eagerly accepted his job offer.

Chapter 6

SHOUP SOUP

All my youthful experience around horses and farming seemed to have paid off, helping me land that new job opportunity. I wasn't a real cowboy, but I did have boots, a tattered hat, and an inclination toward that lifestyle, having long ago outgrown my childhood phase of "playing Indian." So my wife and I moved to Idaho and a small cabin on Pine Creek. This was a small tributary of the Salmon River near the community of Shoup, which amounted to a gas station, a store, and barely enough residents to qualify for a place on the map.

It seemed ideal at the time, as there were no strict schedules and I could call my own shots for work and play. Often I would drive down to the river to wet a line, and one day I was surprised to see a lone kayaker float past. Having never seen such a show before, I had to give chase. It was hypnotic, like watching a ballet dancer, as he elegantly avoided man-eating holes and skirted the edge of catastrophe by mere inches. The potential for mayhem, which has some sort of power over most people, drew me along to see his performance in every rapid.

This was early in the summer of 1971, when kayakers were rare in the West. By the end of his solo run, the lone water-skipper had become aware of my interest in kayaking and introduced himself. He was Ken Collins, a high school teacher in the town of Salmon. Astonishingly to me, he was planning to return the next day and offered to bring along an extra kayak if I wanted to give it a try. He didn't have to ask me more than once. My mile-wide smile was answer enough.

Ken was as excited as me because it gave him a chance to entice me into his world as a possible boating buddy. It worked. Even though I got thrashed and swam a lot during that first kayaking adventure, I wanted to buy a boat immediately. He told me a local physician in Salmon, Dr. Walt Blackadar, might sell me one. It was a kit boat called a Vector, which only required glassing the upper and lower halves together. Little did I know that a kayak would soon be my key to unlocking the liquid secrets of the river world.

Both Ken and Walt worked with me on roll practice along the shoreline near Shoup. Once I learned that technique, I began following them on the water to gain experience reading the river and to hone my skills as a kayaker. It became my obsession, and whenever possible, I was in my boat challenging waves and unfamiliar water. I absorbed Dr. Blackadar's philosophy of staying in the boat as long as possible in a perilous situation and never exiting unless you were near your last breath or imminent danger dictated such action. He said that it was faster to paddle away from danger than to swim for safety and better to wait for the right time to hit a roll than to panic too soon. That became my strategy.

I did not know at the time how lucky I was to have such great mentors. This was before Dr. Blackadar became famous as a kayaking pioneer for daring feats like running solo in Turnback Canyon on the Alsek River in Canada and Alaska. That also earned him a reputation as the "Father of Big Water Kayaking" in the West.

Because there were relatively few kayakers in the West those days and today's instant communication through social media was far in the future, it wasn't easy to find or meet other boaters. One such boater I knew of at the time, but had not met, was Rob Lesser. He had paddled with Blackadar a year or so before I met the legendary doctor. He eventually far surpassed even Walt's exploits in the big-water world after paddling with him in Devil's Gorge of the Susitna River in Alaska. Not only did he manage amazing descents in Turnback Canyon and the

Grand Canyon of the Stikine in British Columbia, but he also bagged some major accomplishments on other continents.

My appetite for adventure seemed nearly as large but did not extend to such magnum-sized risks. However, scale is relative and my experiences were grand in terms of appreciating nature's raw power. My first kayaking epiphany was discovering that it took extreme aggression to work with a powerful river. A timid kayaker was only lunch for the river. Inanimate forces at work in wild currents had to be met head-on with a force of my own, even if pale in comparison.

I loved it. The challenge and beauty of learning to engage the sensuous river on so many levels was as alluring as any pretty woman flaunting her curvaceous femininity. It was like learning a new dance to the beat of the river's seductive music.

As I mastered the basics, the kayak allowed me to continue to gain intimacy with the river by surfing waves and performing other tricks that other craft couldn't do. Things like pop-ups, pirouettes, and enders became a big part of the challenge. Playing in the various dynamics of hydraulic maelstroms became a euphoric obsession. To me, kayaking was a sport that had it all. It was a confluence between body and river that combined the physical, mental, and spiritual dimensions of a deeper human existence in raw nature. The intoxicating alchemy uplifted my soul far above the clouds where mythical angels play in true ecstasy. Nirvana found.

Gaining all this river experience when I did was fortuitous because when one of the river guides that worked for Dave Giles quit, it created an opening for me. I jumped at the sudden vacancy and soon was put to work patching rafts and prepping gear for the upcoming season.

Then, however, my wife became pregnant, presenting us with a big dilemma. Neither of us, or so I thought, wanted to have kids at that time in our life. We were still young ourselves and barely able to keep our heads above water making ends meet. Another mouth to feed was not a cause for celebration, as it is with most young couples. We were confronted with the meaning of creating life as well as the option of abortion.

I am not religious, having little trust in the words and unsupported claims of the imperfect men who wrote scriptures. I consider myself an agnostic who looks for evidence in the search for truth. And while I have little faith in the Bible, even it seems to recognize that personhood does not happen immediately when egg and sperm unite, as some believe. Genesis 2:7 can be interpreted to mean that human life begins with the first breath. Nor can science say when the ensoulment of a human being happens. Lack of evidence for cognition in a developing fetus in the first six months is central to the Roe vs. Wade decision making abortion legal.

Moreover, we felt that rather than adding an unwanted child to an already overburdened human population, it would be better to wait until the child was wanted, and to have no more than two kids.

The choice of an abortion won out, but it wasn't legal in Idaho. However, it was in Oregon, so we decided to go to LaGrande covertly to have the procedure done, and then quickly sneak back to Idaho. Unfortunately, a downside of having lots of relatives is that keeping a secret is next to impossible. Unbeknownst to me, some of my relatives worked at the hospital and got wind of the operation. Game over. Leaving behind a negative cloud of religious and judgmental attitudes, we made our escape back to Idaho, ASAP.

In hindsight, I realize that this was more of a strain to my wife, who came from a religious family and may have assimilated their beliefs, even without realizing it herself. Or she may have been afraid to reveal those concerns to me.

After our whirlwind trip to Oregon, I jumped back into prepping river equipment for the season, under the direction of the lead guide, Don Benedict. I followed him around like a pup to learn whatever I could. I soaked up a lot of river lore, including the fact that a year or two earlier he had been in court as an expert witness to a drowning at Haystack Rapid on the Middle Fork of the Salmon. He had been following close behind another float company that had the unfortunate tragedy. A few such stories, told by veteran guides, built a little fear and anxiety in the new help like me.

The rafts we were using were called sweep boats. They are a popular style of rafts used by outfitters on the Middle Fork, and sometimes on the Main Salmon. A large blade, or sweep, is attached to the end of long metal shafts extending in front and behind the boat for steerage. Unlike oars, which allow an oarsman to row upstream to ferry and to maintain more control to finesse a raft downriver, sweeps could mostly only be used to make right or left turns. On slow stretches, you could turn the boat sideways and row like an oared boat, but that was cumbersome and a disaster in high wind.

While I was enjoying wild waters, however, my wife was struggling with what seemed like menial tasks back at the lodge, where a morally centered Mormon atmosphere prevailed. Because she was such an unhappy camper when I got off the river, I talked my employer into letting her accompany me on the next trip.

It seemed like a good opportunity at the time, but things changed abruptly in the middle of Velvet Falls. The trouble began when I followed Don too closely as his sweep boat approached the lip of the falls. He was entering the far left side, where a subtle nuance of current momentarily stalled another boat. Not wanting to screw up his run, I shifted my raft slightly sideways to avoid nudging him. The main current was too strong for me to get immediately back in line and carried our raft directly over the middle of the falls. All hell broke loose.

The bow punched through the backwash wave below the drop, but the stern sweep hung up in the falls and was ripped out of my hands. Then the river grabbed the bow sweep, too, and soon both were swinging back and forth like two swordsmen battling to the death. Unfortunately, one of the scissoring sweeps hit my wife hard on her thigh.

Meanwhile, the raft was sucked back into the falls and became trapped in the reversal below it. This forced us to run around like monkeys trapped in a lion's cage trying to keep the raft from flipping, all while dodging the flailing sweeps. The current would momentarily subside and almost allow us to escape but then suck us back in again. The action was similar to a metronome as the bow did a back and forth, east-west-east-west over and over again.

A Forest Service worker coming down the trail saw our plight and came running up the west shore, while Don and another guide beached their rafts and came running on the east side.

This was before the invention of throw bags, and our rescuers didn't even have a line to toss us. So I grabbed my knife, cut the stern line, and tried to throw it their way. But as the boat danced back and forth, simultaneously jostling up and down, it felt like riding a bucking bronco. It also made a terrible platform from which to hurl a rope. At the apex of each swing, the rope was always about three feet short of reaching either shoreline. Finally, on my last try before we were both about to abandon ship, I managed to get it into the hands of my fellow guides, and they pulled us out of all the mayhem.

My wife's thigh had a significant cut, which left a scar she could use to illustrate a good story for years to come, but unfortunately, the experience also left a bad taste in her mouth for whitewater boating. That, along with her displeasure over life at the lodge, led to my resigning from a job that I really liked.

Hanging up my oars, my next move was to knock on the door of the Idaho Fish and Game Department in Salmon. Lucky for me, there just happened to be a temporary job opening. Bill Hickey, a senior wildlife research biologist, was working on a bighorn sheep study and needed a bio-tech to gather field data for his project. I was jazzed over such good fortune.

Being with bighorns became my life from late summer to winter. My wife and I were flown into the Flying B Ranch on the Middle Fork of the Salmon. From there, we shuttled our personal gear across the bridge to the Mormon Cabin, which was not far upriver.

With that as our base camp, plus wall-tent camps at Wilson Creek and at Waterfall Creek and use of the Taylor Ranch at Big Creek, I did my field work trying to locate every sheep in those areas.

Camping out when the Middle Fork was frozen over and no rafts were coming downriver provided a quiet wilderness soothing to my soul. Aside from ice cracking like a rifle shot and the similar sound of the ramming horns of rutting sheep, there was little to spoil the welcome isolation and calm atmosphere.

Once that job ended we moved back to Oregon to reside at my folks' cherry orchard. They still lived in Portland, so the ranch house was vacant and offered us a good landing spot as we cobbled together another game plan.

Out went another round of job applications, and I resumed door knocking. A local recreational trailer manufacturing company, Terry Trailers, offered me work. Anything is better than nothing when you need to keep afloat, so I accepted. However, the cookie-cutter type job on an assembly line was boring, and the repetitious nature of the robotic work drove me to the verge of insanity.

My temporary salvation came when a Denny's restaurant opened in LaGrande, and they hired me to wash dishes. When you have a college degree, accepting that kind of work to eke out a living robs life of joy. It was like training for the Olympics and then having the gates close just before opening ceremonies.

Again, fate stepped in, if such a thing exists, and a week later the Forest Service called to offer me a job on an "extra-protection" crew. This basically entailed clearing roads of brush and rocks, and being ready to fight any fires that might erupt in the Wallowa-Whitman National Forest.

During this entire time, I continued to explore rivers on my own by kayak and gained river experience with each new trip. Because others who heard me tell of my adventures asked to go along, I bought a raft so they could join me.

The year before, I had met a guy at Hospital Bar on the Middle Fork of the Salmon. His last name was Pruitt, and he was a well-known member of a long-time family of early river running professionals. I was on a sweep boat and had pulled into his camp to show guests the hot springs there. He was very friendly and enlightened me about rowing boats with oars instead of free floating with sweeps. I paid close attention to his explanations about gaining better boat control and simple instructions on how to build a raft frame to accommodate this different technique. It made good sense, so that is what I decided to do after I got my first raft.

This opened a new world of boating that solo paddling in a heavily loaded kayak did not offer. Once I grew confident with my rowing skills, I invited Forest Service friends to ride along, and we shared many adventures. With several rivers under my belt, my growing interest in returning to guiding in a professional capacity led me to send out more job applications.

A response from the federal Bureau of Land Management in Utah offering me a job as a river ranger on a Southwestern waterway sent my heart soaring. But just as I was about to say, "Yes, I will take the job," my wife told me that if I did so, I would be going there by myself. Deer-in-the-headlight shock stalled my brain, and as the smoke cleared, I was hanging up the phone after saying, "No, circumstances have changed." This may have foreshadowed a divorce looming a couple of years down the road. Abandoning my search for river work, I once again settled for a role in the green-tree bureaucracy.

With my credentialed background and having demonstrated a good work ethic to my immediate supervisor, he eventually helped me land a full-time job as the district's first wildlife biologist.

This all happened well before the controversy over saving the spotted owl moved the goal post for multiple-use forest management in the Northwest. It was when the timber industry was still king. I was excited about doing my part to help save the world, especially the forests, but was to learn that the high ideals of youth may ride atop the wings of unrealistic hope and that what sounds good in theory may founder in reality.

Butting heads with the timber industry and championing changes they were not used to dealing with was like being one of those rams I had watched cracking skulls on the Middle Fork's winter range. No veteran timber sovereign, entrenched with long established habits, wants to hear a snot-nosed college kid dictate where they can or cannot cut a tree.

My job was to coordinate all fish and wildlife needs with other disciplines and their natural resource requirements, all under the umbrella of multiple-use and sustained-yield forest management. One of the first things I did was to map out all existing roads and determine all currently available areas that contained adequate hiding cover for big game. Baseline data is always the fundamental foundation for establishing any good management objectives.

I met constant challenges in group meetings with foresters responsible for finding enough trees to meet the allowable cut mandates, and/or engineers required to get roads on the ground to access those commodities. Often, no reliable data existed to support some of my recommendations, so I would call the Range and Wildlife Research Lab, just up the hill from our office, where Jack Ward Thomas headed a team of research biologists working on the Starkey Experimental Forest.

I would tell them what I needed, and they would offer potential solutions based on their ongoing research and/or adjust their studies to gather reliable information and recommendations needed by people like me charged with real world habitat management responsibilities.

Bio-politics was the real name of the game when it came to compromise among all the various resource needs. It often was impossible to meet minimum fish and wildlife needs once trade-offs had been made, so what sounded good on paper was really an ecological form of corruption.

My workload increased as forest management became more intense, and with no corresponding funds to hire extra help, my field time was reduced, keeping me in the office far more than I felt was appropriate for my job description.

Sitting inside a warm office in the middle of winter drinking coffee and looking at aerial photos did not seem proper when animals were subject to the harshness of nature. Designating areas for thermal and hiding cover, based on an educated guess, was a much more sanitized assessment than engaging habitat face to face. Extraction rates of timber also seemed to be out of sync with allowable-cut targets that were set for district rangers by Washington, D.C., higher-ups who were out of touch with reality. While a 120-year forest rotation in wet coastal regions seemed reasonable, it is inadequate for the drier climes of eastern Oregon where my feet hit the turf. A rotation of 150 years seemed more realistic. One size does not fit all when it comes to varying rates of plant succession.

Cutting smaller and smaller trees became the norm on timber stands meant for even-aged management. Not only did that increase homogenization of the forest, but it also seemed to me further evidence that loggers were cutting faster than replacement, which was not sustainable over the long run.

Ecological diversity produces a healthier forest than heavy-handed mono-cultured management schemes. Ecology runs the natural economy, but money drives the industrial one, and sadly, when the green god rules, it is like running a machine without oil. It burns out the engine. Such dark observations also led to my daydreaming about being on a river somewhere else. I needed to escape the red tape and frustrating dynamics of agency bureaucracy.

That plus my downward spiraling marriage was a recipe for feeling the hammer of failure. I was staring down the cold barrel of divorce, which I had thought only happened to other people. It was crushing to realize how wrong I had been.

It seemed as if my wife had not been honest with me, nor perhaps with herself, as she finally faced her real feelings about children, religion, and family affairs. I also believed that she ended up resenting me for coaxing her into doing things she didn't want to do.

This had a huge impact on me, as my worldview shattered. My folks were model parents and had been together forever, and that is how I believed it would be for me. Divorce was not even on my radar. When that blip snuck across the screen, I had to accept it, but it made me feel like a real failure. It was like getting sucked into a whirlpool and not knowing which way to swim.

Chapter 7

SHATTERED DREAMS AND NEW BOATING FRIENDS

With spinning thoughts about what to do and how to deal with shattered dreams, I began to spend more time rafting and kayaking and escaping into the wilds. My first raft was a 14-foot Hypalon raft advertised as being "World Famous." It was black and had a unique inflatable floor resembling an air mattress. I purchased it from Bill Parks, who operated out of his basement before eventually growing into Northwest River Supplies and a multimillion-dollar business.

I built a wooden frame, following ideas presented to me by Pruitt, whom I had met on the Middle Fork of the Salmon, and made stands for horned oarlocks to accommodate nine-foot oars. Then I had a welder build a metal tubed frame to support an apron that I glued on to the side, just forward of the oarlocks, to wrap around the bow and serve as a spray skirt about 16 inches high to help keep water out. This was way before self-bailing rafts came on the scene.

I braved through many solo trips before I could persuade someone to ride along and join me in my river-centric world. My first raft passenger and willing guinea pig in pushing river horizons was fellow Forest Service employee Joe Shaw, an engineer and road designer. We had a connection because our jobs entailed coordinating road impacts with elk needs, as well as our shared interest in hunting elk.

He was always up for an adventure but could also be counted on as a safety backup when I attempted some crazy stunt in my kayak. Most of my early kayaking was done solo because it was hard to find other kayakers in eastern Oregon at that time. To advance my skills, I continually sought to up the ante in the level of paddling difficulty. As the risks escalated, safety was always a concern, and I was lucky to have Joe as a volunteer to assist when I pushed the boundaries.

One such incident occurred on the Wallowa River a mile below Minam Town, where the Wallowa and Minam Rivers join. It is the launch site for most Grande Ronde river trips. That day I challenged myself to run a nasty looking hole on the Wallowa. This high-water monster would one day become a favorite surfing wave for me and kayaking friends whom I was yet to meet. We named it the Minam Roller, and we spent many days hanging out there, thanks to a convenient access road where we could park.

For that first run, my game plan was to station Joe on the bank next to the hole with a throw rope that he could toss my way if I had to swim. And swim I did when the hole smacked me. The impact felt like hitting the back end of a mule that kicked like thunder. My roll was good but not a match for the river that day, as it gave me quite a thumping and a hard swim.

Meanwhile, a friend of Joe's had seen my boat heading for the hole as he was driving down the nearby road. Out of curiosity he stopped to see what would happen. Little did he know what he would be getting himself into that day, as well as in the future.

The problem with the Wallowa in high water is that there are few eddies and the current is cold and very fast. As Joe and his friend watched, I got eaten by the hole and then was pushed quickly downstream. They gave chase as I was carried around the corner beyond where the road ended. I was trying to swim my boat and paddle, as well as myself, toward the shore.

Being the slower of the two, Joe gave the throw rope to his friend, who sprinted off after me down the river. At the last possible point, just as I was about to disappear into the remoteness beyond the road's end, a line from above landed near my hand, and a total stranger dragged me up onto the bank. I was dead tired, but after catching my breath, I reached up to shake his hand. He introduced himself as Dave Baum.

We became good friends after that, and I invited him on our next multi-day expedition, which spawned many more. Joe, Dave, and I soon began running solo raft adventures. One raft was all we had. No back up. We felt like early explorers and had some epic journeys. They included rivers with obstacles like the Widow Maker on the Owyhee River. The only boating guide for that area that we found to consult described the treacherous rapid as a mandatory portage, but we managed to line it. We felt as though we had accomplished a greater feat than any who had come before us. We didn't know any better at the time.

It was also on that river that we met John Cassia from Idaho, who was kayaking by himself. Seeing that he was very skilled, we invited him to go with us the next week to challenge the Bruneau River. That turned into an epic adventure, too, better left for another campfire story.

Our first trip on the Main Salmon between Corn Creek and Heller Bar came sometime after the Bruneau run, in 1974. It was me, Joe, and Dave, plus a four-legged addition, my dog Banana. I was familiar with the first few rapids we encountered, having seen them from a jetboat while working for Dave Giles at the Corn Creek Lodge, but beyond there it was mostly uncharted country and another exploratory experience.

Our plan was to run the entire section from Corn Creek to Heller Bar, which was one of the longer journeys we had ever tackled. We scouted often and had mostly good runs until we got to Time Zone Rapid below Riggins. The powerful water crabbed an oar and ended up breaking one of my oarlocks. Lacking a spare, we hiked into town and, after questioning several locals, were directed to a mill, where a millwright was able to fix the oarlock, and soon we were back on the water heading downriver.

The millwright had warned us of a place called Snowhole, which caused us to worry for the next few days until we got there. It looked ferocious and we scouted it diligently. Knowing what I do today, I often wonder how we made such a good run on that first frothy plunge. We were inundated by whitewater and flooded by adrenaline as we celebrated at the bottom end. This was the hardest rapid of the trip, and while other rapids gave us serious concern, we made the entire run right side up.

Months later, I found myself facing another boating adventure on the Yankee Fork of the Salmon River. It is a small tributary to the Main Salmon River about 10 miles upriver of Stanley, Idaho. My friend Ken Collins, who first hooked me on kayaking, had invited me to meet a group of kayakers he had lined up to make a challenging high-water run there.

He said it was downstream of Redfish Lake, which I later learned was named after the longest inland migration of sockeye salmon anywhere in the world. Those small, 6- to 12-pound salmon are famous for the males having a green head, green tail, and bright red body in between during spawning. Lakes turn blood red when they show up to perpetuate their kind, and they are the only salmon of the five species that need the periphery of a lake, or tributaries that run into a lake, for spawning grounds.

Unfortunately, the sockeye run was cut off back in 1910 when mining interests in the Yankee Fork drainage got a dam built across the Main Salmon River just below the side creek's mouth. Single-minded extraction interests nearly annihilated this iconic run until the Idaho Fish and Game Department used explosives in 1934 to take out the earthen part of this concrete monster to help restore the unique anadromous fish run. This was the only major dam ever built on the entire 425-mile length of the Main Salmon River, and its ugly history was beyond my consciousness as I kayaked those waters that day.

The Yankee Fork was swollen and high enough to boat, but I was in a bit over my head, having only a fair roll to rely on for self-rescue. At one difficult spot near the end, after almost successfully making the run, I tipped over and had to swim. Holding on to my kayak while another boater tried to get me to shore, we hit a bridge pillar, and I ended up hyper-extending my elbow. No more kayaking for me for a few weeks.

It was quite painful, but enough beer around the campfire that night helped me forget about my woes, and bruised ego. Also, some of these new Idaho kayaker friends knew a few guides, so I asked them if they were aware of any outfitters who had a good conservation ethic and long boating season. I was growing more discontented with conventional life and burdensome bureaucracy, and I was hearing an ever louder call of the wild.

One of the kayakers recommended Martin Litton of Grand Canyon Dories. So the next morning when leaving the river, I stopped at the nearest phone booth and gave them a call. I spoke with a lady named Sally Chang, who was helping her husband, Curt Chang, manage the company's northern division from their home and shop in Lewiston, Idaho.

I figured the phone conversation was all for naught, but a week later she called to ask if I would consider rowing a baggage raft down the Snake River in Hells Canyon the next week. I don't think she could hear my jaw drop, but the "Hell Yes!" answer must have rung in her ears. So I took leave of work and headed off to "Boatland," which is in a hillside area of Lewiston known as The Orchards. There I met the guides and helped them prep everything for the upcoming trip.

With Heaven's Gate on top and Hells Canyon at the bottom, what better diabolical contrast could there be while floating the wild waters of the Snake River? With angel wings to make my spirit fly and a devil's tail to pull my feet into the water, I plunged deep into the river world and a far simpler way of life.

Chapter 8

NOMADIC SPIRITS ARE PRECIPITATED SOULS

Adventure seekers seem to be drawn like a magnet to rivers and the excitement of testing themselves against nature's challenges. In wilderness settings they can satisfy a yearning for freedom from society's restraints. A quest for adventure may free their spirits to soar and help them solve any troubles bothering them. And for some, the sheer joy of taking risks is a reward in itself. For them, no answers or revelations from the universe are required.

Bigfoot escorted me through the gates into the magic kingdom of Martin Litton's Grand Canyon Dory world. There I met Curt Chang, the manager of GCD's northwest division, which had arrived in Idaho only a couple of years before I started working for them.

Martin had been drawn to Idaho after getting a phone call from Floyd Harvey, a local jetboat outfitter who was concerned about threats to Hells Canyon from the proposed Mountain Sheep Dam. Floyd recruited him because he knew of Martin's conservation savvy and reputation as a "no compromise" warrior willing to take a stand against the establishment.

While in college I had heard a lecture by the environmentalist David Brower about the potential drowning of Hells Canyon and was inspired to sign petitions and write to politicians. Little did I know then that Litton was aligned with Brower and that both would be instrumental in saving the Colorado from total drowning by dams. No wonder Floyd sought his help.

Floyd convinced Martin that it might be the last opportunity to get a commercial river running permit for Hells Canyon, and Martin jumped at the suggestion. He purchased a couple of boats and sent Curt with a small crew north to test the waters.

Until joining the Dories, I was unaware of the magnitude of Martin's fame. He was to become one of America's greatest crusaders battling against manmade environmental calamities. His bulldog tenacity to go jowl to jowl against an establishment that was hell bent on subduing nature was what I admired most about him. He was the perfect person to work for, since part of the reason I left the U.S. Forest Service was my own frustrations with the hypocrisy inherent in multiple-use management and extreme timber-flavored policies.

The fight to save Hells Canyon was ongoing when I started with the dories. My first trip with Martin, as a second-year boatman, was in Hells Canyon, escorting some politicians through the corridor to showcase what was worth saving.

At Granite Rapids, which was normally run from the left side, I decided to run the bigger ride on the far right side and began ferrying hard across the river to take that route. Two women politicians were in my bow, and I was soon horrified to see that I was not going to make my intended run. Absentmindedly, in a rookie move, I said, "Oh, fuck!" as we were headed for a giant hole in the middle of the river. Realizing instantly that this would not inspire confidence, I learned a lesson I never forgot. Luckily, I skimmed by the left side of the hole by a hair's margin and quickly made my humble apologies.

I was proud to be working for a legendary outfitter who was in the canyon for more than just chasing a dollar. Martin believed that once something was compromised, it would never return and that it was worth being radically extreme in fighting for preservation. This was a lesson I had learned while working for USFS. All resource disciplines ask for more than they need in terms of multiple-use management, knowing that whatever is compromised is lost and rarely regained.

Martin's championing of an adversarial environmentalist cause united the boatmen in a meaningful direction and contagious heartfelt attitude that bonded them into a close-knit family, more akin to a tribal river clan. We shared a love of rivers and canyons and a willingness to continue fighting for them.

Martin's main operation was centered in a giant warehouse in Hurricane, Utah, where the southern division of boatmen worked on boats and prepped trips for the mighty Colorado. Like Martin, most were from California, and many were ski patrol professionals with virtually no boating experience before being persuaded to hire on to push oars down the Grand.

There are many amazing stories of carnage in those initial days as they learned how to negotiate the chaos of colossal waves and boat-crushing holes. Martin was one of the pioneering commercial river runners in the Grand. He made his first trip down the Grand in 1955 with P.T. Reilly in wooden boats. That inspired him to dabble more with dory boats and to do more trips. By 1968, his commercial venture took off, and clients began flooding to the only company that dared challenge the river in boats that complimented the canyon's beauty.

Curt, one of the early boatmen, had some rafting experience guiding on the Stanislaus River in California before joining GCD in 1968. He guided and helped train the first bunch of boatmen for Martin. In 1972, Martin sent him north to Hells Canyon to evaluate the potential for a commercial venture there. By 1974, Northwest Dories became the northern subsidiary of GCD. Its trips were suddenly in high demand by people who wanted to see the Snake River before it might be lost.

The company had been running out of Boatland in Lewiston, Idaho, for only a year before I arrived in 1975. Having gained much popularity each year, it had expanded its reach to the Main and Lower Salmon,

Grande Ronde, and Owyhee Rivers.

For the first two years of my dory days I guided mostly on Oregon waters and the Snake River in Hells Canyon. Occasionally I would be treated to a trip on the Main Salmon, and in my third season I began leading 13-day trips from Corn Creek to Heller Bar.

Arriving at Boatland to apprentice for a potential position, and having zero experience guiding, had been an intimidating experience. Most of the veteran boatmen ignored me, except for Tim O'Neil. He was friendly from the first handshake and took me under his wing, making my lowly spot as the "new guy" much more bearable. He was soft-spoken, gentle mannered, and smart. Being slightly balding, he looked older than he really was, but he still had a youngish facial appearance.

We soon became close friends, crewing many trips together. He and I often were the last to leave the campfire after tons of stimulating conversations with guests and then between us.

I also learned the ropes under the guidance of Mike Markovich and Steve Dalton. One introductory incident sticks out in my mind from my first apprentice trip with them. It was the same trip my Bigfoot story made its hit, gaining me entrance to the inner circle of guide comradery. After dinner and visiting with guests was over, there was only a little bit of sun left on the river, and the light was magically dancing in the eddy of Tryon Creek. What irony, a heavenly view in the middle of Hells Canyon.

Mike and Steve invited me to join them in a dory boat to circle the eddy, getting a break from work and enjoying some private time. Soon we were smoking some outrageous Colombian pot, stoning out on nature and the power of place. Then they gave me the oars, put headphones playing Pink Floyd to my ears, and I soon zoned out in the pure ecstasy of it all. The feeling of the oars dipping into current, watching the dance between water and light, and seeing the jagged silhouette of a gorgeous skyline make a 360-degree circle around me as the boat turned was all consuming. Sooo ... beautiful! I wasn't just seeing magic. I was feeling it. Such was the addiction of it all.

Earlier on the same trip, I saw Clarence Reece, who may have been leading that trip, heading upriver of our camp at Granite Creek with an ammo can in hand. I was curious, since it was my first trip, why anyone would want to go on a hike lugging such a thing. When I asked where he was going, he smiled and said to shoot some pictures.

To this day, I can still see him standing on that cliff, looking like Charles Atlas with his well-defined physique. He had been a star Golden Gloves boxer and superb wrestler, and had even taken ballet to help with his agility. But no one ever gave him any grief over his dancing because it could be at the expense of their own health.

But the real story, I learned later, was that he was heading upriver to a secluded spot to absorb a little green smoke and enjoy a brief respite from tending to guests.

I became good friends with him, too. I'm not sure why, but I always called him Clarence, even though almost everyone else called him Twerp or Clancy. He was very bright, full of great ideas and pithy expressions, like saying, "Whitewater, go back" when approaching a rapid.

I learned the most from him when on a private trip down the upper reaches of the Owyhee River. It was just him, Tim, and me. They each had an Avon pro raft rowing solo while I kayaked. It was an epic journey that started out in 6 inches of snow, lots of lining, and a few portages, where we all learned some harsh lessons from nature. Clarence's time in the Navy gave him tons of knot-tying experience that came in handy in many ways on that expedition.

Often having only two or three days at Boatland between river trips, guides spent most of the time patching, painting, or maintaining boats, and packing for, or unpacking from, a trip, all without pay. We did so because of our love of boats and rivers. There was little free time because dory boats require a lot of TLC, but sometimes we would get stoned and go to the Sambo's restaurant in town to enjoy some laughs from watching people.

I was always a lightweight in the drug department, but with many trips under my belt I had learned that every trip had at least one guest who smoked pot. I was astounded at how common it was. Attorneys, doctors, every profession seemed to be represented when it came to those who were willing to break the law for recreational use of marijuana.

Another habit that astounded me was the boatmen's meeting that we always held on the beach after lunch and before heading toward our next camp. The trip leader, or TL, would tell guests that boatmen always met privately (in what guides called the back room) to discuss the game plan for the rest of the day. In reality, it was to take a toke or two of green smoke and tell a joke or story or two before going back to the boats and downriver.

It was fun, but I didn't smoke as much as most of the other guides, and never when we had challenging rapids ahead. Some guides actually used it before harder rapids, and I questioned them about how they could skillfully negotiate rapids under the influence. It was nothing I ever wanted to do.

However, they claimed that it helped them, which I had a hard time believing, because being in their comfort zone mattered most. They were so used to being in another worldly state that when they were not stoned, it felt foreign and they performed more poorly. They felt better when stoned, and it seemed they were not far off the mark in executing their skills. They believed they would do better, and it appeared they did.

It's an interesting theory but still questionable to me. I'm not sure that it would hold up as a defense in court in case of a river related catastrophe. Thankfully, we never had any carnage bad enough to warrant testing that out in the years I worked for GCD.

As I gained enough experience to become a trip leader, I had the opportunity to mentor other aspiring river guides, many of whom went on to illustrious careers and fame of their own.

Jack Kappas apprenticed with me on the Owyhee River and was in the bow of my boat, the Clearwater, when I went down the wrong channel of a rapid I misidentified because of high water. Thinking it was a different rapid, I headed down the wrong side of the river and didn't know whether we would make it or not once I saw the boulder garden full of large holes and narrow chutes. It was too late to readjust, so I told Jack to hang on and be ready to high side big time, because we were in deep shit. Luckily, the river let us through.

Many years later, after we all had left GCD for different paths, Jack become the well-known river ranger for the Lower Salmon and Riggins area, based out of Cottonwood, under the supervision of LuVerne Grussing. Jack was a respected figure in the Riggins community, especially in the boating world, but unfortunately alcoholism eventually led to his early death at age 67. Very sad.

Another interesting boatman who apprenticed with me was Vince Welch, who did his first trip with me on the Grande Ronde. An incident that stuck in my mind from that trip happened on the first night, when we discovered we had forgotten one of the guest's sleeping bags. What to do?

A cute female guide who was part of our crew offered to share her sleeping bag with any male guide who would give up theirs to the guest. The guys flipped coins for the privilege and Vince won the toss. Only he can tell more about that part of the story. Sorry.

Eventually, Vince worked his way into guiding many trips in the Grand Canyon before moving on to pursuing his other serious interest in a writing career. He co-authored a book on the life of Buzz Holmstrom, and then came out with a book of his own about the life of another famous boatman, Amos Burg.

Steve Reynolds, known as Wren, apprenticed with me in Hells Canyon. He was very funny and we had a great time together. He also came to my side when I had to deal with some other guides who felt threatened when I became a trip leader.

One image of him still sticks in my mind. It was a time when he was working another trip on the Snake and came floating past my party camped at a place I named Faces, after figures in the shoreline cliffs next to our kitchen area. He was quite far away in the big river's main current, but for good fun, I found some extra eggs to lob his way, trying to splatter his dory. Just by chance, he had some eggs of his own on board, so hatches flew open, eggs were grabbed quickly and launched back my way. People were running, dodging, and hunkering behind rocks as an egg war erupted as their boats floated past. I can still see those eggs flying through the air and splattering like an artillery barrage.

I laugh thinking back about Steve and that encounter. He, too, eventually went on to work in the Grand Canyon, and he was one of the three who made a record-setting 37-hour run through the canyon in 1983 when the Colorado flooded to an all-time high. It was a 277-mile trip organized by Kenton Grua, who rounded up Rudy Petschek and Wren to make the wild journey with him. The entire story is epic and can be found in Kevin Fedarko's excellent book "The Emerald Mile."

The Emerald Mile was the name of their boat. It was another Briggs design and the same wooden dory that had held the previous speed record for running the Grand, also made by Grua, Petschek, and another GCD oarsman, Wally Rist. That 1980 effort was broken in 1983 by more than 10 hours.

I knew all three of the new record holders, but only one, Rudy, who is now in his 80s, is still alive. Kenton suffered a fatal heart attack while mountain biking at age 52. Wren had his own sailboat and cruise company in Hawaiian waters but eventually succumbed to alcoholism, like Jack, and, unfortunately, a lot of people in America. Perhaps he would have been better off if only he had stuck to pot smoking.

I enjoyed working with many other guides during my years with GCD, but as the popularity of river running boomed, our work schedules became more hectic and the family-like feeling we once had was diminished. We were launching simultaneous trips on different rivers, and sometimes even on the same river. The number of guests on each trip also grew to the point where it was difficult to even learn everyone's name. This was too big for me and became the impetus for me to bow out and begin my own company to specialize in smaller trips. I preferred clan size rather than the larger tribes the company's trips were turning into.

And though it might seem a weird way to end this chapter, and despite rarely doing the pot thing myself anymore, it seems strange to me that there is still a political war over pot in this nation. I doubt that marijuana is a gateway to bad drugs, and I believe it is far less impactful than alcoholism. That alcohol was legalized long ago but pot only recently, and only in a few places, is astounding.

Having more than 40 years in the guiding profession, I have learned that GCD did not have a monopoly on pot-smoking guides. Some outfitters now do drug testing, as river outfitting has become more of a corporate affair and legal liability is a major consideration. But guides usually find a way around the system, as do people in almost every other profession.

If I had to ride through rapids in a boat with a guide who was either highly intoxicated or high from good ganja, I'm going green every time. Personally, I prefer the natural high as I float on a river, either by myself or with friends or guests. The current in the water is all the "electricity" I need to get charged up.

Chapter 9

THE GREEN ROOM

One of my most colorful Hells Canyon memories goes back to my second year of guiding. It was a commercial trip and ground zero for the naming of the infamous "Green Room" at Granite Rapids. After much pull and tug with management, we finally finagled permission for one of our favorite shuttle drivers to accompany us on the river.

Everyone called him Rat, though I cannot recall why, but he was cool. His long hair, drawling "far out man" manner of speaking, and happy-hippie, green-smoke-induced vision of the world were always highly entertaining. We were excited to get him on the water and, on the second day, came up with the idea of convincing him to run Granite Rapids in one of our flimsy inflatable two-man Tahiti kayaks. These were brought along for guests who desired a higher level of excitement, but they were a pain in the neck for the guides because they often blew out valves, needed patching, and were a constant babysitting chore.

We thought Rat would love the extra thrill and the fact that he wouldn't have to be in a boat full of inquisitive strangers. We gave him a paddle and some quick instructions before sending him on his happy way. There was a high degree of comedic drama, almost like watching an unsuspecting lemming, high in la-la land, go over the brink of Nirvana. However, the resulting enlightenment was not inspired by anything close to finding Nirvana. It was more like gaining a better appreciation for self-preservation and learning a cautionary lesson against future set-ups and "gotcha" moments.

The lead dory had already run first and was eddied out immediately below the rapid for back-up and rescue. Rat was following the next dory to enter the rapid, and a sweep boat trailed him. I was watching from high on shore, taking pictures before starting my run. Rat dropped bluntly over the hump and into a wall of green and white that totally consumed him and his boat. Fully engulfed! Gone from sight! Then, several yards downstream, the bottom of an orange boat and a bobbing head in a stupor of confusion suddenly popped up.

He was soon rescued, and when out on shore, looking like a drowned rat in drenched shoulder-length hair, he began his story. With soaked jeans and a faded green patch where his baggie of pot had been, he mesmerized us with his account of the ordeal. Over and over, what dominated the telling was his descriptive exclamation: "It was the green room, man!" And from that day forward the name has stuck. Everyone now knows that it comes out with the right water level, and when you are in the V and heading straight for it, there is no mistake. It is "The Green Room," man. Thanks, Rat.

Chapter 10

FROM BIGFOOT TO BAMBI

No baloney this time. One of my most remarkable life experiences happened during the second year I guided for GCD. Having earned my way up to the status of lead boatman, I headed a group of about 30 people and six or seven dories on a six-day Hells Canyon trip.

On day two, I held a short meeting after breakfast and informed everyone that we were going to do something a little different. Rather than continue downriver toward the next night's camp in a tight group as we normally did, I offered all the boatman and guests an alternative. "Do something different, go or do something you have always wanted to do but never had the chance before, or dream up something new," I told them.

They were instructed to go their separate ways until lunch, when we would meet again and continue together toward camp after eating.

I had three guests with me that day, and my choice was to hike a side canyon I had always wanted to explore. It was a place that is easy to miss because a swift current carries most floaters past without them even noticing it. What attracted me was a very narrow, steep-sided, slot-like canyon containing a small stream named Cougar Creek that drained into the main river on the west shoreline.

It is across the river from Kirkwood bar, where we parked to take our hike. Because it was so brushy, we mostly were restricted to wading up the creek bottom. That was awesome because it held several small 3- to 4-foot waterfalls that we climbed around as we continued up the canyon. The heat that day was blast furnace hot, so the cool cathedral-like canopy and cold creek water provided a welcome respite.

Once past the last little falls, we spooked a mule deer doe and saw her scurry around the bend ahead of us. When we turned the bend, she was gone, but what caught our attention was a spectacular falls. It was cascading about 30 feet over a vertical wall formed by an ancient lava flow.

I led the group toward the base of the falls, which required climbing a steep bunchgrass slope with scattered hackberry trees. We headed upward leaning into the severe angle of ascent.

When hiking in rattlesnake country, it is always paramount to pay special attention to the placement of each hand and foot. Part way up, as I was beginning to take a step into the shade of an overhanging hackberry tree, movement suddenly caught my eye. With my survival instincts registering the possibility of a rattlesnake, I stopped immediately and drew back. Too late. I was had. Had that is by the shocking surprise of cradling a newborn fawn in my arms. At first, I didn't even know what it was or how it had gotten there. I had spooked it by almost stepping on it, and as it jumped up to leave, it fell backward into my arms.

It began to struggle and made some bleating sounds before calming down. I turned around, and the person behind me took a picture of it for proof of what we had seen. Then I slowly lowered it to the ground so it could scamper off toward its mother. It soon disappeared, leaving us all in a state of awe. For me, it was a natural high, far better than anything a green herb could produce. I was on cloud nine the entire day afterward. In fact, it was the highlight of my entire boating season. No baloney!

Chapter 11

SALMON FALLS FOLLY

Having gotten through my early years of learning how to negotiate whitewater without ever tipping over a raft, my goal was to extend that record once I began guiding in a dory boat. Like anyone who engages raw nature face to face, I knew that risk is part of the rush and is inherent in the deal made with oneself when tackling adventures fraught with danger.

During my second year working with the dories, I was scouting a rapid called Salmon Falls when I saw a guide for another company approach the drop in a yellow raft. He turned his raft sideways, let it slide directly up onto the huge cushion of water boiling around the middle boulder, and used that to surf off to the left for a really cool entry. Then he dipped his oars, pulled left to stay out of two boat-eating holes, and hit a highway of smooth water for a gallant exit. I was impressed and thought perhaps I might be able to do that in a dory.

I didn't have the courage to try it that day, and after watching the unknown guide's run, we instead ran down the middle and right side of the falls. However, the image of that raft haunted me every time thereafter when I approached Salmon Falls.

The name Salmon Falls is a misnomer to people who have never seen it. Rather than being a vertical falls, it is just a big drop caused by several large boulders close together in a straight line all the way across the river. The resulting barrier forms a natural dam-like impediment that pools water behind it and creates a severe hydraulic jump of several feet below. It's not a waterfall, but rather falling water of sizable consequence that causes a cardiac jump for any boater approaching it.

I was running 13-day back-to-back trips that year from Corn Creek to Heller Bar, and a time came when we scouted Salmon Falls and found it had the right water level to warrant my first attempt at duplicating that amazing raft run that had so impressed me.

It was nerve-wracking because everyone else was taking the traditional lines, and my route had never been done in a dory.

It is hard to breathe when your heart is in your throat, but scattered thoughts are quickly brought into tight focus as the brain prepares to pull off a difficult task. In the moment of truth, when one passes the point of no return, adrenaline-soaked muscles prepare the body for fight or flight. Once past the horizon line of entry into the madly frenzied froth, flight was no longer an option, and fate took over.

My boat rode up onto the cushion, momentarily stopped, as did my heart, and suddenly slid off the left side toward the menacing holes. My nerve toxins kicked in as I dipped oars and pulled hard. There was enough time to surf off the face of the last wave and make it to safety below. I was ecstatic. It was so cool, and that became my standard route for the next few times I was at Salmon Falls with the right water level.

Young guides, or younger people in general, often have more hormones than brains. My wife calls it testosterone poisoning. It is probably some sort of function left over from times when early people had to explore new country in search of more plentiful fish and game to eke out a living. Some kind of fuel is needed to push people forward into high-risk endeavors when otherwise they would be either too afraid or complacent to move on.

Scientists say people who need high adventure have low levels of serotonin and must do these things to up the amperage. Whatever the reason, I had such energizers coursing through my veins during my Salmon Falls runs, and I enjoyed it immensely.

Unfortunately, my days of bouncing safely off the cushioned boulder were numbered, and my record of no tip-overs was about to fall. On that fateful day, I had two guests, a small woman and a large man. Neither had a good sense for moving fast, or moving at all for that matter, as the boat came up on its side and teetered on the edge of equilibrium.

I had made the top surf off the cushion, sliding around and down to face the big hole and wave, but I missed a critical back stroke with both oars. So instead of surfing to the right side of the wave face, the river sucked me into the hole and turned us up on a side in a heartbeat. Time stood still and it was a slow-motion tip-over, or so it seemed, as I was as high as a high-sider could get, to no avail.

I also remember thinking at the time that had my two passengers been high-siding with me, surely the boat would have crawled out of the hole. That is how slow the tip-over was. My worst mistake, aside from missing crucial oar strokes, apparently had been in not giving proper high-siding instructions and not stressing the extreme importance of being ready to act before the plunge.

Fortunately, we didn't get trashed and just went for a swim. I immediately climbed up to the bottom of my boat and hauled the big guy up with me while other boats rescued the woman. Then we grabbed my flip lines and righted the boat.

While it was a very good recovery, my goal of keeping a clean record of a right-side-up boating career faded into the land of impossible dreams. While harshly humbling, it was a good experience for learning first-hand how to deal with that kind of mishap, and it eliminated any pressure for maintaining such a lofty goal when I arrived at the top of difficult rapids in the future.

Chapter 12

DANCING WITH THE DEVIL AT FOOL'S ROCK

What does the Devil's Slide have in common with Colt 45?

Nothing.

Water and alcohol do not mix, especially when that water is funneling through the second deepest gorge in America where solid cliffs on one side and a rock slide on the other pinch the longest free-flowing river within one state down through a narrow chute maybe 50 yards wide. On a normal day, you could shout at someone on the other side of the river and be heard quite easily, but on July 2, 1978, the thunderous roar of the monster rapid there was so loud you couldn't even hear yourself think.

The Devils Slide is only a nemesis of a rapid in high water on the Lower Salmon River. It disappears entirely in low flows of less than 4,000 cubic feet per second. While some may need the liquid courage of one can after another of Colt 45 beer to muster up enough steam to run a rapid when it becomes fearsome, it in no way helps keep a raft right side up. Such was the case that day when I was working for Grand Canyon Dories and we were on a high-water commercial trip that landed us where we didn't want to be.

The water flow was at 35,200 cfs, which renders the Slide something akin to a giant fire hose blasting tons of water at high velocity through a small orifice. The physics term for this event is called the Venturi effect – or nozzle effect, as I like to call it.

The guide roster for that trip included three company dory guides and one guest guide hired to run a baggage raft, an Avon Pro. Clancy Reece led the trip in a glass dory, the Ne Parle Pas; Barry Dow rowed a wooden dory, the Copper Ledge Falls; and I had a twin glass dory, the Redwood Creek. For saving face, I will refer to the rent-a-guide as Colt 45 Chip. He thought we dory people were snobs who worried too much about getting our delicate little boats through a rapid he thought looked more like just some good big fun and no big deal.

This rapid was formed around 1950 by a giant rock slide that tumbled into the river from the western shore. Legend has it that people in a cabin six miles away felt compression waves caused by the magnitude of the slide, but it's likely that a slight earthquake caused both the slide and the tremors.

In its aftermath, that giant rumble left behind the potential for the mighty force of a high-flow rapid we now had to deal with. It is a class V rapid when above flows of 25,000 cfs, but that day we were looking at getting our three dory boats and one 16-foot raft through the nastiness of it all at 35,200 cfs. This is the story of how Fool's Rock got its name on a day when all of us running the god-awful gauntlet would have rather been somewhere else.

We were on a five-day Salmon River trip that had launched June 29 at Whitebird, only 30 miles upriver of the Slide. While the Whitebird gauge on our launch day was at 36,800 cfs, it was predicted to drop, which was the reason we were given the green light to conduct the trip. We were told that if the river did not drop enough, management would send in a road crew to pick us up at Eagle Creek so we could avoid running the apish water.

Barry was the only guide to have run the rapid earlier in the spring in flows around 34,000 cfs. At that time, he was with some other guides to determine if later commercial trips would be feasible at that flow. They had hairball runs and barely made it, so it was determined to be too marginal for commercial guests at that level.

By the day we arrived at the Slide, it was slightly higher than what Barry and his crew had faced on their trial run. However, management miscalculated and did not follow through with plan B. They underestimated the river and believed that there was only slightly more water and that it was within reason to run. They did hire a jetboat and pilot, the famed Everett Spalding, to meet us at the rapid to ferry women, kids, and anyone who didn't want to make the run around the rapid and then to serve as a backup for the guides bringing willing guests through the Slide.

The Eagle Creek access road 15 miles upriver of the rapid offered our last chance for an escape route via a bumpy backcountry road to avoid the mighty maelstrom waiting for us below. Riding over a class V road would have been preferable to dancing with the devil on class V whitewater.

The morning of that fateful day, we four guides were in good spirits. Having guessed the river level was still too high to run, we prepared for plan B, thinking our worries were over.

Once we packed up and left camp, we thought we would be seeing our shuttle rigs when we got to Eagle Creek. We waited for a long time, expecting rigs any minute, but they never came. Soon our spirits took a dive as we realized we would have to continue down river to meet the Devil.

By the time we got to Blue Canyon, we decided to do lunch at a nice sandbar at the entry to the steep-walled gorge. However, all of us guides were so worried about the hydraulics ahead that we could not eat. The sky was blue with lots of sun as guests ate their lunch rather nervously, while we guides tried not to reveal our hard-to-hide fears and put on game faces that probably revealed far more than we wished to convey.

When we were once again on the river, a few clouds began to stream in from the canyon's western rim. As we neared the Slide, the clouds grew darker and more ominous. Lightning flashed across the sky and thunder crashed deafeningly as we pulled into a micro eddy on river left to reach our scouting point. It was as if the Devil was warning us with a pitchfork and a vehemently loud voice. The entire scene was unworldly weird as we secured our boats, then climbed a precipitous slope and a jumbled mound of elephant-size boulders to see what the river had in store for us.

From high above, we could see another large boulder that would offer a better vantage from which to scout. On top it had a small depression of pooled water that held a couple of dead salmon, which in itself was not a good sign. Though we didn't know it then, fish biologists now believe that flows above 30,000 to 40,000 cfs impede salmon migration. The velocity of the current is so strong that even the powerful anadromous fish that live in such chaos must pool up to wait for lower flows to make their passage.

As leader of the trip, Clancy spotted that same salmonized rock and announced, "Anyone who wants to run this rapid is a fool, so those of you that want to run, meet down there on "Fool's Rock."

Having gotten a closer view of the rapid after reaching that rock, I had an eerie negative epiphany. It was the first time I had ever looked at a rapid and tried to determine the best placement for being in an upside down boat. I just wanted to survive the run and get flushed on through it, rather than being thrown into the giant whirlpools on river left or caught in the maw of the two giant ocean-like waves rolling parallel to each other on river right. They recycled in a continuous back-loop upriver and into the matrix of mayhem just slight of center. We dubbed them the "Things" for lack of a better name to describe something none of us had ever seen before. It was uggggly.

As we three dory guides conferred to determine a good game plan, the rent-a-guide thought we were just prima-donna dory elitists making a mountain out a molehill.

Meanwhile, since there was no sign of the jetboat that had been promised, we had to figure out what to do with the women, children, and men who did not want to run the rapid. It was a bleak situation, until finally the jetboat arrived with another dory crew. The cavalry had come. Some of them began to escort guests through the maze of rocks on a class V hike to bypass the river's outrage and reach the jetboat awaiting below. This gave us fools on Fool's Rock more time to figure out our foolish runs.

All hikers safely below the rapid, the jetboat was maneuvered into position to assist any of our boats, which would be run one at a time, should we need it. And all but one did.

Barry ran first, with two men in the bow, so we could see what would happen and alter our runs, if possible, depending on his experience. He made a river-left stern entry, which is called "powelling." This term was coined after Major John Wesley Powell's pioneering trip down the Grand Canyon, because he faced downstream and called orders out to his boatmen, who rowed downriver with their backs toward the rapids. Even though boatmen today row with the bow facing into the rapids, anytime they have to turn around and pull sternward with their backs facing downriver, they use this meaningful reference.

Barry aimed for a very slight soft spot in the largest diagonal entry wave, which funneled its power into the middle of the rapid, where the bigger, uglier waves were exploding. He hit it just right, but the wall of water kicked like a mule and knocked him into the stern of his dory. Luckily, some angel wings helped his boat through to the backside of the wave, staying right side up. As he climbed back to the oars, the giant hybrid eddy-whirlpool below spun his boat into a 360-degree circle faster than the blink of an eye. He missed hitting the wall by less than a foot, which would have made kindling out of his wooden boat, and it scared those of us watching as much as it did him.

Once Barry regained control, he just managed to make it to shore below the next rapid. Then cowboy Chip mounted his raft to make the next plunge, lemming style. But when he rounded the corner and saw the full magnitude of the rapid, he froze like a deer in the headlights and immediately flipped on the same wave faster than you can say, "Oh, shit." The jetboat gave him an immediate assist by holding the raft in place so it could be righted before getting swept into the next rapid.

I was next with three guests. After watching all this carnage, I decided to go for a middle run. The idea was to hit a marginal V in the middle where several waves converged into a vortex of sheer energy. My intent was to enter the center between two giant waves so they would hit me from opposite sides at the same time, offsetting each other, and squirting me through right side up in the process.

But when I rounded the corner with and saw the depression Barry had made, I hesitated, which is my 20-20 hindsight analysis of what went wrong. That moment cost me focus time, and I ended up being only a couple of feet from hitting both waves simultaneously. Instead, the right wave hit the bow first and sent us all flying. We were blasted by such power that it felt like someone on shore had pushed a plunger to explode a dynamite charge under the right side of my bow out there in the middle of frenzied chaos.

I was able to grab hold of the leg of one of my guests who was still clinging to the boat, and soon we were both up on the bottom of the tipped over dory. The jetboat came by to hold us in place while we righted it and recomposed ourselves to run the next rapid and eddy out a little below Barry. In my mind, I can still see an image of Barry as I went by. He sat on the shore visibly stunned, just shaking his head side to side in disbelief.

Neither of us could see it, but we soon learned that Clancy had more or less duplicated my run and had the same result. Invisible gremlins on the cliff side had exploded another round of dynamite and blew his boat over, too. When all was said and done, we had flipped three of four boats. That was, and still is, my worst record for consecutive flips in one rapid during a career of guiding multi-day trips on remote rivers.

There were still plenty of big-water rapids yet to run before getting to the Snake, but, with adrenaline pumping, we made them all and reached our final night on the river at Cottonwood Creek. It didn't take long to get there with the river flowing at such extreme velocity, but our night was made more difficult because the firebox we used for cooking had been lost when my bow compartment flew open during my flip. We had to cobble together a stone fire ring for cooking, which deepened the curses we aimed at management for their shaky decision not to pull us out.

We were pissed, but several beers helped, as did our recounting of carnage tales far into the night. The telling, like a never-ending feedback loop, seemed eventually to ease our post-traumatic stress. We fool's who survived the Slide had formed a bond thanks to the unforgettable experience that was burned deep into our minds. To this day, I salute Fool's Rock every time I get near it, no matter what water level, raging or mellifluous.

Chapter 13

OLD-TIMERS WHO PAINTED THE CANYON WITH THEIR CHARACTER

During my first couple of years with the Dories, I mostly lived in Hells Canyon, but when I got the opportunity to guide more on the Main Salmon, that became my home for the summer.

From a marketing standpoint at that time, before the American psyche was revved to a hyped-up super pace, longer trips were easier to sell. So our normal trip took 13 days to cover the 200 miles between Corn Creek and Heller Bar. For me, being an ardent lover of wild places, it was a dream job. To be out in such grand country for such long periods, often with back-to-back trips, made living on the river a virtual reality.

I was also fortunate to be there at a time when some historic figures, who are now gone, lived along the river. I am grateful to have had that opportunity, and reflecting back on their passing is a stark reminder of my own sound-bite relevance on this cosmic orb and of how my time is draining away at too fast of a pace.

A benefit of history is that it gives people still living a chance to examine how much the land has been changed by the action, or inaction, of those who came before us. Like the wind that blows dust across the planet, the natural drift of humans across the landscape is also an agent for altering the environment, for better or worse.

One memorable character who drifted into the canyon environs was Frances Zaunmiller, who was living by herself when we first met. How I came to make her acquaintance is an interesting story.

Tom Rambo, a boatman on one of my trips, had brought along a gift that he was eager to pass along to her. The week before, during a company trip that I had not been on, Tom had flipped his dory at Elkhorn Rapids in some very high water.

He had gone into the middle of the mega boat-eating hole at the bottom of Elkhorn, and the ensuing flip broke off the entire stern area of his dory. A woman sitting there by herself, still gripping the gunnels, suddenly found herself adrift amid a chaos of turbulent water.

After the anguished and suddenly isolated woman, along with miscellaneous gear, had been safely retrieved, camp was immediately made and repair work commenced. The problem was figuring out a way to make the boat float long enough to get it out of the canyon without sinking. Tom hiked all the way to Frances' place and pleaded his case.

Sympathizing with him, she offered him the only thing she had to help remedy the situation. Her old sewing machine had a piece of wood large enough to patch up the back end of his boat, making it seaworthy again and saving his bacon. So he was determined to pay his dues with replacement wood for her machine, and I was with him when he hauled it from the river up to her place.

She was quite the independent woman, and not overly friendly, it seemed to me. However, the thing I remember most was her showing me a cougar skull that had a .22 bullet hole in it. She told me she was the one who had shot it, and I think there was an underlying message to her story: Don't mess with Frances Zaunmiller. She was a tough cookie but fell victim to throat cancer, dying in 1986 at age 73.

Another, perhaps more famous, character who drifted into the canyon and stayed was known as Buckskin Bill. That wasn't his real name, and he was very different from Frances, who sought privacy in a more hidden location. Sylvan Hart's place was right along the river, and he actually enjoyed company.

The first time I met him, I asked how he had found this ideal spot on the river and how his unique structures had come about. He first led me over to a little cellar and told me it was a tornado shelter. Having come from Oklahoma, where twisters are a fact of life, he wasn't taking any chances with storms out west. So he dug in, not knowing that funnel clouds hardly ever occur in Idaho, especially in the state's deep canyons.

He also had an interesting sniper's roost, fortified by logs and armed with guns on turrets, to protect him from the U.S. Forest Service, which he feared might try to take away his land. He was a good bit paranoid, to put it mildly, as is the case with a lot of folks who purposely escape civilization and live alone for long periods of time. He mostly lived off the land, and not always within all the rules and regulations of the outside world, so some of his fears may have been justified.

Often when we would camp across the river from his fortress, we would row over in the evenings and bring him to our side to have dinner with us. He loved the attention that his storytelling drew, and he was a big hit with guests. We later would row him back home in the dark. The next morning we would gather up firewood to take to him as a gift and would hike with guests up to his cabins, where he'd entertain them again. He loved it.

The first thing he always did was to pick out a good looking young lady, lead her inside one of his little storage buildings, and dress her up in a buffalo skirt or some other off-the-wall attire. Then he would parade her out in front of everyone in his version of a Salmon River fashion show.

He would also show us the oddities he had collected, such as pickled cougar kittens, and provide elaborate explanations for them all. He was especially proud of his gun collection and liked to demonstrate how they were made and how they functioned. All were meticulously handmade from scratch, including beautiful mahogany wood stocks that were inlaid with ivory-like bighorn sheep horn. He arranged the intricate artwork so that it all told a story like a pictograph on a rock.

He also had a set of giant skis that looked to be about a mile long, six inches wide, and an inch thick. Outrageously, he claimed that the fancy, skinny skis used by present-day skiers could not hold a candle to his homemade contraptions.

Many of our boatmen, who were professional ski patrol members when not working as river guides, had to bite their tongues while chuckling to themselves. They all laughed as he talked about his escapades on such monstrosities in extreme mountain conditions. Although they were extreme embellishments of astonishing journeys possible only in la-la land, they were fun to hear and were never to be forgotten.

Unfortunately, good times and good people don't last forever. Buckskin passed away in 1980 at age 74. It is told that during a graveside service along the river that he called home, a few of his favorite bighorns came down to grace his farewell ceremony and pay tribute to their fallen buddy. Such is the connections we form when we communicate in the earth's language.

Chapter 14

KAYAK MAGIC

In the fall of 1976, after guiding all season, I invited my friend Dave Baum, (aka "the General") to a private trip on the Lower Salmon with a few of my GCD guide friends. From a dory boat he watched as we kayakers surfed our brains out on every wave we could catch. All our tricks inspired the same bug in him, and he was determined to get into such an intriguing sport. He couldn't see why I should be having all the fun, so he solicited my help in getting him a boat after our trip.

However, he needed two boats because his wife, Anna, wanted one, too. After they took my advice and got kayaks like I was paddling, a TJ-1 (Tom Johnson) glass boat, I worked with them on roll practice and some paddling basics before hitting the river. They continued practicing on their own and soon became accomplished kayakers and my best buddy-boaters when I wasn't guiding. Many trips and resulting stories ensued.

After Dave had more experience and a dynamite roll, I took him to Captain Lewis Rapids on the Snake River. It was a short distance below Heller Bar and contained some giant surf waves. They were hard to catch but an awesome ride when the planets aligned. The downside was that a super strong roll was required, because there was a major Maytag effect when you were upside down.

We surfed all afternoon, and on one run, a GDC crew coming off a commercial trip stopped along the road to watch us. As they did, Dave's dog jumped into the river, perhaps in an attempt to retrieve him while he was surfing. The dog got ate but rolled up and eddied out near the road. The watchful guides, never missing an opportunity for a good harangue, hollered out, "Hey, your dog had a better run than you did." We all got a good laugh over that one.

Later that night, as Dave and I sat around the fire drinking whiskey and enjoying the full moon, we wondered what it might be like to surf Captain Lewis by moonlight. Jack Daniels talked us into it, so we abandoned camp and headed off to attempt our hare-brained idea. We agreed to do just one surf and call it good. Luckily, both of us surfed the face, didn't flip, and paddled safely back to shore unscathed. Johnnie Walker, or was it Jack Daniels, kissed us goodnight. Awesome.

A year or two later, we expanded our private circle by adding another boater, Spencer Grogan. He was one of my students when I taught kayaking at Eastern Oregon State College. As the institution's first kayaking instructor, I had access to its indoor pool and the nearby Grande Ronde River to use as teaching tools. It was an ideal setup for coaching students, in addition to being an opportune place to entice new blood into our kayaking group.

From my time teaching kayaking I learned that while some students could master good technique in the pool, not all had the cool-headedness and special psychological makeup needed to be a real-world river kayaker.

Besides having a serious thirst to boat with us, Spencer was one of those who did not panic when his head was under water. I knew this was true after he told me about a bad rafting experience he had with his dad and other friends on the Owyhee River, before he ever stepped foot into a kayak. The Owyhee mishap ended with him being forcing to swim through the god-awful tunnel created by a giant leaning slab of rock at Whistlebird Rapid. His story impressed me because I thought it was next to impossible to survive that swim, and if he could do that, he had the right stuff to be a kayaker.

Besides doing a lot of boating together, we shared some outstanding overland adventures. On one such trip, Spencer led me on a descent into one of his secret places, the location of which I can't even remember. It was like a land-mass island surrounded by a circular river canyon in the middle of the high desert. Sounds weird, but having seen it, I know it to be true. It was almost like discovering the ultimate place for an eternal river trip. Round and round, no start, no end, the perfect perpetual motion machine. The vertical walls on both sides and all around the island were maybe 300 feet high. We had to descend a side chute barely possible without technical aid to get to the bottom. It was dreamlike, and since I can't remember how to get there, it seems even more so now.

Unfortunately, after a couple of years of kayaking and exploring together, another calling lured Spencer to a different world and we lost sight of him. It was sad because he was a fun-loving and like-minded comrade for sharing wild escapades.

After that, Dave, Anna, and I spent a lot of time boating the Grande Ronde above LaGrande, and we would always call one another when the river jumped up and granted us another excuse to get on the water. We also made many side trips to the Salmon River because it always had good water, even when the Grande Ronde became too tame for us. But there are many other reasons why the Salmon River is such a seductress.

Chapter 15

ROLLERCOASTER, SKOOKUMCHUCK, AND SPACE ALIENS

Speaking of the cosmos reminds me of another day spent surfing waves at Rollercoaster Rapids on the Lower Salmon River. Being between trips as a commercial guide, I called Dave and Anna to coax them into driving over from Oregon to meet me on the river. All it took to get them to agree to make the rendezvous was my telling them about a place where we could spend all day just playing the same waves and not worrying about a shuttle.

It was a beautiful bluebird day, and the surfable waves were optimal. The eddy that enabled our recycling access to them required a bit of a workout, but it was well worth the strained effort.

In our long boats, which are considered dinosaurs today, we managed many great popups and pirouettes. It was just as much fun watching each other as it was to catch a wave ourselves. Enders that resulted in upside down kayaks, wildly flung braces, missed rolls, and other humorous modes of carnage were all part of the entertainment.

By the end of the day, we were spent as we dragged our boats up the beach to load them onto our rigs. To grace our day, we were treated to a very close encounter with a golden eagle that flew by. Perhaps we looked like wounded prey to a hungry raptor as we staggered around the water's edge?

Once packed, we drove through hot dust on a primitive road to join the main highway and proceed up the river to a good campsite for the night. Skookumchuck wayside was our destination. It had a restroom and a sand beach the size of a football field for daytime recreational use by locals and tourists. We were lucky because there wasn't another rig or person in sight that late in the evening.

For grilling burgers, Dave had a "trick" bucket setup that contained the coals and kept the beach clean. After finishing dinner, we stoked the fire and sat in the dark talking under the twinkling stars of far off worlds.

This beach is located along the highway between Riggins and Whitebird, and though the road is a main artery connecting south eastern and north western Idaho, it does not get a lot of traffic. This was especially true in the late 1970s when we were there. Aside from an occasional semi-truck putting in long hours, nary a vehicle passed by. We felt pretty much alone and loved having a camp all to ourselves.

Before heading off to slumber land, we sat visiting and pondering a wide variety of topics. I threw out a "what if" scenario for contemplation with a question: If a spaceship landed on this beach and made contact with us, would you tell anyone else? After we had spent a few minutes discussing what we might do, we suddenly heard, and then saw, two dark forms approaching us. It was surreal.

It was a young couple. Since we had seen no other cars, bikes, camps, or people on the beach since our arrival, this was eerily strange. "Where did you come from?" I asked. They replied, "We are from Mars," and then they turned around, walked back into the night, and were never seen again.

We were temporarily stunned, then had to laugh. Perhaps a clue to what had happened was in the name locals had given to the campsite: "Smoochandfuck." The young couple probably had been having a romantic encounter in the privacy of a willowy alcove before we arrived and decided to stay hidden. Overhearing our conversation, they couldn't resist messing with our minds. If we had intruded on their lovemaking, maybe they felt justified in fucking with us in turn.

If so, it was a brilliant scheme, and even to this day, I often think about it when I'm on some lonely beach gazing up toward otherworldly places in the la-de-da-da of outer limits and du-du-du-du of the twilight zones of distant space.

Chapter 16

WILD MAN RICK

Dave called me one day to say he had found another person who might have the "right stuff" and interest to become a kayaker. Rick Hamilton did, indeed, qualify as being crazy enough to fit in with us. It didn't take long to size him up on the river and learn how bold he was. He soon became our "hole tester," jumping into questionable mayhem before we were willing to do so and earning the nickname "Wildman Rick." We became hard-core kayaking buddies and had lots of memorable experiences together.

One time, Wildman Rick and I decided to run a tributary of the lower Grande Ronde River called Joseph Creek. It was named after Chief Joseph, the Nez Perce leader who was born in a cave on the lower end of the creek and had a winter camp near the mouth at a place called the Narrows.

We started from the mountain viewpoint on Highway 3 between Enterprise and Boggan's Oasis, not far from the Rim Rock Café. The weather was sunny and nice enough that we stripped down nude while carrying our kayaks on our shoulders during part of the descent. We eventually had to trudge through two-foot snowdrifts to reach the river far below in the canyon.

I always wondered whether the Nez Perce had a trail to follow along the river bottom when they moved between their winter camp along the Narrows and their summer camp at Wallowa Lake. But after seeing the cliffs and impassable places along the river bottom, once we reached it, I could see that their trail must have been more on the top where we started.

We floated about 35 miles in one day. There were some challenging sections, which were not terribly difficult but were strenuously long. Aside from stopping to scout a few times, almost everything could be read from our boats. Barbed wire, strung across the creek in a few bad places, was our biggest worry and something we had to use hawk eyes to see to avoid becoming trapped.

It was an epic voyage, and we were ecstatic to think that we were the first kayakers to have ever done this run. Rick led most of the way, though we did take turns, and at one point a cow elk swam the river in front of us. I got out to scout a few things that Rick felt comfortable reading from his kayak, and in doing so I got to see interesting things on land that he missed because he was totally focused on navigating past the perils of near-blind runs into the unknown.

About a month later, we learned that Whit Deschner and his lady friend had made the run a week before us. They gained access by road into Swamp Creek a couple of miles above our launch site. At least we could take comfort in the fact that our adventure was more challenging because just getting to the creek by the descent we took was a major accomplishment.

For me, the trip also helped to connect pieces of my mental puzzle concerning the entire saga of Chief Joseph's time, clarifying how various aspects of the landscape helped shape the tribe's history. Our trip to Joseph Creek was intriguing and made me appreciate all the more why the Nez Perce people so loved this land.

Chapter 17

DOCTOR DEATH

I can't remember for sure how I first met Paul Daffer, but I suspect Wildman Rick had something to do with it, as they were good friends before I knew either of them. Paul was the next extreme personality to join our kayaking circle. He soon acquired the nickname Dr. Death, thanks to a story only he can tell and not because he was the kind of doctor you would call in a medical emergency,

He also lived in La Grande, Ore., not far from Rick, and I can still vividly remember the first time Rick brought him to Riggins for introductory kayak lessons. We met in town and then headed far up the Main Salmon River, where I was to be part of the instructing team. Plan A was to help Dr. Death learn how to negotiate rapids, work on his roll, and learn to surf.

When we stopped our rig high above the river to road scout Vinegar Creek Rapids, Paul soon lived up to another reputation as a "ruttin' bull elk." As luck would have it, two rafts had stopped to scout the same rapid from the opposite shore far below our eagle-eye viewpoint. The rafters were all women and all were nude.

Dr. Death fought us for the binoculars, which we were using to check the rapids' entry tongue. He tripped over his own tongue trying to scope out a quick line to get through the rapids and catch up to the oh-so-alluring women. Plan B.

Once we got on the water and escorted him through the rapids, we eddied out to wait for him so we could demonstrate proper surfing technique, but he was nowhere to be seen. He had flashed past us like a dog in heat, intent on catching up to a different objective. It irked us a bit, as we had offered to help him improve his boating skills, giving up an opportunity to surf our brains out in our favorite play spot at the Cats Paw. However, he was more interested in honing his "elk in rut" skills. Not that it wasn't tempting for us, too, because we were all single at the time.

Rick and I didn't want to look too pathetically obvious and/or desperate, or violate the women's privacy. That didn't matter to Dr Death. After all, a "ruttin' bull" has only one thing in mind. All else is only a bothersome distraction.

By the time we caught up to him, he was hanging on the side of one of the rafts working his magic. Some women appeared to be annoyed while others seemed to revel in the humor of it all. About then, the town sheriff just happened to be driving upriver, which was unusual because it was not his common beat. Shockingly, he quickly grabbed a bullhorn and began bellowing out loud demands for the women to put on their clothes. Really? What a yahoo. People were out having a good time far from civilization, feeling the freedom of wind and water, only to be slapped in the face by the hand of self-righteous authority.

They grumbled, grabbed some clothes, and began sheltering their curvaceous bodies so as not to corrupt the morally challenged Barny Fife-like cop. We yanked Paul back out of his "rutting daze," bade farewell to the women, and headed downriver to catch a few more waves before calling it a day.

Rick, Paul, and I became good friends and over the years had a host of wild adventures, from "real" elk hunting to other epic river trips.

Chapter 18

FLOWER POWER
FINDING A RIVER WOMAN OPEN TO TIPI LIVING

Dave and Anna continued boating with me any time we could get together. Knowing that I was a bachelor, they eventually brought one of their women friends, Karen Wells, over to my tipi and introduced us. She worked at a local flower shop where she arranged bouquets that helped beautify many people's lives. We hit it off immediately, and a serious relationship soon bloomed for us.

While I made many lasting friendships with men and women guides during my dory days, the growing river company was getting so large that it made me uncomfortable. When I began coming off 30-person, six-day trips without having gotten to know every guest by name, I realized it was time to move on. I still wanted to be a guide, but in a smaller, more intimate way.

The far north had always fascinated me, so I planned a trip to the Tatshenshini River in the Wrangell St. Elias World Heritage Site near Haines Junction, Alaska. I invited my new tipi partner Karen, Dave and Anna, and two guide friends with whom I was considering going into business. They were Barry Dow, who brought his brother, and Tim O'Neil, who brought his girlfriend to round out our party.

We had a great trip on the Tat, but it brought me to the realization that I did not want to be part of a new three-person river company. My dad had always warned me that people often lost friendships after going into business together, and I was afraid it could happen to me. Not wanting to chance losing these friendships, I decided to go it alone.

That was in 1979, the year I bought my own dory and my last year working for GCD. Jerry Briggs, a famous boatbuilder from Grants Pass, Oregon, built my first dory. The hull was a design he had modified with input from Martin Litton. It was called a Grand Canyon River Dory. I added my own touch by drawing up a blueprint for a deck design that would make the boat totally self-bailing.

Up until that time, all the GCD dories had bailing tubes for the boatmen's foot-well, but after a wet ride, guests still had to bail water from their own foot-wells. I believe my dory was the first totally self-bailing one to be put into commercial use. A few other guides quickly followed suit with similar self-bailing modifications. And rafts, too, were soon being made to eliminate the need for bailing.

On our Alaskan trip, we had cut the floors out of conventional rafts to make our own self-bailing rafts, far before they were being made commercially or were available to the public. But not having the inflatable floors that are in use today, our rafts plowed water and squatted deeper in the water, making them harder to row against the current.

Deciding on a name for my new company was a challenge. The answer finally came to me in 1979 during my first viewing of a total solar eclipse. At precisely the time the sun turned black, the name Eclipse Expeditions came to mind. It seemed appropriate because one phase of my life was being eclipsed as I moved into another. Inspired by the solar synchronicity of Alaska, the place of the "midnight sun," being the launching site for my new river venture, I named my boat and company.

However, my outdoor life and rowing experience far outweighed my business acumen. This was new territory to me, and I figured that if the service was good, customers would somehow magically show up. Wrong. Even the name of my company was misleading when it came to marketing. It mostly attracted questions like: "What kind of eclipse-seeking expeditions do you run?"

After that first raft trip in Alaska, I returned to Oregon and began guiding on the Grande Ronde River during the fall elk season. It was much harder than fishing trips or whitewater floats, but easier than dealing with horses used by hunters to pack elk out of the high country.

In the spring I did fishing and whitewater trips, as well as adding the Owyhee River in southeastern Oregon to the mix of trip offerings. That desert river normally only has flows ample enough for good boating from early March through mid-May. Trips are dependent on annual snow packs and the whims of weather conditions.

By then, Karen had joined me in living a tipi lifestyle, which was a major feat for me. It's hard to find a woman willing to embrace that kind of hard-core, outdoor lifestyle year-round. I was elated. She was a neat lady, eager to learn, and together we made a good team. Life suddenly improved by leaps and bounds.

In 1980 we did a trip on the Noatak River above the Arctic Circle in Alaska. It was the first time I had to admit to myself that a river could be boring. Six days of flat tundra on a river with no rapids, wall-to-wall mosquitoes, and 360 degrees of sameness was mind-numbing. However, it also came with a consolation prize worth the boredom. We encountered a caribou migration along the way and found ourselves engulfed by about 20,000 animals as they swam around our raft on a river crossing.

My first thoughts were of what it must have been like to see the buffalo when they thundered across the western plains by the millions. Secondly, it was exciting to appreciate that awe-inspiring wildlife sightings of similar magnitude can still be experienced today.

By the 1981 season, we had gotten a 16-foot drift boat from Bruce Koffler, a builder in Springfield, Oregon. My dad suggested we name it the Wapiti because he knew that was one of my favorite animals. When I later took it to Alaska, where it became one of the first drift boats on the Kenai River, I had an interesting epiphany.

Karen and I were on our way to the Kenai in a passenger van with the quite conspicuous drift boat on top. While driving along the Matanuska River, we saw a commercial rafting group running some roadside rapids, so we pulled into a wide spot nearby to watch them. One of their shuttle drivers who was there saw our boat with the name Wapiti painted brightly on the bow. He looked back upriver at the rafts bouncing through the rapids, glanced again at the name of our boat, and jokingly said, "Oh, I get it, when that boat goes down through the rapids, it goes wapiti, wapiti, wapiti." My epiphany was to change the name of my company to Wapiti River Guides. That name at least told what our service was all about, and the driver's descriptive comment became an easy guide to explain how to pronounce the word "wapiti."

Karen and I chalked up a lot of river miles and fun expeditions over the next three years. Rivers we ran included the Copper, Chitna, Nizna, Tazlina, Nenana, and Tokositna, as well as Lake Creek.

Unfortunately, despite all those outstanding adventures and time together in the far wilds, a dark cloud seemed to sweep over us. Our relationship began to deteriorate, though it was more her idea to break ties than it was mine. Her discontent with me threw me for a loop, and I tried to figure out why.

She could not have children, and I still didn't feel a big desire to have any, so I had stopped thinking about it. Perhaps that issue should have been addressed. Adoption could have been a viable alternative. Either way, I had always thought it would be nice to have a family with kids who would gravitate to guiding and keep the enterprise a tight-knit family affair.

I had not asked for her hand in marriage, so perhaps that was it. Or maybe it was my extreme outdoor lifestyle. Did I compromise enough? What was it? It was another gut-wrenching experience and psychological setback that hit me hard. I felt like a failure. Knowing that I was the common denominator in two failed serious relationships and a few semi-casual ones over the years began to tear down my self-esteem yet again.

What to do? What was wrong with me? How could I become a better person? What needed changing? What was I willing to compromise on in future relationships? I told Karen I would marry her, give up rowing, and go back to conventional wildlife work, but she knew I would not be happy if I did. Her response was quite convincing, and I knew she was right. I would only come to resent her if I gave up the river world.

Just as my first wife grew to resent me because she had to give up too many things that defined her preferred lifestyle, I could appreciate wearing that shoe when it was on the other foot. That realization didn't make me feel much better at the time, but it did help reshape my life and put me on a path to better define how I could attain happiness as a human.

Chapter 19

FOLLOWING MY SHADOW

After my painful breakup with Karen, I continued running my company and hired various other guides on an as-needed basis. But after five seasons in Alaska, I longed for the Salmon River of Idaho. My mind was occupied by the thought of trading clouds, silt, and glacial flows for sun, sand, and warm water. Needing to get my body to where my mind resided, I kept looking for some sort of opportunity to make that happen. It was time to employ intention to actuate the old adage that whatever the mind can conceive and believe, it can achieve.

Dave (The General), Rick (The Wildman), and I (The Chief, as they often called me) would often travel to Riggins from the Grande Ronde Valley, which the Nez Perce and Cayuse called the Valley of Peace because blood was never shed there and it was a place to meet, race horses, and trade goods. We took our kayaks to Riggins to hang out on the Salmon River, where we spent most of our time surfing waves, and on one trip we ran into some interesting characters.

After we finished surfing the Machine Wave on the north bend of town, we headed downriver to find our next play wave and saw a raft pulled up on shore not far below. This was in about 1985, before raft traffic on the river became an everyday occurrence. Back then, seeing other like-minded river people was incentive enough to check them out, and having spotted a pretty woman near the raft, we wasted no time in paddling over to say hello.

Who were these people and what was that suspicious smell?

It turned out to be Mike and Connie Kennedy, along with their close friend Bruce Elmquist. We discovered they were local guides who had pulled in for a temporary smoke break. This gave us some commonality in more ways than one.

As we shared stories and a little herb, we quickly became friends. A few years later, Bruce became my main guide and friend as we worked together and enjoyed a lot of awesome adventures. During that time, Mike and Connie ran trips for other companies and occasionally assisted me and Bruce. We also managed to take a lot of private river trips together, including tons of high-water runs at Ruby and many fast-paced dashes on the busy current of the Little Salmon River.

But after bidding them farewell on the day we met, Dave, Rick, and I continued downriver. As we surfed, I kept visualizing ways to get a permit to lead trips on the river and find a way back to my "spawning grounds."

With more time and distance away from unfortunate experiences with women, my luck began to turn for the better, and a series of events fell into place to help facilitate my intention. An Oregon outfitter whom I had met in my early years on the Owyhee River, Don Merrill, wanted to sell his Lower Salmon River permit.

This was most fortunate for me because most western rivers are so highly regulated that the fixed numbers of outfitters that can legally run commercial trips on them are maxed out. The only way to obtain a special-use permit, which is required for any commercial activity, is to buy a business that already has one. Only the business can be sold, not the permit, but the permit is always transferred to the new owner. Supply and demand rules, so with supply so scarce, demand boosts the price significantly.

Don had suffered the loss of a guide to sad circumstances on an Owyhee River trip in 1984. The college-age guide misidentified what he thought was an edible plant and ate poisonous water hemlock. Don hiked out of the canyon for help, but it came too late and the guide could not be saved. Distraught and badly shaken by this tragedy, Don decided to get out of the river profession.

Presented with such a good opportunity, I borrowed money and paid him $7,000 for that part of his business. So it was back again to my old Salmon River stomping grounds, and I began looking for a place to stage my whitewater trips. It was 1987, and Riggins was just beginning to get its reputation as the Whitewater Capitol of Idaho. With a goal of getting my river-running sign up on the main street, I drove from Oregon and began searching for a good location.

With me was Jay Silver Tongue (J.S.T., for short and my name for him), who had called me earlier that year to introduce himself and express his interest in helping me with marketing in exchange for my teaching him about guiding and introducing him into the river world. He presented himself as a titan of salesmanship and indeed had a silver tongue.

We went to Riggins to seek a site we could rent that would serve as headquarters for the company. From my kayaking days, I knew that there was a big lot next to the post office, so I called there to find out who owned it and whether they might be willing to rent us space. They gave me the phone number of the owner, Gus Carlson, and I called him to arrange a meeting the next day.

Gus was a long-time resident who owned a lot of acreage in the canyon. When J.S.T. and I showed up at the doorstep of his old log cabin across from the city park, we both knew we were in trouble as soon as he opened the door. My first impression of him was a bit on the scruffy side, and the feeling seemed to be mutual. Seeing my bearded face and long braids, he said, "You sure ore a woolly bugger, aren't ya?" Then he looked at John, who admittedly was a little on the plump side, and said, "Looks like you could use some time on a shovel, too." Things went downhill from there, and we bid him farewell not only without a rental but also with more than a hint that we were not very welcome around his neighborhood.

After knocking on several doors, we finally found a great location in the middle of the town near City Hall. I rented a hole-in-the-wall storage room from local businesswoman Charlene Workman for $75 a month. It was available because another company, Whitewater Express owned by Casey and Becky Benson, was moving its ancillary gear out of the space.

This 12-by-15-foot room had one door, one window, and an ideal main street frontage. There was just enough room to store oars, lifejackets, and river gear. It was between Charlene's office and a one-garage fire station, and it had an ideal roadside spot to park my wooden dory to attract business. It soon became a semi-landmark in town, catching the attention of travelers going by.

All traffic between Boise and Lewiston had to pass by us on Highway 95, the only main road that bisected the large expanse of remote mountains separating the two distant cities where much of the state's population was centered. This was several years before the town installed cement sidewalks at the behest of local business people who wanted Riggins to be like every other stereotypical American small town.

At the time, other outfitters were on the edges of town in both directions from my location. Whitewater Express, Epley's Whitewater Adventures, and Northwest Voyageurs were to the north, while Discovery and River Adventures were to the south. A few others were farther out of town.

J.S.T. knew an artist who came up with a new logo for Wapiti River Guides, and he helped me create a new slogan, "Big Fun, on the Big Rivers," for advertising purposes. Then I began training him as a guide so he could get out on the rivers where we were offering trips.

We did some Grande Ronde and Salmon trips together, and in the fall season, he dreamed up a side business for himself, selling elk hunts on private lands in the Lookout Mountain area of eastern Oregon. He hired me to supposedly manage the elk on the property and to guide hunters seeking to kill them. Theoretically, there would be a sustainable number of big bulls to harvest. It sounded good, and he paid for some aerial surveys, but in reality the elk population was managed by the state game agency. So any bulls of trophy size that we allowed hunters to harvest on private property often spilled over from other areas. The idea that we had much control of them was farcical at best. But as a marketing scheme, it sounded good to potential hunters.

However, storm clouds on the horizon eventually roll in. I knew John stretched the truth a bit when enticing people to sign up, but it wasn't until I was guiding an elk hunter whom he had grossly misinformed that my own reputation came into question. I was not willing to sacrifice my good name because of his outright embellishments, and I had to draw the line. His far-flung fabrications were like a snake biting its own tail.

J.S.T. and I parted ways and he eventually started his own river business, which he promoted in newspaper articles that claimed he had been guiding for many more years than even I had. That was laughable, and disgusting to me.

His best friend was the telephone, and he could talk a good show. Without doubt he was far better at marketing than me, and it didn't take long for him to snag people and build his business. My best friends were my oars, and for me the best show on Earth was out on a river. Sometimes it is just simpler and wiser to pay attention to your own shadow.

Although I had spent three summers as a guide on the Salmon River between Corn Creek and Heller Bar from 1977 to 1979, my moving to Riggins was my first opportunity to live beside it year-round. I was very happy to be there on the high shoreline in the middle of town.

Chapter 20

THE RIGGINS RIVER RUSH - CROWN JEWELL AND WHITEWATER MECCA OF IDAHO (1980S - LEGACY OF GENERATION ONE)

The outstanding beauty of Riggins begins with its site, which stretches for about a mile along a narrow river bar composed mostly of white sand, loamy soil, cobblestone gravel, and erratic boulders. Scattered bands of ponderosa pine sit atop the substrate, while scraggy-limbed hackberry and mountain mahogany trees crowd each other along steep-sided shorelines. Both sides of the river rise sharply skyward from the edge of the river bar to form a narrowing V-shaped canyon pleasing to the eye of all except those with claustrophobia.

While empty sagebrush flats are to the east, the west side is where the population is concentrated, which, geomorphologically speaking, gives rise to our claim of being the "longest town in America."

Being at 1,800 feet of elevation, Riggins' most dramatic geologic feature is its proximity to the severely saw-toothed Seven Devils Mountain Range, which is nearly 10,000 feet high and separates the Salmon and Snake River watersheds. Those charismatic trenches offer a unique allure with their labyrinthian depths of more than a mile, resulting in a rain-shadowed, banana-belt weather pattern that includes mild winters and intensely hot summers. The bonuses are views capable of stealing the breath away and river waters in which to cool off.

The Salmon River, serpentining its way through all this immensity, was not new to me as a river guide, but becoming a fulltime Idaho resident was. It felt weird being the new kid on the block, even though I had more river experience than most of the other outfitters who had hung out their shingles before me.

Luckily, my good friend Clancy Reece had preceded me and had played a significant role in shaping the early Riggins area guide scene. He managed the original Salmon River Challenge, a guide service started by Jerry Kooyers, a vastly experienced entrepreneur from California.

Jerry was an avid big game hunter who was first drawn to the Salmon River country around 1966 because he was enchanted by the wild wapiti there. However, he also had an interest in mining, and in 1978 he bought a gold mine from a legendary female dentist in Council, Idaho, and created his own mining company. He also bought property upriver on Elkhorn Creek, where in 1979 he built a ranch from which he also operated as a registered Commodity Trading Advisor. In addition, he bought his present residence in Riggins from Bruce Oaks, a local jetboat builder. In the transaction, Bruce included rafting equipment and both power and float boat permits, enabling Jerry to create Salmon River Challenge.

An attorney for the dentist from whom Jerry had bought his mine finagled his way into Jerry's mining company and introduced him to another edgy character, Jim Galeen. With little practical river experience himself, this seemed opportune to Jerry because Jim, who had purchased river permits for Hells Canyon and the Main Salmon from Myrna Beemer's outfitting business, proposed that they join forces.

Their relationship didn't last long because Jim's girlfriend soon left for Alaska and he followed her, farming off his share of the rafting business to Jerry. It languished for a time, until a chance encounter in 1981 set in motion a revitalization.

It was at his ranch that Jerry and his wife, Geneva, first met Clancy, who was hired to install a wood stove and chimney. Accompanying him was a helper, Ron Howell. As they worked, the conversation turned to river stories, and before leaving, Clancy was hired to manage Jerry's river business. Ron benefited too, because he became one of the first river guides to be trained by Clancy.

Being a dory guy, Clancy talked Jerry into buying five glass dory boats from Lavro Boats, a builder in Monroe, Washington, to add to his fleet of rafts. Next came the hiring of a menagerie of wannabe guides and transforming them into what turned out to be the area's first bona fide company specializing in day-trip business. Thus in 1981, Riggins became ground zero for a pioneering group of hard-core guides who were willing to take a job for $35 a day without benefits, aside from a chance to work in a beautiful environment conducive to good health. This helped launch the conversion of a tiny logging and ranching community into a river town.

Change, of course, can create strife, and there was some initial tension between the new people who looked to the river for their livelihood and the long-time residents whose ways of making a living were dependent on trees, grass, and minerals.

After the local lumber mill, located at the confluence of the big and little rivers, burned down in 1981, the resistance to change lessoned and new growth began. The mill was not rebuilt, partly due to the shifting economic tides of the time and the altered face of progress in the community.

Another source of upheaval at the time was the controversy over federal efforts to protect the endangered spotted owl by setting aside millions of acres of forests to preserve the bird's habitat. It was a tipping point for addressing an out of balance timber industry whose timbering operations were running rampant.

Natural "capital" is as important as industrial riches, an essential fact that is so often missed by the dominionist worldview that permits unrestrained consumption of natural resources while ignoring the fundamental ecological processes that allow the natural machine to keep running. It's like using a chain saw without oil. It ends up burning out the cutting chain.

Fortunately, the attitudes of most locals evolved, though some sub-surface animosities still exist. One must remember that this transition began in a time when it was common to see bumper stickers in Riggins that said, "Save a Salmon, Spear an Indian."

By 1982, soon after Jerry struck gold by offering day-trips, other copycat outfitters who were attracted to the color of green cash began staking their claims to river profits. Just as gold had lured the first miners who eventually turned a vacant river bar into a town, big rapids drew in a new adventure-seeking crowd, and before long Riggins was being proclaimed the "Whitewater Capital of Idaho." It became an iconic beacon to thrill seekers and a whitewater mecca for river-running enthusiasts.

Like the merry men of Robin Hood, Clancy's motley band of seditionists began to take from the rich and give back to nature. Water is the ecological oil that drives everything from the bottom up, and soon people with money were willingly paying guides to show them a good time on the river and thereby contributing, knowingly or not, to a more empathetic perspective of nature.

Besides Ron, those early corrupters of the status quo included pioneering Riggins guides such as Mark Hollon, Dave Bicandi, Bob McClure, and Steve Schultze. Gresham Buama and Brad Eiggen guided only briefly, and Morgan Owens died in a mining accident in the fall of 1981.

Mark was fresh out of high school when he signed on as a guide. He had been born in California but came to Coeur D'Alene at age 2. His family lived quite ruggedly in the back country nearby, hauling water like in the old days. They moved to Whitebird when Mark was a high school junior, and it was a real culture shock to have running water and more social conveniences.

He pursued outdoor interests, and while panning for gold down by Pine Bar on the Salmon River, he saw a raft go by. He couldn't get the thought out of his mind about how exciting and fun it looked to be. So a year later, after graduating from Grangeville High, he went to Riggins to seek guide work.

Entering the "Best Little Oar House" in Riggins, as the sign the guides had put above the boathouse door said, he saw a cloud of smoke and felt like he had entered the world of Cheech and Chong. Fortunately for him, help was needed, and Clancy hired him on the spot.

Although the company at that time ran mostly longer trips in Hells Canyon and on the Main and Lower Salmon, it also began offering day trips, which would help make Riggins a tourist destination and enrich the community. The 1981-82 seasons jump-started Riggins as a big-time draw for day trips.

The next year the company ran an ad in Outside magazine that attracted Norm Klobetanz, who was from Pennsylvania, along with Mike and Connie Kennedy, Bruce Elmquist, Cory Chase, and Jeff Peavey.

Norm, was an English teacher who found nature pulling him west to become a student of the wilds. After drenching his veins as a whitewater guide, he took to steelhead fishing along with Ron Howell. They were at the forefront of the first service to guide anglers in pursuit of those red-sided river denizens. After leaving SRC, they temporarily guided for other companies before starting their own outfitting business. However, they dissolved that venture after a couple of years and went their separate ways.

Several years after marrying Frank Mignerey's daughter, Norm took over Frank's river photography business. In 1982, Frank had established the first service for taking rafting pictures at Time Zone Rapids and then selling them to outfitters' guests after their trips. Over the years it bloomed into a thriving venture, but competing photographers eventually came to the river, depriving Frank of his monopoly. After having helped

Frank, Norm started his own company, Suncloud Productions, specializing in outdoor digital photography and a broader array of services.

Meanwhile, Ron branched off in a different direction. He began building hard boats and created a company, Idaho Driftboats. Near the same time, he began working as a fly-fishing guide in the McCall area, and he eventually bought out the owner of a McCall fly-fishing shop. He is the owner of Fly Fish McCall, a fishing guide service.

Jeff also had an interesting river history. He grew up in the Lewiston-Clarkston Valley on a farm along Tammany Creek. By 1970 he had saved enough money from selling his 4-H animals that he was able to buy his first raft from a local Army/Navy store. It was a four-man survival raft with paddles. He somehow persuaded his parents to drive him and a friend to Doug Bar to launch for a five-day float. They had tons of fun and caught lots of fish, but it was really Jeff who got hooked. The world of nature worked its magic.

Four years later he bought a better raft, a 10-man World Famous, and fashioned a homemade 2-by-6 wood frame to set it up for rowing instead of paddling. My first raft was the same overrated model, which I also equipped with a similar homemade frame.

Besides the attraction of rivers, he was inspired by Del Roby's outdoor films, leading to several runs on the Snake and Lower Salmon. It was on one of those trips that he met Clancy and Snake River Jake (Jim Wyatt). From Clancy he learned about Grand Canyon Dories and the operation they had in Lewiston.

He soon checked them out, and then spent two years trying to talk them into selling him one of their boats. Persistence paid off and he eventually bought an old boat named the Malibu Canyon. Interestingly, I had been on several trips that included that boat.

One day in 1981, Jeff was working on the old boat in his front yard when Clancy, who was shuttling for another trip, pulled up. After a couple of beers, he told Jeff he might be able to get him a job rowing boats with a new company called SRC, if he didn't mind working for $35 a day. Saying he jumped at the chance is a far cry from describing his exuberance over the opportunity, and soon he was a river guide.

Several of these first-generation guides also became addicted to dory boats, thanks to Clancy. He also instilled in them many of the old Grand Canyon tenets that had been hammered out during the golden era of dory boatmen that was jump-started by the grand master of it all, Martin Litton. Martin's love of rivers led him to name his boats after wild places that had been lost or compromised by the hand of man. His efforts to open the public's eyes to what we are collectively doing to our planet rubbed off in many ways and directions, and that awareness was passed on through Clancy into the bloodstream of the Riggins guide community.

By 1983, with the business in the red, Clancy and Jerry no longer saw eye to eye. It was a typical clash between ownership and management, with the owner's decisions being at odds with, and trumping, the manager's high ideals. It is far easier to make decisions when you are not the one holding the purse. It is like rowing someone else's dory down a rock-strewn riverbed with a high risk of putting a hole in the boat.

After Clancy resigned, Mark and Jeff presented Jerry with a new plan to get the business back into the black, and they offered to take Clancy's place if they could co-manage. Jerry put his feet up on his desk and said,"Sounds good to me."

Unfortunately, that didn't last long either. By 1984, only a year later, Jerry was compelled to hold yet another pow-wow in his living room with Jeff and Mark. By then, Jerry had learned more about the habits of river guides, who were governed more by freedom than loyalty to the king. It seemed there was a controversy about some extra food that came off of commercial journeys and a question about its availability for guides between trips.

The Kooyers family is also devoutly religious and did not appreciate some of the more questionable behaviors of the stereotypical guide, which added a tint of insult and increased frustrations. River "religion" is different from organized religion. Deciding that he needed a new source for more reputable river guides, Jerry looked to some local bible circles for better behaved folks.

By 1985, Jerry turned the business over to his son-in-law, John Cook, but problems persisted and things soon went south. With financial conditions of the rafting company worsening, Jerry, who had no real deep roots in the river world, wanted out, so he sold everything in order to devote more energy to his family, following Jesus, and writing.

Pat Merek, a local who had been a mill worker, bought the business and its Salmon River permit. He retained the company name, Salmon River Challenge, and some of the first-generation guides, who continued to conduct trips and helped train additional guides.

In the free enterprise system, the smell of potential fortune travels far and wide, especially when relatively new discoveries are made. Copycats are never far from the nip, and river rats are quick to cash in on the cheese. The river business is also a bit like musical chairs, and trying to unravel the history of all the ownership changes is a bit like trying to untangle a backlash in a Level Wind reel.

There were a few other outfitters offering float trips on the Salmon River before Jerry began the more serious day-trip business, including Olin Gardner (Idaho Guide Service), Ted Epley (Epley's Adventures), Chuck Boyd (Salmon River Experience), Glen Foster (Teton Expeditions), Charles Ferdon (Dissendat Expeditions), and perhaps Brent Epstein (Mackay Bar), but their trips were mostly of the multi-day variety.

Some were running trips based from other places like Moscow (Boyd) and McCall (Epley). Olin ran operations from his North Riggins residency, but in 1985, Chuck and Ted had yet to locate in Riggins. Only Teton Expeditions, Dissendat Expeditions, Mackay Bar, and Whitewater Express were in town during the same time as Olin. They followed

Jerry's lead with the day-trip idea, or they sold their companies with that prospect used as a carrot to attract buyers. Dissendat was sold in 1987 to Rich Cook of Wild River Outfitters, and Teton Expeditions was sold in 1989 to Rex Black of R&R Outdoors. Mackay Bar migrated out of town and upriver to near the South Fork.

A few jetboat operators were in the Riggins area at that time, including Red Woods and Sam Whiten of River Adventures, as well as some others, before and afterward, whose ownership changes resembled a game of musical chairs. One ancient mariner of jetboat professionals was Paul Filer, who moved to Riggins in 1969 after having built a successful sportsmen's lodge at Shepp Ranch.

In 1985, when John Cook broke ties with Jerry, he went to work for Salmon River Experience when Chuck was still based out of Moscow. The next year, John's father, Dan Cook, bought out someone else and started his own company, called Discovery, but resold it in 1989 to Lester Lowe, who continued under the same name.

Also in 1989, Olin sold his Riggins base site in town to Ted, who then began to pursue the shorter adventures from there, instead of traveling from McCall. As more time passed, the sales of various outfits resembled flipping pancakes in a hot skillet.

The common thread among all these other outfitters was that they were rafting specialists and did not use dories. After the Kooyers company transfer, SRC let go of three dories, keeping only a couple for trips, and focused mostly on rafts. For the most part, the companies centered around Hypolon rafts were of a different mold than the hardcore dory boat enthusiasts. It takes a special breed to want to row a hard boat that requires more specialized skills while also facing risks of flipping or wreckage that are not a problem for a raft.

But from an owner/outfitter's perspective, the biggest reason to push Hypolon is economy. Rafts can be piled several to a stack on one trailer, and more people can be crammed into rafts, making the guide-to-guest ratio more profitable. Dory boats also have higher maintenance costs, not to mention additional trailers and rigs to haul them. Bottom line: It's all a matter of profit margins.

However, from a non-financial point of view, the biggest difference between the two types of craft might best be described by paraphrasing Martin Litton's perspective: "It's simple, dorys are beautiful, rafts are ugly."

A couple of years after leaving Jerry, Jeff Peavy had a chance to purchase a Lower Salmon permit from Bill Bender. Jeff kept Bill's name for the company, Northwest Voyageurs. Being close friends with several of the first-generation river guides, he employed many of them.

That first year, Jeff did not have enough money to run everything, so Bruce Elmquist agreed to be a partner in the venture. In 1986, they bought a place on the north corner of town from what turned out to be a local white supremacist. The Peavy crew didn't know it until they were cleaning the place and discovered papers of a disturbingly nefarious nature. Basically, it was a manifesto of accolades praising the virtues of the "white race" while spewing vile proclamations about the evil declivities of the "mud race."

It seemed to be alluding to the native Indian people from the viewpoint of historic missionaries who perceived a struggle between an omniscient Christian god and demonic savagery. It's an undercurrent of ugly racism still to be found among a few local bigots, who reflect a hatred that is not easily flushed away in a country founded on a dominionist worldview. It was an eye-opening effrontery to Jeff and crew, who had a much more liberal worldview and community spirit.

After a year or two, Bruce sold his interest to Bill Terry, who in turn sold it back to Jeff two years later. Jeff continued to build up the business, adding more river permits, including trips to Costa Rica and India. He also gained the first mountain bike permit in Idaho and offered the first backpacking trips in the Seven Devils Mountains.

During that growing stage, Jeff also made a couple of strategic location moves. He sold his North Riggins site to Chuck's Salmon River Experience around 1988 and moved to the middle of town. He later moved to Lucile, before it all became too much and he sold out to a wealthy city businessman who had been bitten by the wilderness river bug while he was a guest on a Hells Canyon trip. The new owner had caught the fever that induces delusional dreams of what it might be like to be a glorified "river outfitter." He kept the same NWV company name and ran it for a few more years before eventually selling out, too.

SRE eventually become the biggest outfit in town, with many guides, lots of trips, and hordes of rafts that looked like an armada of lemmings heading for the falls on the daytrip section. But unlike their cliff-jumping prototypes, which followed each other into oblivion, these whitewater lemmings survived their encounter with the fun rapids.

The original Northwest Voyageur guides were the folks I most identified with when I found my Riggins landing spot in '87, and I hung out with them when not guiding. Bruce, Mike, and Connie became my best river friends in town, not only because we all loved the river so much but also because Mike and Bruce had also succumbed to dory fever and ended up with their own boats. The elegance and dance of a river dory is hard to explain to people who have never been courted by such sirens of exquisite design.

Bruce became my "first call" extra guide when I needed help on trips I couldn't do by myself, as well as a companion when attending sport shows where we promoted our river excursions. He had an interesting personal history too, having originally come to town on horseback after working stock for various ranchers in Hells Canyon and the surrounding area. Like me, his head had been turned by the lure of the river, and we also shared a grassroots appreciation for living close to the land that feeds us all.

Mike and Connie also ended up helping me at times after Bruce died unexpectedly. He came home one day, sat in his chair, and had a fatal brain aneurysm. It was shocking to all of us flabbergasted friends because he had been in good shape and had no known problems.

Connie was the first female guide in the Riggins area, but it took her a while to get her foot in the door. When she started working for Jerry, the Christian-oriented Kooyers company had a policy that did not permit female guides to do overnight trips with male guides. Because Mike and Connie were married, they didn't have to worry about temptation outside of wedlock, so she was eventually permitted to join multi-day adventures.

Together, we pushed the limits for big-water dory boating and also pioneered new raft runs on the Little Salmon River. A now famous rapid called Oh Shit was named by me and Connie when we simultaneously uttered that exclamation as we saw the huge waves for the first time from the bow of Mike's raft. We had not seen them as we scouted from the highway while looking for upriver put-ins that would add more miles of fun to our trips.

Unfortunately, all of our time running the Little Salmon and fine tuning our routes was negated in the big 100-year-size flood that hit in 1994. It washed away houses, caved in banks, and eroded away parts highways, leaving Riggins cut off for about a week before road repairs could be made. It also completely changed the rapids. It was like boating an entirely new river after the flood.

I was joined in the second-generation wave of guides to be lured into the Riggins river vortex by adventure seekers like Dale Turnipseed, Kerry Brenan, Jeffrey Geoff, Steve Fiedler, and Scott Lindsey, to mention a few of the main characters with whom I became friends. Many of them worked for me at various times, as most guides in a small community must be opportunists to feed their families.

After my comet first cratered-out the Riggins rental site in 1987, I remained there until 1990, before buying a place immediately north of City Hall where the Wapiti Whitewater Epicenter shop is now situated. I was fortunate that my parents provided some financial aid, which helped with the down payment and got me off to a good start. Trying to rat-hole money while renting is difficult and a situation to be minimized as much as possible.

Another nice thing about the new location was that it had a good place to set up my tipi overlooking the river. I had gone through three previous lodges while living in Oregon. The first one was a 16-footer, then I progressed to 18 feet, and finally a 26-foot mega-lodge. When a canvas tipi is set up year-round and not protected by shade, the sun is so harsh on fabric that it eventually deteriorates beyond fixing. Sewing works for awhile, but then the canvas gets too thin to hold stitches together. Gluing patches eventually fails, too, and replacement is the only remedy. In Riggins, I went through two more lodges, but it was nice to get back to a semblance of my old ways.

These days my old rental space, after much remodeling, has morphed into a fishing tackle store named The Hook Line and Sinker, along with an ancillary business, the Riggins Liquor Store. It is now owned and operated by Charlene Workman's daughter, Rexann Zimmerman. Evolution in the business world is a curious thing, and it's hard to predict what will come next.

Over time, Riggins bloomed into a major recreational destination for a multitude of outdoor pursuits. This led to a revolving door of many part-time guides, mostly college kids working seasonally as a stepping-stone before moving onward to other career paths. The more ephemeral attitude of the younger guides was far different from that of the more serious career-oriented, full-time guides. This contributed to a changing dynamic in the social fabric and atmosphere in town. While the transitory young folks often were more interested in achieving social status from being recognized as a "Guide," the career guides were more focused on providing the best experiences for their guests by continuously improving their own people skills.

The transformation of a mining/ranching/mill town into a recreational hub reminded me of my time doing wildlife work for the U.S. Forest Service and having to contend with timber interests who boasted that recreation could never hold a candle to the lumber industry. It was their justification for trying to secure policies more favorable to their industry and minimizing restrictions placed on them that would give other interests a chance to gain their objectives, too.

Wrong. Exhibit A: Riggins.

While those extractive, more subsidized industries still exist on a smaller scale, the dominant theme in town now is based on pass-through, less impactful, conservation-oriented services. As tourism came into full bloom, it put a different color to the town. Flowers may not be green, but money is, as is the color of a more earth-friendly environmentalism that serves both capitalism and nature.

A standard joke in the outfitting business is: Do you know how to make a small fortune in the outfitting business? Start out with a big one. Though tourism is often a less obtrusive economic pursuit, there still exists a lot of avarice in the river world Altruism is a rare virtue in the race for success.

There are always a few empire-building outfitters who lust for the palatial zenith and aspire to the profession's alpha position. This overzealous entrepreneurial spirit is not uncommon in a lot of businesses in America today. "Give me liberty or give me death" is a battle cry that people died for to keep capitalism and free enterprise alive. In the land of the free, chains and shackles are despised, even when they take the form of restrictions to help curb complete exhaustion of natural resources. Our two-party system of government continues to fight over how much free reign to give industries that gobble up resources.

Early on, and admittedly at my own peril, I stubbornly refused to participate in the unrestrained growth patterns indicative of the country's march toward corporatocracy.

In addition to a human population problem, our country has an extreme over-consumption addiction, and I recognized long ago that I did not wish to contribute to more of the same. All people need to make a choice between joining the "camp" that creates problems and the other that cobbles together solutions.

I chose "Camp Solution" and a lifestyle goal of running a sustainable business not based on continual growth. Just how much do I really require from this world anyway? The constant need to acquire more is an addiction trap that many people fall into without ever realizing it.

While savvy politicians eventually came up with a new "sustainable growth" paradigm shift to try to sway the uninformed, I never could understand that shadowy oxymoron. Like jumbo shrimp, it is a convoluted concept filled with dubious holes and twisted language to describe the same aims: more unregulated extraction. Growth is growth. We live on a limited planet. Something doesn't compute.

Capitalism is touted as the worst concept for industrialization, except for all the rest. Unfortunately, long-term success tied to extraction has an end point on a planet with finite capacities. It's simple math that defines the laws of nature. Sustainability can never work if it is always based on exhausting the very resources that are the foundation on which it is built.

The only reason there is anything left for current generations is because those that came before us recognized the need for more rules and regulations. No one ever likes relinquishing control to others or having their liberties restricted, but the alternative is even worse.

> ***Only when the last tree has died***
> ***and the last river has been poisoned***
> ***and the last fish has been caught***
> ***will we realize***
> ***we cannot eat money.***
>
> *Cree Indian proverb*

Chapter 21

PURPLE HEART AT EYE OF THE NEEDLE
(MAY 20, 1990 -- 12,961 CFS)

Eye of the Needle. How bad can a rapid be with an innocuous name like that? It didn't take long to learn that answer on the day it flipped my dory upside down. Nor would it be the last time this powerful rapid impressed its cosmic message on my conscious.

Even though I always had the highest respect for Eye of the Needle's role as a nemesis, it didn't seem to matter. Over the years, that Mixmaster of chaotic whitewater just seemed to have my number, as in "your number's up." I always pay attention when approaching this beastly rapid.

It all started on a trip in 1994 with my one boat, one guest, and two dogs. Most outfitters will not do a one-person trip, as there is no money in it. But for me, it was early in the season, I had nothing going on, and it never took too much of an arm twist to entice me back out on the river. Almost any excuse would work.

My only guest was Sarge, a 205-pound decorated Vietnam vet on vacation with me on the Lower Salmon River in the cooler weather of April. Sarge (not his real name) never wanted his wife to find out what happened to him on this trip, so I was sworn to secrecy about his identity.

He was quite a conversationalist and it was sometimes hard for me to answer back and focus on my rowing at the same time. At least, this became my excuse for the wall-crashing incident on the first day. With us in my wooden dory boat for the four-day trip were my two dogs, Inua and Metoo. The river was about 15,000 cfs when we started, but it was dropping. The water was snowmelt cold, barely above freezing. As we drifted along through an easy class II riffle, I was too busy responding to Sarge's banter when I should have been concentrating on the cushion of water piling off a cliff at the rapid's tail-out.

What I didn't know until too late was that at this flow, the cushion I would normally use to surf off the wall, was not happening. The rock wall had an extreme undercut that enabled water to gurgle beneath it without creating a pillow.

Suddenly, the current was pitching me so close to the cliff that I could no longer use my right oar. Kawhack! I smacked sickeningly hard into the solid rock wall. You might say my dory kissed the wall, but if so, it was more like a French kiss. The abrupt engagement with the immovable object put a disheartening small hole in the side of my boat. Luckily, it was a few inches above the water line, just below my right oarlock. Since this was the first time I had punched a hole in my boat, it also put a hole in my heart. I made a quick repair of the initial wound with a duct tape Band-Aid.

The next shock of the trip came on the second day when one of my Weimaraners, Metoo, got bit by a rattlesnake. We were too far in the wilds for a timely evacuation, and I had no anti-venom. Fortunately, the bite was on her right rear foot, the farthest point from her heart. It made her legs swell, but surprisingly, she recovered in about three days. I made her as comfortable as I could on my boat and in camp, and she did as all animals do naturally. They mostly lay down, rest, and do nothing. If only we humans could also appreciate their inner wisdom.

The western Pacific rattlesnakes in our area are smaller and less toxic than many of the larger, more dangerous species elsewhere. I still wouldn't stick my finger in one's mouth, but their bite is not as consequential as that of their more venomous relations.

Laying low when injured is a lesson humans should take to heart, as exemplified by a guy on a private lower gorge trip who surely didn't know about the wisdom of wildlife. After he was bitten by a rattlesnake, he paraded around with his swollen hand in the air like it was an esteemed badge of courage or macho sign of manhood. Rather than conserving energy, he continued to clamor over the boulder-strewn shorelines on long hikes to scout rapids. I think I can still see the word "idiot" written by the wrinkles on his forehead when his image streams across my memories of his moronic parade.

Another unusual scenario evolved on day three. I hoped we had left our bad luck upstream. Wrong! As we were floating the river's primitive road section, more weirdness began to happen. This is where an expeditionary type road comes in from the Eagle Creek drainage and follows the Salmon River for about 2 miles. It ends at a remote cabin in an Idaho Fish and Game Management area. The access road provides a difficult motor route for sportsmen who don't like tearing up the terrain driving into the area.

Once again we were busy chatting when Sarge looked far downriver and saw a person doing something along the shoreline. He wondered what. "Probably fishing," I offered, as that is what most folks who drive into this area like to do.

As we went back to our conversation and drifted on, a rifle shot cracked the silence, jolting us to attention. We looked up just in time to see someone aiming a rifle at us. Oh great! Here I am on the Salmon River with a heroic soldier who had given me an ugly account of his near brush with death in a Vietnam battle in which he earned a Purple Heart, and now he's being shot at on his vacation in Idaho. Along with me.

Luckily, I soon realized the shooter's attention was not focused on us. He didn't even know we were there, so I began hollering at him. As my adrenaline subsided, I could see it was a young boy who was aiming at a fish in the water. Unfortunately, we were in a direct line, and with his shooting angle, a bullet could have skipped our way.

Hearing my earth-shaking shouts, he became conscious of our close presence and lowered his rifle. Apparently flabbergasted, he turned and ran up the bank to quickly disappear. He must have realized we had caught him in an illegal act, and he probably panicked when he realized he could have hit one of us in his folly.

A little farther downstream we could see another dory boat with two people. One guy was rowing, one was fishing. When we caught up to them, it turned out to be two river acquaintances. The man oaring was my old friend Clancy Reece, with whom I had worked several trips during our time together with Grand Canyon Dories. In fact, I had been with him on the famous trip from hell at Devils Slide on the Lower Salmon when we all contributed to the famous carnage that is now part of campfire river stories old dory boatmen like to tell.

The second guy was another "wild and woolly" boatman, Jon Barker, who is a good friend now though I did not know him well at that time. He was busy fishing in the bow as I made my approach. Clancy and Jon went on to experience many adventures of their own, providing great storytelling material, but those tales are theirs to tell, not mine.

As we approached, Clancy asked, "Hey, want some company at the Slide," greeting me with his typical dry humor. Both remembering that fateful high-water run, we prepared to head toward the same rapid at another very respectable river level. The waves would be kicking gigantically, so we realized it was a fortunate coincidence to team up again to run this formidable rapid.

After scouting, he ran first as I watched from the boulders above. His entry was too far left and he ended up clipping a rock and putting a small gash in his glass dory. This is known as "bad form" in boatmen's lingo, and it may even have been an expression invented by Clancy. He was very quick witted, but not similarly quick enough on the oars to avoid being crunched that day.

I capitalized by learning from his misfortune and had a good run. Whew! It is always a relief to be on the downstream side of the Slide at high flows. Once below, we briefly celebrated being right side up, bid farewell, and parted company.

I ended up camping at Robbers Roost, the old name for a beach that newbie river guides call something else now. It is about a mile above the confluence where the Salmon dumps into the Snake River. Only two more big rapids separated us from the Snake, and they loomed soon after our departure from camp the next morning.

Day four was our last, and we had a long 21 miles to float. We were up early to get a good start and on the river by 8 a.m. It began to sprinkle rain as we pulled away from shore. However, it was not that cold, and we were warm in our rain suits and knee-high rubber boots. This was our whitewater dress code for keeping dry in the rapids.

The first rapid was Checkerboard. It was big and fun. Then came Eye of the Needle, our final barrier before entering the Snake River. "Hang on, Sarge," I hollered as we began to thread the needle. At this water level, it consists of huge waves and a most violent eddy line. Did I say "MOST VIOLENT" forcefully enough?

I was still oaring when Sarge let go of his grip on the boat to turn around and tell me, "Nice run." But unbeknownst to him, we were only through the big waves, not the nasty eddyline. It is a beastly nemesis and the extreme bottom-line for staying upright in this gnarly rapid. Or, more accurately, "bottoms up" for many ill-fated floaters who have succumbed to it over the years.

The tremendous eddy fence at this flow is created by a massive differential line, where upstream and downstream flows rub against each other and form an abrupt, violent edge. Not to mention deep whirlpools of frightening proportions and coffee pot boils fit for a mythical giant's brew. It causes extreme havoc to any boat that ventures there.

Before I knew what hit me, the boat was dancing on its side. Had Sarge been hanging on, I'm pretty sure we wouldn't have tipped. As it was, his 205 pounds was thrown to the low side, along with both dogs, as I jumped to the high side with my 140 pounds. Sarge's side of the boat won. Right then and there, we joined the Salmon River Swim Team.

However, I did not lose contact with my boat and was not in the water more than 10 seconds before I was able to climb up onto the overturned bottom. But Sarge had lost his grip and was free-floating. Even though I had stressed to him over and over how important it is to never lose physical contact with the boat, he was caught off guard.

This "never lose contact" policy is even more important when on a one-boat trip, where no other help is at hand. Self-reliance is the name of the game on wilderness adventures. It's part of why people sign up for risk-taking experiences.

Anyway, my dogs were both gone, and I could not see them anywhere. I feared they had drowned but was too busy trying to save myself and Sarge to let that terrible gut-wrenching feeling affect my own survival actions.

I hollered at Sarge to swim to the boat. "I can't," he said. "Yes you can," I hollered back. "No, I can't" and "yes, you can" went on for about three more repetitions. Failing that plan, I gathered my stern line and tried to heave it toward him. It was too short by about 3 feet. If he would have taken one swim stroke, he could've grabbed it, but he didn't. I could not reach him.

Nor could I tip my boat right side up by myself because it was too heavy for one person to flip. I needed him and his weight to overcome the inertia of the heavily loaded boat. Instead, we floated about a quarter-mile down to a sand bar near the Pullman mine. Slightly downstream of the beach is a rock wall several yards long that forms the divide between the Snake and Salmon Rivers.

At that point, he was near shore and about to grab a rock to pull himself out of the water. I told him I would flag down a jetboat and return for him as soon as possible. Then I was on my own, heading for a collision course with the peninsula of massive basalt. I wanted to use my feet to keep my boat from banging the wall but decided that might break some bones. Instead, I just cringed at the moaning sound of wood scraping along several yards of rock. The result was a damaged portside gunwale that looked more like a waterborne porcupine with spines of splintered wood.

Bouncing off the wall, I was cast into a bit of soft water in a triangular pool at the foot of an apex jetty forming the crux of confluence. In lower flows, it is calm water. But in this flow it was more bath-tub size, minus the warm temps. I immediately dove into the pool with the stern line in hand. My idea was to pull the boat into the pool. The river had other ideas. I could not break the current's strong grip, and I had agonizingly come to the end of my rope. It was my last connection with a hope for salvation, as the boat surged away with the pull of the river.

Hand over hand, for 75 feet, I worked my way along the line back to the overturned boat and climbed onto the bottom again. I decided to secure my oars, which were strapped with short cordage to the gunwales and were floating alongside the boat. I grabbed the first oar and tucked it under a safety line that encircles my boat at mid-level, but the other oar broke its line and began drifting away from the boat.

I dove back in, swam to the oar and leap-frogged it back to the boat. Climbing aboard again, I secured this oar on the opposite side of the boat. Then I heard one of my dogs. Her wailing, a god-awful sound, was coming from somewhere nearby. At first I thought she had followed me downriver on shore, but then discovered she was trapped under the dory.

I leaned over the side of my boat and hollered at her through one of the self-bailing tubes, which are channels for water to drain from the footwell of my decked-over boat when it is right side up. "Hang on, girl, I'll get you when I can," I yelled. There were a couple more whimpers and then silence. My guts twisted tight as I feared the worst, but I was jolted back into my own survival mode because the boat was about to enter another rapid.

Just then my ammo can with $300 cash and a $500 camera broke loose from the cam strap holding it to the footwell and began floating away. I made a grab for it, but it was a foot beyond my grasp. My energy was draining, and I had to conserve it for the next wall at the foot of a long train of giant waves.

The box was gone. I was going up and down in monster waves. They were smooth with no curls, and it would have been fun right side up. However, they were funneling me toward another dangerous spot, where the main current met with another basalt jetty. Most of the water deflected away downstream, but the rest created a huge whirlpool that was very strong with a deep depression in the middle.

Should the boat enter it, it would become trapped in the Forever Eddy. I prayed not to go into it. Luckily, my boat hit the wall and bounced downstream at the last possible second as the whirlpool pulled at it in the opposite direction.

There was little respite because I soon was entering another big rapid that rolled along for a couple of hundred yards toward the Oregon shore on river left. Each time I went up a big wave, I tried using the extreme angle to flip my boat right side up, but it was too heavy. When the current carried me within 10 feet of the shore, I dove in with my stern line and swam quickly to land.

My plan was to snub the line around a rock and pendulum swing the boat toward the bank. However, all the rocks were too rounded off from eons of relentless current to secure the line. Being once more at the end of my rope, I jumped in and again began hauling myself 75 feet along the line to my boat. Reaching it, I climbed aboard and began surveying the shoreline for better rocks. I was still within 15 feet of the bank in fast current but no waves.

I spied some good rocks with angular edges about a quarter-mile downstream and again dove in with the stern line, swimming hard for shore. This time the plan worked. My boat swung into shore and became wedged on a boulder, still upside down. I tied it off and quickly returned to the carnage to look for my dog.

As I attempted to submerge myself under the bow, my life jacket almost got tangled up on the oarlock with my head still below water. Luckily, I narrowly escaped that dangerous situation. I took my life jacket off to try again. Keeping a death grip on the boat as I slipped under it, I found my dog still alive. She was cradled on the oarsman's seat and had plenty of air from the drainage tubes.

With Inua under one arm, and hanging onto the boat with an adrenaline-empowered death grip, I avoided being swept back into the current and soon clamored up the rocks. Inua was happy to see me, and I hugged her big time. I still get tears in my eyes every time I float by this place and remember our embrace.

The rain was still falling. I had lost one rubber boot, and it was still early in the morning. The nearby rock overhang provided good cover from the weather. Inua and I kept each other warm under the big boulder. With thoughts of Sarge, who had been left behind, churning in my brain, I felt serious compassion for outfitters who had lost guests on commercial river trips.

However, I knew Sarge was a survivor. He would fight hard for his life, as he had in Vietnam. I formulated a plan to get back to him if no jetboat showed up. It involved hiking the Oregon side of the river far enough along the Snake to where I could swim across it, climb over the top of the steep mountainside, and drop down to the Salmon to look for Sarge. Luckily I heard a jetboat approaching as I was visualizing this plan. Woohoo!

They pulled up not far from me, and I shouted over their idling engine sounds, describing my dilemma and Sarge's situation upriver. They immediately ripped loose on the throttle and roared away. My intention had been to go with them, but they were so quick to leave that I missed the chance. A half hour later they returned with Sarge. He was cold, but alive. Miraculously, my dog Metoo was also with them. I was elated.

They towed my boat downriver to the first available sandbar, at the foot of a massive cliff overhang called Nez Perce Cave. After beaching, it took five of us to flip the boat right side up. One oarlock was bent beyond use, but that was fixed with the help of an axe they had. Once we recouped, they bid us farewell as I profusely thanked them.

When they were gone, I opened the hatch, grabbed a propane heater, and headed for the cave. Sarge hung out there with the heater as I returned to my boat to bail water from the compartmentalized hatches. They're not totally leak proof, and my boat was about half full of water. I grabbed my bilge pump and had begun pulling the plunger to withdraw water when another jetboat arrived. It was one of the biggest boats on the river, from the largest jetboat company in the canyon, Beamers Hells Canyon Tours. The boat was so huge that the pilot talked to guests via a microphone.

As he stopped in mid-current, I heard his voice booming over the microphone. He asked if I had lost the ammo can he was holding in his hand. "Yes, yes, that is mine," I hollered over the roar of his jets. So he powered toward shore and pulled up next to me.

I was still up to my knees in my boat, dressed only in a loincloth, bilging water out of my boat. Surely, I was quite the sight to his party of about 50 people, and I could feel all of 100 eyes on me.

He gave me the box, I thanked him, and went back to bilging without saying another word. His curiosity got the better of him and he broke the silence to ask if I had flipped my boat.

"Yeah, that sometimes happens out here on the big creek," I replied. An elderly couple intently gazing my way caught my eye. "Say, I have about

15 more miles to float and have room for a couple of more people. How would you like to go with me?" I asked them. "Oh, no, no, no!" they replied.

I told them an abbreviated account of what had happened to us, and they soon sped off, so I could finish my job. Before long, Sarge and I arrived at the Heller Bar takeout where a warm rig awaited. We'd survived a nearly Purple Heart river affair.

Chapter 22

SALMON RIVER TRIPLE DIGIT CLUB

Only a few people can claim to have run the Main Salmon's legendary Ruby Rapid at flows over cfs, but you can count me as one of them.

Around 1994, big-water runs finally began to be welcomed with anticipation by local rivermen rather than being dreaded like a fearsome monster to be avoided. Even so, not all guides were drawn to the challenges of high-water boating. Really only a small handful of adrenaline-junkie guides were addicted to what my later-in-life wife, Barb, termed "testosterone poisoning." Not that only the male gender was represented on the river on the historic day of May 18, 1997, when records kept by the U.S. Geological Survey show the river to have been at 101,000 cfs. More than one female, perhaps in need of an estrogen boost, were drawn to the white chaos that awaited that day.

Some enormous rapids have such a variety of chromosomal hydraulics in their DNA that the different parts deserve their own names. Like a human body whose organs contribute to the whole, a rapid's reputation is given life by its internal aspects.

Such is the case for Ruby. I began referring to five different areas of the rapid by making up my own names for them. At the top of the rapid is what I call the Gates of Ruby, where large diagonal waves on both sides of the river serve as entry walls that must be punched to meet the next set of even larger diagonals. The larger ones converge in the middle of the vortex in what I refer to as the Pencil Sharpener. It can flip a boat upside down just like the corkscrew action of a pencil being twisted in a grinder. Once those obstacles are successfully negotiated, sometimes a Mystery Wave surges up from the side or stern of a boat quite unexpectedly. It cannot be read ahead of time, but it demands a quick response.

If that doesn't mess with your boat, then I normally head for the Freeway, which offers a safe passage just a hair right of a long train of several consecutive standing waves. Catching the Freeway is imperative because a hundred yards downstream of the Pencil Sharpener is the Pancake Wave, which can flip a boat faster than Aunt Jemima turning pancakes. I'm not sure who named this wave. It could have been me or Mike Kenney or someone else. Mike and I both have some memory lapses from getting smacked by whitewater punches over the years.

These descriptive names offer a cautionary hint of what boaters can expect to see at high flows, but on the day the river ran over a hundred grand, the Gates of Ruby and the Pencil Sharpener were a tad more user-friendly. But only a tad. The Mystery Wave had disappeared, but the Pancake Wave was still there, only bigger.

The appearance of the rapid that day was hypnotic. It was like looking at the Himalayan Mountains, with the bottom wave train containing more than a dozen white-capped peaks separated by deep valleys of dirty brown, debris-filled water. Once past the Mixmaster-like entry, it was mostly a straight shot through, with a side step to avoid the Pancake Wave. However, once they entered the V leading into the rapid, each raft was caught in the river's inescapable grip, which sucked everyone into a battle with irregular waves and random jostling akin to a birdie being batted back and forth in a violent game of badminton. It was a liquid rollercoaster ride threatening to go off the rails, and we were in for a thrilling ride.

101,000 cfs
What the Hell Were We Thinking?

Why are people drawn to this kind of experience?

Since I began boating on the Salmon River in the Riggins area in 1975, that was the only day I have seen the river over 100,000 cfs. It was a day I will never forget, with waves resembling the big rollers ocean surfers seek to challenge. While river waves are different and smaller than the 100-foot giants the ocean can stir up, size is merely a relative perspective because all waves have in common a primal force of great power and energy.

All energy in motion in nature is expressed as some kind of wave, be they optical waves, radio waves, electromagnetic waves, shock waves, ocean waves, or river waves. But the real beauty of river and ocean waves is that they are pure energy made visible in a manifest physical form that holds an undeniable, extremely strong force of attraction. To deny its power would be like telling someone not to think of a white elephant in the room, knowing that doing so would have the opposite effect of burning that exact image deep into the mind.

The attraction of giant waves and the power of the river may never be fully understood, even by those who have felt it. They just feel it and have to go. Explanations just get in the way. Surf's up! That is all that matters.

Of course, not all guides like high water. When I first came to town, only a small core group, besides myself, were excited for high water, and the higher the better. Some companies were too intimidated, and a majority didn't have high-water experience. However, most of them slowly drifted into the high-water scene, motivated by competition for a piece of the action and a dollar.

On that unusual high-water day, nerves were only a little quelled when we stopped on the road to survey Ruby and study every nuance of where critical moves would be needed to make a successful run down through the mountainous swells breaking on top like snow avalanching down precipitous slopes and do our "slam dance" as Mike Kennedy liked to say.

This day the waves were bigger than I had ever seen on the river, but fortunately, it looked like an easier run than some at mid-flow levels where one learns what "slam" really means. As is often the case, things had looked smaller and easier from the road than when we got there and found that our years of professional judgment had underestimated by more than we could know.

So how was the river ride when it went over a hundred grand? Here is the actual transcript of my journal of that day and our run:

"The Day of the 100,000 Club"

Quite a parade of boats today. NWV had a commercial trip that Mike took. But of course the high-water entourage showed up for support and to engage in the extra electricity brought on by the power source – the Salmon River.

Ruby was high and mighty today, and the extra amperage was felt by the tiny boats as they surged toward their separate destinies. It was more like a parade as just about every kind of craft was represented. Bruce rowed his Majestic Sky blue Maravia, Mike in his NRS self-bailer, a trainee in a new Incept raft, Coop Glenn in his renewed glass dory boat, me in my dory, Mike Harp in his cat boat, Sue in her cat boat, and 3 kayaks: Greg (or Craig?), Scott Draper, and Ian (?).

There was also a safety boat in the water (an Incept) below Ruby.

Bruce led off and had a good run. I believe Coop went next, but he did not have quite as good luck. The Pancake Wave lived up to its name and flipped Coop. They did manage to recover fairly fast. The safety boat did not respond – it was waiting for guest boats.

Mike ran next and he had a good run ... practically hitting the road, he said, after yesterday's flip. He made a very conservative run today.

I ran next. This was my poorest run through Ruby this season. I entered pushing forward as usual. Then I turned sternward for the Pencil Sharpener ... actually the diagonal on the backside of the Pencil Sharpener was what I was planning to surf into the Freeway below it. However, it was bigger and more powerful than I thought it would be and it tweaked me. Had to lean to the right side (as I was sternward and my right side was to the wall) to keep the boat from flipping. Lost my right oar in the process. Tried frantically to get it back in the oarlock, but part of the tie-in line had wrapped around the horn and messed with me.

However, I did manage to get the oar in, then grab the other oar, and, with both, turn the boat sternward to ride up the mountainous waves on the roulette highway. It was a helluva ride going up those waves backward.

I was rowing as hard as I could and thought that any of those breaking waves could gobble us up. Fortunately, none of them, including the Pancake Wave broke on us too severely, but close. About halfway down (past the Pancake Wave) I was able to get turned around and continue on down bowardly.

But, I was heading directly for the wave that had flipped Mike yesterday, and I could see it was building for us, too. It broke big time on us. I hollered for us all to go forward. It hit hard, but with our high-siding and a bit of luck we managed to save it from presenting the bottom to the sky.

That was one hairball run. Ursala (She Bear) and Travis Hollon rode with me through that one. Him in front, her in back. It worked great again, even though I blew my entry.

Glen came next and saw what happened to me, so he made sure he entered a bit more left than what I did. He had a good run, though I did not get to see it. Mike and Sue followed suit, having good runs, right side up anyway. And that more or less means a good run.

The kayakers had good runs, too, I heard. Except Greg said he ran right dab into the Pancake as it broke on him. It flipped him despite his anticipating brace. The river turned upside down on him, he later said.

Lake Creek was big. I ran down the middle, even though the left run was tempting. Half the boats went each way. Both dories went middle. It was a nice ride.

Lower Catspaw was big and ugly. Real ugly. We got messed with, but not severely enough to high-side. But close.

The next big swirly stuff in that next lower rapid was also huge and ugly. We got tossed around a bit there, too. Ugly!

Such was my diary account, but other things I also vividly remember was just how powerful the boils and whirlpools were, and how the current between the monstrous rapids was nearly as challenging as the whitewater mayhem we had bitten off that day. To those who get smacked in the face by them, the wild forces of nature are extremely humbling and command a ton of respect for their awe-inspiring character.

Years Later ...*

What lingers longest in my memory bank as I picture the ride that day is how big the waves were and how long the boats remained out of sight from one another as we all bobbed about like corks on a line in that helter-skelter mayhem. Most striking was the view of the boat in front of me, as it dipped over the top of liquid mountains, completely disappearing for what seemed like forever on the downstream side. Only when climbing the next wave did the boat re-appear, but then disappeared again over another high peak in a process that repeated itself about a dozen times. The crest-to-crest time span between wave peaks seemed like it took days to traverse rather than just a few seconds. It is a weird paradox of the slow-motion effect of fast-moving events. It is also part of the magic of the mind tricks big waves play.

Chapter 23

WHEN ALL HELL BROKE LOOSE
THE LITTLE SALMON RIVER FLOOD OF 1997

Happy New Year! What better way to start off a new year than to jump onto a raging river at flood stage? OK, not everyone was lining up to partake of such opportunities. Admittedly, it might require some degree of craziness and extreme thirst for adventure to consider such a stunt. But I'm not alone in being pulled by the stronger forces of nature, like a moth to the flame, as I gathered with kindred souls that first day of January 1997, trying to figure out if and how the extreme flows could be negotiated with good planning.

Although many of us had run some pretty big water on the Little Salmon, 5,800 cfs was the highest level I had tackled before that day. But the river was pushing so much water down the canyon when it crested that it exceeded what the USGS river gauge could calibrate accurately. Technicians had to take manual measurements and make best-educated guesses as to the flow. In the official records, the day's level was recorded as 10,500 cfs. I suspect that was a low estimate, as the river was off-the-wall powerful and eventually scoured out the river bed, changing the channel in many places between Boulder Creek and the Riggins city limits bridge.

On its first day, the new year came crashing in on a far grander scale than any tumultuous party humans could conjure up. Fortunately, a few of us local guides did not have bad hangovers from wildly welcoming the transition from '96 to '97.

It was a most unusual set of circumstances that set the stage for the Little River flood that proved to be epic in its aftermath. The main trigger was an instantaneous Jekyll and Hyde weather change. With a large blanket of snow covering the entire region, a sudden low pressure cell with high temps and torrential rains scurried across the area. That combination was a recipe for the extreme geologic change that resulted.

I saw houses and other structures falling off high banks into the river, roads being inundated with water and mud, and tons of debris floating on raging currents. Bridges were taken out at Pinehurst and the Winchester grade, isolating Riggins from the rest of the civilized world for about a week, with no power or phone service.

Before the buildings began caving into the river and all hell broke loose, some of us took advantage of the situation to chalk up some memorable river runs. Following is an excerpt from my river journal describing the conditions and our attempts to navigate a portion of the extreme flows. Clarifying information about my diary entries is inserted in italic type.

Jan. 1, 1997 Happy New Year "copy of my hand writing diary"

Talked with Dick Pullin on the eve of the New Year about his "slide" experience. Him and Mark Hollon heard the mudslide (which took out all their landscaping between the house and shop – and moved one of his rigs) as it came.

They said it sounded like a horrific freight train and they didn't know which way to run cuz they couldn't tell where the noise was coming from, up the river from them or up the hill.

Dick was worried about losing his home if things worsened. He came into town to stay with Mark. *(He lived just upstream of Fall Creek, west of the highway, but the entire house was removed when they constructed the new highway a few years after the flood.)*

Day 1 *(Jan. 1):* It had rained hard for the last day or two. Weather had warmed up, and the snow blanketing New Meadows was making a quick exit (about 1½' of snow on level along highway in Valley area).

Dick had mentioned the river was higher than he had ever seen it. So I was sleeping later than usual when Glenn Upperman called and wanted to know about running the Little River – cuz his creek was roaring. *(Glenn and Lisa were living up Cow Creek maybe a mile or two up from Lucile.)*

I got up (9 a.m.-ish) immediately and jumped into the hot tub. The main river was not up terribly (maybe 30,000-ish) but I could see logs and lots of debris in the river. It also appeared that the mouth of the Little River was crankin'.

So I didn't stay in hot tub long – I figured I better go check the river. Got in the car and raced off. As soon as I could see the creek, I realized I was looking at a horrendous spectacle. Higher than I have ever seen it. Raging! Scary!

At Rapid River it looked ugly. Three big holes – two magnum right together (where I pirouetted in the raft last year) and a third where Doug Dennis swam last year. It appeared there was a run if everything went perfect. *(stretch of river immediately below mouth of Rapid River)*

It would be a powell right, immediately turn and pull guts out left to miss a gaping corner pour-over. Looked very marginal to do. And a swim could be really terminal.

At Miners Jct *(turnoff at main highway that leads to Miner's Supply shop)* they were directing traffic and letting people know of slides covering the main highway. I drove up to the first one (Grouse Ck?) and took pictures – it was past the rest stop but before tavern. *(Grouse Ck is the next trib just upstream ¼ mile from Sheep Creek Rest Stop.)*

Came back and went up Pollock Road. The hump rock where Dwayne swam last year was very spectacular. *(what guides now call Jelly Bean Rock – located immediately above the bridge that crosses the main highway near Miners Jct)* Amazing! Lots of amazing sights. Stopped and talked to Nancy Black. *Salmon Lodge – near bridge that crosses the little river just upstream of back road to Pollock*

Water was getting close – threatening the bridge even. I walked out on it (after driving over it) and could feel it shake a hair. Rocks were rumbling down the channel. Awesome!

At Carol Darraughs *(next to bridge that crosses Little River just below Rainbow Bend and ¼ mile above mouth of Indian Creek)* water was piling up each bridge pillar – splashing on the road. Absolutely no room for a raft to go under – a foot or 1½ feet from hitting the bridge. I was guessing the bridge could go out.

Drove up to as far as the next slide – Rattlesnake Creek. *(¼ mile below main highway bridge crossing Little River near Pinehurst)* No way around this one. Mud 5' thick over the entire road for 50-75 yards. Rattlesnake Creek pouring through the middle of it.

I took pictures here and other radical places. Huge wave in front of Red Woods house. *(west side of Little River maybe a mile above Carol's place)* Mudslide around new house at our "catch a breath" eddy. *(maybe a mile below bridge at Carol's place)*

I checked everything out in terms of running it. The only thing that looked reasonably safe was from about a mile above Wick's Bridge. A good spot to drive and put in boats. *(about 1-2 miles upstream of Riggins)*

Went home found Doug Dennis and Glenn, both of which I wished to talk to. After Doug talked to Glenn, he gave me the phone and I urged Glenn to get his raft and head up.

Meanwhile, I went out and readied my driftboat. Glenn, Lisa, me & Doug were going to run. When we got up to Wick's Corner, we decided to walk down and scout. Just as we stepped onto the bridge, a huge cottonwood tree upstream uprooted and came skyward and thunked up against the bridge. Like an ominous omen – the bridge shook a little, the branches creaked and groaned. Temporarily, we didn't know what was going to happen.

But it stabilized and we walked across. The entire run looked difficult. Precision the key. Waves to break and stay away from. Current unbelievably fast. Guess it to be 15 mph.

There was a diagonal to break upstream of the bridge in order to miss an ugly pour-over not 6 seconds below, then a diagonal to avoid coming off the fence line at our big eddy stop. *(only giant eddy river right just below Wick's Bridge)*

Immediately we would try for the right channel (of island), but if missing it (and a good chance of that), it would be a hard pull trying to maintain inside curvature on the 90-degree bend. A series of waves/holes on left side would be swim city.

Then at Delbert's Drop there were huge crashing waves to break thru – so as to miss an ugly, ugly hole caused by the big boulder below Delbert's Drop. It appeared to be only about 6-7 seconds of time to get right of the hole. *(This is the rapid on the S-turn corner below Wick's Bridge and out of sight from the main highway.)*

Although if worse came to worst, it might have been possible to skirt the hole on the left.

Herein I decided to abandon the driftboat and volunteer to paddle assist Glenn. Me & Doug in front, Lisa in rear. All stroking fortuitously.

So we went back and drove farther up just to look. When we were at the cushion rock (Dwaine's Swimming Hole) near bridge/Miner's Cutoff, the police stopped us and said there was a big earth dam about to break and a potential 15' wall of water to follow. *(cushion rock now called Jelly Bean)*

I didn't believe it, but when we got back to my rig (at Wick's) Glenn pretty much decided not to run. So we came home. I was disappointed although the river was a reckless torrent and intimidating as hell.

Day 2 *(Jan. 2):* Called Glenn, but he had commitments in Lewiston. Luke showed and he was the only person willing to run with me. Doug Dennis left for a job. Norm wasn't interested. Geoff definitely not interested. Kerry not the slightest interested. Wouldn't even look up from morning paper to look me in the eye and say no. Smily Dave had a kidney infection.

Didn't call Bruce E. because Glenn was unable to get him by phone yesterday – and I knew (if he was home) he was stranded due to mudslide on highway and Pollock road washed away. *(Bruce lived up Denny Creek, across and up from Pollock.)*

The cat crew was up at French Creek. *(on big river)* So it boiled down to me and Luke. (In my raft).

Note: Wick's still looked too wicked to chance with only one paddler and high-sider.

Even though the river dropped a foot, it was lapping up on the highway at bend above storage sheds (yesterday), though not today. *(guessing the river to be over 8,000 cfs that day; storage sheds located at new bridge behind Kerry Brennan's new tackle shop)*

We put in at Terry Farmers place. *(This is the only cabin on Windy Corner – between highway and river, maybe ½ mile above city limit sign.)* Just out of the chute and the first diagonal stopped us momentarily and surged us onward. This river was awesomely powerful. Moves had to be initiated far in advance, as we were swept along frantically fast.

I powelled left at storage sheds so as not to run the middle of the wave train – due to a very large bottom wave peaking high and steep. I did catch the edge of it though.

The next wave train – perhaps the biggest was at the city limit sign just on the bend below Mike marker rock. *(Mike Kennedy's Rock that he used as an indicator of river level is just below the "Nozzle" – the name I gave the rapid created March 29, 2005, when Hailey Creek blew out across from Squaw Creek.)* This was a great ride – though I hair-lined the right side of the wave train to be cautious.

At the Riggins Bridge *(old bridge)* there was a gargantuan hole caused by rock on left, just upstream of bridge. *(This is the old bridge before the new one was put in 200 yards upstream of it in 2014?)* I clipped the edge of it. A very big wave train right under the bridge was also an awesome ride. From there down it was fast and fun, nothing tricky.

The entire run probably took only 10-15 minutes.

It was so much fun we did it again. This time I let Luke row. He did great. We bypassed the diagonal that toyed with us the first time. Then he took on more of the wave train behind storage sheds than I did. But it felt good.

He was a bit right of city limits wave train, but still had huge ride. I only got splashed over my head once or twice. Sticking out over the bow with a paddle.

We did one more run. By then we saw Kim and Kirk. They didn't want to go with us – but shuttled and said they were up for tomorrow. Also, then the Canyon Cats would be back. (Roy & Karen).

On our third run I hit everything down the middle. It was an awesome ride. The best rides being the storage shed waves and the city limits wave train. Luke was buried in the storage shed wave.

It was like Grand Canyon wave size, but faster current and a much more reckless fury feeling. Logs and debris, flood water running rampant.

Day 3 *(Jan. 3):* Up early and up the road to check out Lake Ck. Roy got in last night and said it had blown out. Sure enough, the creek had raged down the canyon, wiped out the bridge to Rhetts place, washed out road, and filled in left run by the big boulder. *(Rhetts – house at mouth of Lake Creek)*

Lake Ck rapid actually looked worse. It appeared to be a nastier run. Ruby was kicken', probably 30-35,000-ish.

Then I drove up to check out Wicks Corner and take some photos. It still looked marginal for running. But I decided to run my driftboat down from Terry's. All I needed was one rider. Could not round up anyone. Not even Luke. They all partied till 4 a.m. – so didn't get up till noonish. Roy, Kirk, and gals went to Knuckles to get his catboat. Was almost dark when they returned. Norm came over and offered to shuttle for me, but I was a bit leery without someone to bail – just in case I needed it.

Too bad the Oregon boys aren't here. We have had no electricity or phones (other than locally) since New Year's Day. So I couldn't call them. *(This was also before internet access.)*

As I think back over the years, and consider myself still lucky enough to be alive, I like to think (hope) I have gained a little wisdom from all the adrenaline-soaked experiences that have enlivened my allotted time on the planet.

When I contemplate all the extreme runs, first descents, and unusual river exploits, I recall advice my dad gave me when I was competing in sports. It applied to both winning and losing. He said to just remember that "there will always be someone faster." I was a runner and wrestler, and it applied well for both, as well as everything else in life.

It brings to mind the times we used to drive along the North Fork of the Payette, before anyone ever ran it, thinking it was impossible at the time. Our standard line was: "Even Dr. Blackadar wouldn't run this."

Of course, extreme boaters do it almost routinely now. Kayakers jump off waterfalls, treacherous gorges are challenged that require extreme climbing skills in addition to river-running expertise, and natural selection still weeds out the good and the bad with serious consequences. But it all still reminds me that no matter the accomplishments I may manage to achieve, there is always that sub-4-minute miler stepping up to the starting line.

So rather than basking in any kind of grandiose sense of self in comparing my feats to those of others, what's far more important is the race I run against myself. It is more about how I relate to the river and to life, while here to engage them, that really matters. The best thing about the more extreme events that I live to experience is that they give me even more respect for the power of nature and appreciation for all life.

Chapter 24

THE KILLER PILLARS

In 1997, the Idaho Transportation Department implemented plans to replace the Goff Bridge, which is also known as the Time Zone Bridge, just north of Riggins. It was constructed in 1935-36, replacing an earlier steel/timber bridge built there in 1911.

I never could understand why it was necessary to erect the new version, which I call the "Golden Gate of Riggins." The official justification was to alleviate safety concerns over cracks and weaknesses in the old structure. Instead of mending the problem areas, the state opted for an entirely new bridge, along with a highway extending through the middle of town. To me, it seemed to be a "pork barrel" project to provide temporary jobs, which would soon evaporate and many of which were filled by outsiders.

With a $12.4 million price tag, the project, which got off the ground in May, was much more expensive than what a fix to the old bridge would have cost. If we can put a man on the moon, repairing an aging structure should be simple. But based on results, there are fewer mistakes in space travel.

It soon became apparent the engineers had not foreseen some potential problems. One huge oversight was their failing to consult with some of us local people who knew the power of the river and its potential for wreaking havoc. They apparently had never heard of the Precautionary Principle, which holds that an action should not be taken if the consequences are uncertain and potentially dangerous.

We outfitters running day trips on the river had grave concerns and requested a meeting with the project leaders once we learned of their construction plans, which did not take into account hazards to boat traffic. One elephantine menace we foresaw was a huge barge placed at the bottom end of Time Zone Rapid to facilitate various bridge building activities. It would occupy considerable space on the water.

When we warned Transportation Department officials and building contractors about potential high-water problems, they pretty much poo-pooed our apprehensions as overinflated paranoia.

Before the big chiefs of industry would heed our concerns, the river, as if to prove our point, kicked into high-water gear, and soon the raging torrent ripped loose the cables securing the barge to the bank. The huge iron barge, maybe 20 yards wide by 60 yards long, headed downstream like an out of control whitewater river craft following the river's whims on a path to destruction. Luckily no one was on board.

The worst looming threat was to the pillars of the bridge that crosses the main river at Lucile. Should the barge go that far, it would be unlikely to avoid hitting them and causing serious destruction. Fortunately, it was sucked into a giant eddy 200 yards upstream of the bridge, near the old Northwest Voyageurs boat shop, which is now an RV park and private residence.

I don't know how they got it back to Riggins. It surely was a costly affair, though far less than what it could have been if the barge had not eddied out where it did. After that, the officials paid attention to us outfitters, and new meetings were held to coordinate bridge construction with our float trip schedules.

Besides the main problem of the barge's placement at the foot of the rapid, an additional issue was the positioning of inch-thick steel cables used to anchor it to both sides of the river. One cable stretching across the river was only 2 feet above water level and a real peril to any kind of float traffic. The plan was to manually raise it with a system of winches when the construction crew saw approaching craft.

They also padded the upstream side of the barge and provided a large climbable net over the side to help in the rescue of anyone in a river craft that hit the barge. It all sounded tenuous at best, but that is what both sides agreed to in our safety meetings with the project leaders.

Another major problem with the barge's location was that it reduced the margin of error for boats passing the pillars of the old bridge, which could not be removed until the new structure was opened for the traffic that the original bridge continued to carry.

In super high flows, they were very ugly and hard to miss. We called them the Killer Pillars. There were two heavy-gauge cables between the two pillars used for support that looked like a giant X from an approaching raft. It was like a bullseye into mayhem, but this was one target we tried not to hit.

Time Zone Rapid is a real menace in flows above 30,000 cfs, even in normal conditions without an extra obstacle to avoid. It contains many large and capricious waves, many breaking on top, several changing as giant boils and whirlpools flex muscle and push them around. Add the barge and Killer Pillars and that menace turns into a dreaded monster. Huge boils and the main current banging into the Killer Pillars were difficult to avoid and quite nerve wracking. I saw more than one raft postage stamp the X, spilling people into the river like ducklings scrambling for safety. The river's forgiveness may be the only reason no one died there before the new bridge project was completed.

My scariest run occurred one day when I had two ladies in the front of my wooden dory, the Eclipse. We had come around the corner about 300 yards upstream where the entry to the rapid begins. In low water, there is a nice sand beach for a lunch stop on river right, but that day it was covered by high flows.

As I was scouting my run and looking far downriver to be sure the cable was not in our way, a shocking sight hit me like a brick in the face. The cable was stretched tight across the river in the middle of our run and impossible to avoid, and no crews were doing anything about it because they had not seen our approach.

As panic poked its head out of the water like a sea monster, I immediately began frantically rowing in search of any nuance of slower water I could find in a world with no eddies. Only the outside of the main current was slightly slower, which might minutely prolong our fate with an ugly destiny below.

I told the ladies to wave their arms to try to get attention of anyone downstream. Luckily it worked. Guys began scrambling as fast as they could to raise the cable before we would crash into it. I was still strenuously rowing against the current, mostly in sheer survival mode. Only 40 yards before we got there, they managed to raise the cable just enough for us to barely sneak under. Whew! Game almost over, aside for the Killer Pillars waiting hungrily below.

Gears shifted back to frantic rowing speed again as I weaseled my way around them and caught my breath below. Continuing onward after that, an old reoccurring thought that I sometimes have in lower flows came to mind:

"As I float down the middle of the river, I see the green mossy shoreline as a messenger of the river's testimony to its essence. The high-water mark above the green is a reminder of the river's sleeping, waiting only for the passage of time to yet again arouse from its slumber. Once returning to that upper level again, the river rises up to its quintessential power to reveal its strongest beauty."

Below the menacing rapid, I thanked the river once again for allowing us safe passage through its quintessential power. Our experience surviving the barge beast and Killer Pillars turned out to be the real beauty of the river that day in 1997.

Chapter 25

SERMONS ON THE SALMON

Why are some humans so intent on saving the world? I, too, want to save natural areas and promote integrity in how we use them, and I'm willing to share my views with others. However, I am not one of those who point fingers at anyone who has opposing views and threaten that they will burn in hell for not believing as I do.

Some people think they are heaven sent, and are hell-bent, to save the world from the devil. I encountered such a character on the river during a Labor Day weekend trip. The river was very busy that day, with lots of rafters and river floaters of all stripes.

Under the bridge at the bottom of Time Zone Rapids, on the left side, was a lone man holding up a sign with some apparently applicable psalm and yelling, "Repent," to all who passed him. He seemed to think that everyone floating by, whom he knew nothing about, had a soul needing to be saved. I couldn't resist responding to the lone savior's righteous advice and hollered back, "Jesus loves you, everyone else thinks you are an asshole."

I was so pissed off that it didn't dawn on me then that I, too, might have sinned at times by thinking I needed to save people from themselves when it comes to how humans treat nature.

While I can differentiate between good and bad influences on landscapes and track down culprits responsible for bad ecological behavior, God shows little sign of caring how we treat the Earth. Therefore, we humans had better take responsibility for the task at hand in this world. The results of our actions are measurable and plainly visible on nature's tablet. They are written in our own handwriting upon the land.

That stream-side zealot's stern warning, shouted in his loudest voice, could not drown out the voices of nature that surrounded him. Those are the voices I pay attention to, and even the deaf can "hear" them, because they sing out soundlessly and communicate directly to the soul.

Chapter 26

DISMANTLERS EXTREME SPORTS CLUB AND PULLMAN POUNDERS

While high-water adventure was the main pull that brought a crowd of "wild" country people who were my friends from northeastern Oregon to the Salmon River, they also heard the siren's call of the summer sun, warm water, and lively atmosphere in the canyon. They included a broad array of athletic people who liked to have a good time.

Someone, perhaps Doctor Death, started the Dismantlers Extreme Sports Club, which was quite an appropriate name for people who were good at downhill skiing, river running, and many other outdoor endeavors. There also was a common bond formed by the consumption of tons of alcohol capable of dismantling those who drank as hard as they played.

Sometimes, I would run up river to reserve them a campsite a day or two before they arrived. Some would caravan in, while others straggled in at unimaginable times, depending on saloon side stops or some other temptation too enticing to resist, all resulting in the difficult task of finding a designated driver.

When it came to dismantling their campsite in the morning, after the previous evening's extreme partying, it looked like a war zone littered with altered-state casualties strewn across the beach. I was an honorary club member, though I never felt like I was quite as hard core in the consumption department. Heck, I barely met their extreme qualifications for membership. However, I admit there were times I felt highly qualified as I partied with them, although I can't remember everything that happened on those occasions. By the way, did I mention the short name for the club: the DISMANTLERS?

We had a lot of fun during those high-water adventures, with thrills and spills, yard sales, hole plundering, stupid human tricks, stellar runs through the white chaos of giant wave trains, and heroic efforts to gather up ducklings that went too far over the black side of the horizon line. Because most were wise enough to save the drinking and green smoke for after making a run, there never were any truly stupid stunts on the river, just solid fun and high adventure.

However, once the rapids were behind, the party started. It normally went on all night long, or until sleep or passing out brought an interlude until the next day, when everything was repeated by those who had survived the night and could rally their crew and gear for more challenging runs. Not all were as good at recovering as they were at partying.

It seemed quite crazy to me that none of these friends, other than Rick, had done much, if any, river running before I met them. When I was living in my tipi on the family cherry orchard in Cove and first met them, these folks mostly just thought I was that crazy guy who did dangerous things like running wild-ass rivers.

We were all young people in our mid-20s at the time, and everyone had somewhat of a niche they were noted for, like fly fishing, elk hunting, or downhill ski racing. Nearly all had a high level of athleticism and were gregarious, which made them such a great bunch with whom to share adventures.

After getting their own gear and joining my world, they soon found that it wasn't as "crazy" as the one they had left behind. They found sanity in the river's medicine, which was far more addicting than anything that could be imbibed or inhaled.

One year when the Dismantlers came to Riggins to run the river and party hard, I had a commercial trip with a group from Washington state that proved to be somewhat of a twin extreme sports club. It might better be named the Extreme Drinking Club. Most of these people were from the Pullman area, where they worked farms and had occupations similar to those of the Dismantlers.

They had signed up for a day trip with me and had asked permission to bring a few beers. My mistake was to say yes, not knowing that their spelling of "few" was "way too much." There were three boats and guides helping me that day, including Rick, and we had our hands full trying to contain the overly enthusiastic Pullman people. We kept reminding them that we had plenty of time to party after the trip, and luckily we survived the day with no major mishaps on the water.

After the river leg was completed, Rick and I arranged to round up all the Dismantlers to meet the Pullman group in downtown Riggins to party together. Well, that was the night the Pullman Pounders earned the second part of their name. Wow. They could pound them down, drinking just as hard as the Dismantlers. We all danced up a storm and drank till closing time at Summerville's. Tim and Vickie Heath were the owners then, and it was the place to be in those days.

Everyone had a great time, and by the next morning the Dismantlers were once again dismantled and the Pounders pounded, evidence of pretty much a tie in the game of hard partying and hard recovering.

Ah! The good ol' days! Most of the Dismantlers are pretty much dismantled now, but still functional with new hips, joints, and a wide array of replaced body parts. Sadly, it all reminds me of the scene in the Monty Python movie "In Search of the Holy Grail" where the knight keeps fighting even with both legs and arms cut off. Ever struggling, never giving up. Such is the trademark of good athletes and good memories.

Chapter 27

BIRTH OF THE BIG WATER BLOWOUT

In the two years after the epic high-water event that spawned the hundred grand club at Ruby Rapid in May 1997, more and more local guides were drawn to tackling such runs. By 1999, Matt Laine, one of the up and coming youngbloods, had cooked up the idea of creating a more official, organized high-water celebration every year to entice business for guides and outfitters.

Those of us who had been running higher flows were looked down on by a few other outfitters who thought it was too dangerous. However, they lacked whitewater experience comparable to what the core group had accumulated over many years. So, aside from running extreme flows just for the fun of it, we wanted to demonstrate to the public that it was a reasonable thing to do, if treated with proper respect. By promoting extra safety procedures and screening guests to qualify them physically for participation, it all seemed very legitimate.

Having done a lot of leg work, Matt got the first event off the ground on June 5, 1999. He talked us outfitters into donating free river trips to the public to help promote it and river-running business during the high-water season. Red Bull Energy Drink helped sponsor the event and set up a giant Star Canopy at Spring Bar as its headquarters. People could sign up for trips there with the outfitter and guides of their choice, then boat the river, and be shuttled back to the put-in at trip's end.

The day was highlighted by a loosely organized, helter-skelter whitewater parade that included different craft; dicey, cutting edge routes through rapids; and occasional carnage that was always a crowd pleaser for the riverside gawkers and photographers on hand.

People were amped up by a day of electrifying action on the river that recharged their human spirit. After the runs, alcohol flowed with about as much cfs as the river, as people made it to the Seven Devils Tavern for the rest of the activities, which included a Dutch Oven Cookoff, live music, and replays of videos showing the day's river carnage. The fun extended into the nighttime with noise as loud as the roar of the rapids, as people pounded the floor with their dancing feet and pounded down a large quantity of beer. Some may have even remembered it all the next morning.

By the year 2000, I had acquired what I used to call the UFO – unidentified floating object. It was really called a Hydro-Bronc and was basically an inflatable hamster wheel about 10 feet in diameter that could be propelled across water by a person inside walking or running on a mesh treadmill. It required a lot of stamina, even for people who were in very good shape, and was not suitable for most people. It required the use of arms as well as legs for balancing and to get it moving without rolling to the side. It could go anywhere because it couldn't be tipped upside down, but it could spin fast enough when caught in a hole to keep a human lying down in the water gulping for air and getting tired while trying to escape the river's grip.

For those who dared, it was an out-of-this-world ride in an alien-looking UFO, and for some it was a way to emulate Jesus and walk on water. It provided big fun during what had become known as the Big Water Blowout and a big draw for the carnage-crazed crowd of buzzards gathered to watch at the serious rapids.

I thought it was going to be a unique option to add to our company's fleet, as we were the first outfitter in Idaho to make it available for public use. However, it turned out to be a surprisingly hard sell because it was too demanding physically for the average person. I ended up passing it on to a private high-adventure seeker for his own pursuit of the outer limits.

By 2003, the Big Water Blowout had evolved significantly and took on new meaning. It was decided that a trophy, called the Big Water Bruce Elmquist Memorial Cup, would be awarded annually to a different high-water guide in honor of Bruce, whose shocking death from a brain aneurism had saddened the entire boating community. Bruce was one of the original core of high-water boaters. Though he was too humble to ever wear the title "Big Water Bruce" very well, it was a nickname used by some of his friends who knew how much he enjoyed the magnum intensity of the river's power every spring.

The Big Water Blowout trophy was named for him as a way to remember his legacy and friendship to those who knew him and to serve as a beacon to the spirit of adventure for new guides and all other boaters who like high-intensity nature experiences. The cup is held for a year by a guide, who then chooses another guide and passes it on to continue the tradition. I believe that would please Bruce, who perhaps is still running rivers of stars in the heavens.

I believe the trophy was the brainchild of Matt Laine. At the time, he was one of the younger guides in town, working for other outfitters, but eventually he became one himself, as owner of another company in town, Wild River Adventures.

Chapter 28

ESTROGEN EXPRESS AT THE SLIDE
JUNE 30 – JULY 4, 1997

JUNE 30:	28,700 CFS
JULY 1:	29,700 CFS
JULY 2:	29,900 CFS
JULY 3:	26,600 CFS
JULY 4:	24,400 CFS

5-DAY TRIP
GUIDES: ME, SUE TALBOT, AND URSULA VICARO
GUESTS: HOLLY, JACKIE, KATHY, AND JEANIE (ALL IN MID-40S AND FROM EASTERN U.S.)

What do you get when you combine six women and one man at the Slide in high water? Short answer: peak intensity of estrogen power. It was in June 1997 BF (before Barb), and we were a group of three guides and four women guests scouting the Devils Slide again. I had my dory, the Eclipse, and had hired two female guides to help on the trip. Sue Talbot (alias "The Trickster") rowed the Itsiyiyi, my aluminum Kofler driftboat, and Ursula Vicaro (alias "She Bear") rowed the Periwinkle, my 15'6" Aire raft. My nicknames for them reflected something about their character that struck me, and all were given in fun and endearment. They had their own names for me, too, and maybe some I don't even know about. It all adds to the good-natured fun had by those who enjoy the river world together.

However, along with the fun come some tense moments in the guiding world. Such was the case with the river flowing at about 30,000 cfs when we embarked on this epic journey. It is a nasty level, producing wildly chaotic snarl that made us all as jumpy as a frog in a blender waiting for the power button to be pushed. The agony of anticipation is sometimes almost overwhelming.

In general, as the water level rises at the Slide, it gets more difficult. However, some intermediate flows can be more or less difficult than the water reading would indicate. They can produce unusual conditions that are more radical and difficult than lower or higher flows. Because of the Slide's remote location, no one runs it every day in higher flows, so it is less well known than other sections of the river with easier access and more opportunity to run. Therefore, like a magician's new trick, the rapid always has an element of surprise each time you find yourself staring at it from "Fool's Rock." Trying to decipher how the trick works to make it through the torrent is a challenge.

Remote runs in the wilderness and extreme backcountry have added difficulty because the nuances of a rapid's human-like "personality" are less well known. Cfs readings in the mid-20,000 range, like we were seeing at the Slide, are among those infrequently encountered levels leading to uncharted adventures.

A male leading a trip with all women faces an added challenge, but there is lots of joy at the same time. This group of women had been with me before and were really a hoot. There was no shortage of humor on every trip they had ever booked with me, and my guts hurt from laughing so much by trip's end that it took several weeks to recover.

But we weren't laughing that day as we saw the Slide, which seemed to have a sly, devilish laugh of its own that we didn't trust. Telling ugly Slide stories the night before might not have been the best strategy to quell already high anxiety levels in that pool of female hormones, but it was too tempting for me not to embellish, even if I might pay for it later.

One such story I told was about surfing my dory down the face of the giant V wave at about 23,000 cfs a year earlier in April 1996. That was on a BLM interpretive trip for river professionals and agency folks, and I had two women guides in the bow of the Eclipse. One was Sue, who had recently started working for me, and the other was Lisa, who worked for Northwest Voyageurs, the same river company we were teaming up with on the Estrogen Express trip.

When I started down the gut, all went well until I hit the apex of the largest wave in the middle of the vortex. It stalled us, spun us around, and then slid the bow straight down into the trough to surf just like a giant kayak. But unlike throwing a huge eddy turn and topping out over the wave like smaller yaks can do, we turned sideways, then flipped.

I always coach people not to lose contact with the boat, as it is good floatation in the turbulence of whitewater. But I was surprised by the power of this rapid. I had lost my oar but managed to grab the lifeline, a quarter-inch nylon rope that goes all the way around my boat. I had a very firm grip with both hands, but the river shook me far more violently than I would have ever guessed. It felt like being a human flag in a hurricane. First it sucked my right hand free of my death grip, then as it tugged at my stronger left hand, and I was on the verge of losing it, too, when the river relinquished its power and I managed to get my other hand on the flip line and crawl out of the water onto the bottom of my boat. Lisa was still hanging on to one side, and Sue, who had gotten sucked down into the Maytag zone, had been saved by a safety boat nearby.

Once I was on the bottom of my dory, I helped Lisa up and we flipped it right side up and made a good, but shock shaken, recovery. What a demonic wake-up call to the power of that hellish "fire and brimstone" of a rapid.

Flashbacks aside, there we were again on "Fools Rock" trying to tame our butterflies before entering the ugly maelstrom doing its thing far below our eagle-eye scouting perch. As nervous as I was for myself, I was more apprehensive for my crew. I had never done the Slide at this level in a driftboat, and here was Sue prepping herself for something beyond what I had ever done. Then there was Ursula, who had a raft but was not as experienced as Sue, who had her own hard boat and a list of other river accomplishments before ever teaming up with me. It was part of why I had great confidence in her, though still nervous because of the gravity of potential consequences for open boats.

We had tons of flotation in the open driftboat, which is absolutely necessary to keep them from going to the bottom of the river should they get swamped with water or flipped. As is my normal standard when running rapids, we had flip lines already in place on each of our craft. We were prepared for an emergency.

Following is what happened, as recorded in my journal:

5-day Salmon Trip. June 30 – July 4, 1997
Guests: Holly, Jackie, Kathy, and Jeanne (all from east coast; all in mid-40s)
Guides: Sue Talbot in driftboat (Itsiyiyi), Ursala Vicaro (She Bear) in raft (Periwinkle) and me in my dory (Eclipse.)

Flows: backtracked later

June 30:	28,700 cfs
July 1:	29,700 cfs
July 2:	29,900 cfs
July 3:	26,600 cfs
July 4:	24,400 cfs

July 3 (day 4) Day of the Slide

The water has been high and questionable. However, since NWV is doing a 3-day trip and we can team up at the Slide, it seems feasible.

July 3. Well, as the Slide Day became a reality, we found the river to be at near the 30,000 cfs mark and the rapid at a very ugly level. It looked quite bad. Almost as bad as the 35,000 cfs level.

Mike was leading the NWV trip and had a bunch of kids on the trip. They hired Jacque Barker to run the big pontoon through with the kids for safety. Also, Scott Draper ran the big NWV J rig, too. Another good safety boat.

The ironic thing that happened was that Barker ended up running the rapid without his motor and missed pulling in to pick up the kids. Just the evening before, he had pulled into my camp at Billy Bar to chat a bit.

I asked him if he ever had trouble with the motor not working. He said that they switched to electric starters and had never had any problems. Well, they turned off the motor in Blue Canyon for a moment of silence before running the Slide and then could not get it started again until below the rapid. Fortunately, they were able to remain at the bottom of the rapid for safety.

There seemed to be much chaos at the scout, with Mike trying to get kids and people hiked down to the J rig below, after it had a big, but good, run down the gut, then eddied out immediately below the whirlpool eddy on river left. To speed things up I opted to run my flotilla down the rapid next, one at a time.

Holly and Jackie were with me, but Jackie got scared out and decided to walk around. So, it was me and Holly. I decided to try "powelling" the left side. There was a big diagonal that fed into the maelstrom and ugliness at the V where everything explodes into frenzy. Above that diagonal funneler was another smaller diagonal that needed to be busted.

As it turned out, the first diagonal was not as steep or nasty as I had anticipated. But the big one was so huge that it pretty much just surfed me over to the Vortex of Chaos.

My original plan was to row out more toward the middle to get momentum built up going left. However, I did not get out far enough and was not able to achieve those ends. I entered a little farther right than I had intended. Needed to be about 6-10 feet a little more inside at my entry.

When I got surfed over to the shoulder of the Vortex, it stood me up so high that I got that same feeling I had when I surfed that very same place last year (though at a slightly lower level). Only this time it let me through right side up and did not suck me into the trough.

I did have to high-side though, as did Holly, and lost my left oar in the process. I let go of my right one, too, so was basically oarless and at the mercy of the waves and current.

The next wave just behind the Vortex was also huge and required high-siding. It spun me around somewhere in those big waves, and my boat did a 360-degree dance. It was dangerously close to the rock wall, missing it by about 3 feet or so. I finally managed to regain the oars. One was outside the boat and hard to retrieve, as the current was sucking it under my boat. But, soon I had it and was cranking wildly to make the eddy just above the J-rig.

The boils bounced me around the entire time, and a few moments almost sucked me out and downstream. It was a very tiring eddy to wait in.

Mike came through next with paddle assist. They, too, got thrashed and had to high-side ... out of control and did bounce into the wall. Glad it was a rubber boat. However, he was right-side up ... recovered and made the eddy below the J-rig.

Then Joe came through and also got thrashed. High-siding and in survival mode. Paddle raft with stern mount. They made it. However, they came crashing into the side of my boat as they were still celebrating when they should have been paying attention. Then made the eddy below me and above the J-rig.

Forgot to mention that the J-rig ran first – before my run. Scott said he was going to do the left run but ended up going right down the middle. It sent water flying everywhere as he hit the Vortex. But he shot through in good shape. The raft contorted its way through the sloppy maelstrom of kickass waves.

Next came Sue. I was really nervous for her and Ursula. I was pretty nebulous in visualizing the Itsiyiyi in that water. It was Sue and Kathy. She pushed into it, not "powelling" at all. She was too worried about taking too much water over the stern.

It was the right thing to do. She had a hairball run. Both high-siding and getting thrashed like the rest of us, but making it. It was unbelievable to get that little driftboat through that gargantuan water and monstrous waves – a damned amazing feat. I was really happy for her.

Now we were down to two rafts left to run. One from NWV and Ursula and Jeannie. Scott ran his J-rig over to Barker's rig on the other side of the river – picked up Jacque and then they came back over to our side, and Jacque ran Scott's rig up to where Scott could jump off and hike back up to the raft. The other NWV guide got a bad case of "Slide-itis" and opted to let someone else run his raft through. This was a guy who has been rowing since the '60s and has never or only once or so tipped a boat. Of course, they lined Lava in the Grand when they were there. And according to Mike, it sounded like this fellow avoided any hard stuff. It helps your record better.

Then came the petite Panimanian Duo (both small women with South American roots) in the light Aire Craft. From my perspective, I could tell that She-Bear's entry was a little too off. I knew she was going to flip before it happened. And she did. But at least she was left of the Vortex and in the right spot to flip.

They pretty much just got washed straight through. They did not get pell-melled into the wall or sucked into any bad eddies. Also, most importantly, they maintained contact with the raft all the way through.

Scott ran next, behind She-Bear, and had the best run of any of us. He had three other men with him. Brian, someone else, and the guy who didn't want to row his own raft. Of course, Scott did have the advantage of watching the guinea pigs first, but he still made the right corrections to get through with boat oars in his hands. He said he changed his attitude on the entry so that he was able to get farther inside than the rest of us – avoiding getting surfed into the vortex as did all the rest of us.

I believe he had more of a sideways angle (as it appeared from downstream). Pulling hard for the left bank and hitting the diagonals a bit less than perpendicular. He also had a heavy raft, with paddle assist from big guys.

They were close to She-Bear, but too far for rescue. I was the first boat to get to the upside down raft. Joe was next. I got Holly onto the raft to help the gals flip it. They almost had it once, but then lost it. They needed more weight.

Mike's raft was there and Joe's was there. Several men from Joe's raft got on to help. Finally they got it over, and Ursula regained the oars and got into the next available eddy downstream. This was about a quarter to a half mile below the Slide. Below the next immediate rapid on river left.

One bad thing that happened during the ordeal was that Jeannie got trapped underneath the raft and water by a line when one of the guys fell on top of her when they were trying to flip the raft. It tangled her for long enough that it put a pretty big scare into her. Though she did not make a big deal if it. Luckily, one of the guys helped her up.

We all then went down to eat lunch together and tell war stories. It was quite the exciting day.

Lunch was on the beach that I had intended to camp at, but I did not recognize it or realize that we had come so far in such a short time. I didn't recognize that mistake until we were in the boats and heading down the next rapid. Checkerboard. So I pulled in to camp there, even though I do not like the parking due to ocean-wave beach action.

The gals dubbed this Sue's Right, Gary's Wrong camp. Seemed fitting.

This was an epic trip, as I look back upon it, and only time and more experiences with female guides and guests has continued to reinforce my discovery long ago: Never underestimate the power of estrogen. There is good reason our planet is referred to as Mother Earth.

Chapter 29

ONE BREATH AWAY FROM DEATH – ONLY THE "EYE" KNOWS
NEARLY A KNOCKOUT
(JULY 11, 1997 -- 21,700 CFS)

Another day, another time, another trip. Two boats this time, my dory the Eclipse, rowed by me, and Periwinkle, my 15.5-foot Aire raft, being rowed by Ursula (She Bear). My two dogs, Weimaraner sisters Metoo and Ruby, were along for the adventure, plus we had three guests. Ruby was Inua's pup and was there in her place.

This trip was a family affair for a man and his two sons, who were all big people. Both kids were high school football players, very athletic, and in great shape. That turned out to be a good thing, because they became heroes before the story was over. At least to me.

After a nerve-drenching ride at the Devils Slide, where our near carnage gave She Bear and me more pre-mature gray hair, we found camp for the evening.

Early the next morning we launched and soon faced off with the Eye of the Needle, the rapid that had been more than a match for me during my trip with Sarge seven years earlier. As had happened there before, and faster than you can say, "Oh, shit!," my boat was slapped in the face again. Bottom treatment, round two.

It was nearly my last breath, and the closest I have ever come to drowning. I had had other close calls when I was 2 years old at the ocean with my dad and at age 6 while fishing with an uncle in the Eagle Cap Wilderness. In each case, an opportune hand, perhaps with some sort of divine guidance, had pulled me to safety. Or so it seemed.

When you suddenly find yourself out of control heading toward oblivion and then unforeseen assistance plucks you from sure disaster, it indeed feels like there is something in the far beyond touching you with its power.

No hands from the beyond were available this time as I was stuffed under a ton of water. At the last second, when I thought my time was about to expire, my head popped to the surface. But I only managed one short guppy-like breath before the current drew me down again. Many people in near-death situations report their entire life flashing before them. Not me. I was cussing out my stupid life jacket. It was brand new and was a great design for kayaking because its trim cut allowed freedom of movement. But it only had about 16 pounds of flotation, which is not enough for extreme whitewater conditions. My head would have been above water more often with only three or four additional pounds of flotation.

We had almost made it through the rapid when the eddy line surged and put the boat up on its edge. The two strapping football players were in the bow. Their dad, also a big hulk of a man, was in the stern.

The flip was too fast for anyone to high-side. That is how menacing this rapid can be with its blasting energy and element of surprise. "Shock and awe" rings true here. Suddenly I was sucked down with violent force. I held onto my only connection to the boat, one oar. It was tied to the gunwale but had snapped in the carnage. As I was hurriedly climbing the oar to reach the boat, I was horrified to discover I had lost my linkage with it.

Frantically, I pawed and clawed for the surface against an unseen force of resistance. Yikes! It was like some cosmic power was holding me hostage and putting pressure on my soul. My lungs were close to bursting when air mysteriously met by the lips. After a quick inhalation, I was sucked under again. But not for long, as I popped up once again.

This time, my head was above water long enough to see that I was being sucked back upriver in the eddy. I saw Ursula in the raft, heading downstream. Unbeknownst to me then, she was heading for the father, who had been in the stern of my dory. He was being carried downstream in the main current. I hollered for help, but she didn't hear me and was intent on saving him.

Then I saw my capsized dory with the two football players hanging on its side. It was three feet away, going down river, beyond my reach, as I was heading back toward the very boils and sucking whirlpools that nearly drowned me the first time through.

Swimming against the current as hard as my failing strength could muster, I managed to get close enough to the boat to get a finger under the safety line, but I could not hang on. Fortunately, one of the kids was close enough to grab my hand and pull me to the boat.

I caught my breath, then climbed up onto the bottom of the boat and helped each of them up, too. With their help on the flip lines, we soon had the dory right-side up again. We climbed aboard, got oars into the locks, and headed downriver to find the raft. I also opened the hatches to let my two dogs out of their dark world, which had been turned topsy-turvy upside down, then right-side up again.

I had put them inside before the rapid because they were safer there than facing the possibility of getting sucked down in the ugly whirlpools percolating violence had they been on the deck.

She Bear had saved the other swimmer and was waiting for us in the nearest eddy she could catch, just above the confluence with the Snake

River. More "Purple Heart" material? No, not this time. More like a "purple help us" experience.

Such times help one appreciate fully how wonderful the air we breathe tastes. Perhaps that is why I take such deep breaths every time I approach this rapid, while thinking seriously about the possibility of "my number" being up.

I will keep returning to run this river knowing that the Eye of the Needle awaits. Having once been so close to crossing over to the other side, whatever dimension that may be, at this particular place on Mother Earth, I will always wonder if she will be calling my number when I arrive.

Will my next run end up being my last breath? Only the Eye knows, and it will probably always cause me considerable angst as each oar stroke leads me closer to the tongue of this powerful, yet beautiful rapid.

Chapter 30

FOLLOWING NATURE'S LEAD

For a single man immersed in the outdoor world year-round, trying to find a romantic mate is a challenge, especially at middle age. Over time, my trial-and-error search for a lasting relationship led to various encounters with the opposite gender, but most ended in long-range disappointment. My living in a tipi, even in the winter, while also running rivers, hunting, fishing, and avoiding cities severely narrowed the potential for finding love. Add to that the limitations of living in a small town with fewer than 500 people, and finding a woman is akin to discovering the Hope Diamond.

Since the odds of finding a female with similar long-term interests in the bars of Riggins were miniscule, I decided to try something different. Why not follow the example of nature and copy the bull elk? Since my company, Wapiti River Guides, was named after that majestic animal, it seemed applicable. The bull elk bugles to advertise his availability to cows during the breeding season, so why not try that. Time to follow my friend Doctor Death's "ruttin' bull elk" strategy for finding a mate. So I did. This was in 1997, before the Internet was available in Riggins, so I sent in an ad to the Idaho Statesman newspaper in Boise. It read:

"Escape the City, DWM, many moons, otter disposition, coyote

heart, strong medicine. ISO earthy, country minded, good medicine Woman."

This didn't get as much response as my previous ad, which partly read, "Robert Redford lookalike (from the knees down)," but it did get better results and eventually landed me my present wife (of 20 years as of 2017). Barb, who lived in Boise, had never answered an ad in a newspaper before and only answered mine because her friends talked her into it. After she kept reading it over and over for about three weeks, her friends said it was obvious it interested her, so why not get on the phone.

Barb finally worked up the courage to give me a call, and we had a nice visit over the phone. Though I was willing to meet her half way between Riggins and Boise, I told her that I was a river outfitter and would offer her a free day of rafting as a safe way to get acquainted. If it didn't work out, at least the river trip would be worth the price of gas to get to Riggins. She took the bait, and I reeled her in.

As it turned out, we had a lot of similar interests, a common respect for the Native American worldview, and a deep-seated need for greater elbow room and distance from the treadmill of city life. We dated for several weeks, until things got serious enough that she gave up her full-time (with benefits) job with HP for a temporary (no benefits, aside from outstanding landscapes and river views) guide job, which we still joke about.

I set about showing her the ropes and getting her feet wet with a personalized on-the-job training program down the Salmon River. She took the big plunge by purchasing a 14-foot Aire Ocelot cataraft, which I suggested would be quite forgiving and perfect for someone with zero experience learning river-running skills. She became adept at rowing but was never comfortable with big rapids. She was more content camping out along the river, enjoying the natural beauty of the surroundings, and sharing it with interesting guests. We spent a lot of time together on the water and enjoyed a simple canyonland lifestyle.

After the previous summer on the water, Barb began guiding for me in 1998. She was 50 years old, and although she had always wished for such an outdoor opportunity, an earlier marriage, kids, and work prevented her from any such option. I was her crack in the door opening the way for joint adventuring. Not many people begin a guiding career at that age, and she deserves a lot of credit, at least in my mind, considering the sacrifices she made and challenges to be met. It was a major lifestyle change for her that required a lot of courage. We enjoyed a lot of fun together on the river, and she gained my respect and my heart for all that she went through during our early years together.

At that time, we needed additional guides to help with commercial trips. Fortunately, my niece, Sena, was old enough and interested in learning the ropes of guiding, as was her boyfriend. Nepotism? Sure, why not. Family time together can't be beat. Never have had kids of my own and with only one sister, her daughter and son became my surrogates, as well as a potential guide pool. While I did gain a stepson, Justin, from Barb's previous marriage, his differing life direction ruled him out as an option.

Sena's older brother, Sven, was my only nephew. He also would have made a good guide, as he did learn how to row a boat and was a gregarious person with the ability to draw people like a moth to the flame. But he was too busy with other pursuits when we needed help.

Sena had a charming personality, and people appreciated her spontaneity. She was a shining example of the "likeability" quality that is so important for a guide. Negotiating rapids is a requisite skill that almost anyone can learn, but personality can't be taught. You are what you are. A guest's experience on a river trip is highly influenced by the guides who orchestrate the adventure. When considering guides for employment, their attitude and ability to engage positively with people are my most important criteria.

Sena's boyfriend, Dieu, whom she later married, also had an amiable personality and respectful attitude toward humans and nature that people liked, including me. He also had a different perspective from another culture. His parents, who were of Vietnamese and Chinese descent, brought him to America at an early age, having survived a dangerous boat journey that included an encounter with pirates.

Barb helped me train Sena and Dieu when they joined the Wapiti summer guiding clan during their college days. My sister did not want her daughter to be a guide because she thought it was too dangerous. Yet, ironically, before Sena took to the oars, she had had a near death experience while working at a care center for the elderly.

One of the patients had mental issues and delusions that caused him to think Sena was his ex-wife. Apparently because he hated his ex, he tried to strangle her in Sena's body. Sena was saved only because she barely managed to push a panic button next to the bed to summon help. It took several people to pry off the patient's two-handed grip around Sena's throat. We never had such a potentially dangerous problem on the river, which proved to be a safer place than the seemingly innocuous care facility.

Once free of her mom's apron strings, Sena began spending time on trips with Barb and me. It proved to be fun as we shared in her training. A big part of a rookie guide's education is the mistakes made that facilitate learning. While sometimes those character building experiences can seem quite harrowing, they also can contain some humorous aspects that lend themselves to future stories.

An example of river carnage providing future campfire fodder happened at a rapid called Lorna's Lulu. At least that is what we "fogs" (fucking old guys) called it before the BLM erroneously re-named it when they came out with their first river guide of the area in March 1995. Their name for it was Bunghole and Lower Bunghole, which is what all the "fngs" (fucking new guys) and general public use these days.

At a moderate water level this is a two-stage rapid with upper and lower sections. However, they trade ugly faces at changing water levels. In higher water (above 10,000 cfs), the upper is bigger while the lower washes out, but as the water drops, the upper tames out as the lower gets decidedly bigger and wilder.

In this instance, when the upper was the bigger rapid, Barb and Sena were on the 14-foot Aire Ocelot catboat. Barb was rowing with Sena in the bow. After entering the rapid, they got too far left, and Barb got off her line on a big wave just above a bad hole. Both were thrown from the raft, which did not flip. Sena was closer to the cat and managed to crawl back in and tend to the oars. Meanwhile, to avoid going into the hole, Barb swam for my dory, not far below.

When she reached my dory and grabbed the side, she expected to be pulled aboard, but I tried to coax her into swimming back to her raft. I explained that if she was to be a guide, people expected her not to abandon them in the river to seek help elsewhere. Naturally, I ended up helping her into my dory and rowed over to reunite her with Sena. As the story morphed afterward, the tale eventually became that I had to step on Barb's fingers to keep her from climbing into my boat and made her swim back to the cat.

Another time, one of my cousins and his son came for a five-day trip on the lower gorge. It was back when our Porta Potty system consisted of a 5-gallon bucket for solid waste, while used toilet paper went into a Ziploc bag. We would burn the bag's contents in the evening garbage fire. This was before the development of scat machines that could also take toilet paper with the crude mix.

Evidently my cousin didn't understand the original "nature call" procedure, so one night when Sena and Barb grabbed the plastic bag to pitch its contents into the fire, it was a little heavier than just tissue. My cousin apparently thought I'd said everything went into the bag. Once past the bad smell, we all rolled on the ground laughing over the humor in it all. Never a dull moment in river-land.

Like the constant flux of things in nature, so too is the coming and going of river guides. Sena and Dieu followed suit with the typical stepping stone employment that many seasonal guides experience before they find more stable and profitable careers. In their case, that meant marriage and better paying jobs with more security. It was sad for me, as we had a lot of great times together on the river. It also meant a huge face-slapping change in a young couple's world, as they began "life after kids" or, as I like to say, "life after guiding."

Unfortunately, not long after that Barb took a bad fall off the tailgate of our vehicle while unloading it after a five-day lower gorge trip. She hit her back on the tongue of the dory trailer, necessitating a trip to the emergency room in Grangeville. It was a life-changing turn of events. Sadly, it pretty much ended her rowing career. She gravitated into more office work and talking on the phone to entice more business, in a new world without working oars.

Like the heavenly planets that rarely line up, so life choices don't always line up with the right opportunities at the appropriate times. When it comes to lofty goals and ambitions, many plan A's are superseded by plan B's. Thus, to paraphrase an old adage: "Better to aim your bow at the sun and hit only the moon than to aim at the moon and hit only a rock." The original plan is never set in stone.

Chapter 31

ROMANCE ON THE RIVER: AS THE OARLOCK TURNS

What better birthplace for budding love affairs to grow than the ambience of a secluded river setting in the beautiful wilds of nature. Simple and pure. Where primal juices can flow as rampantly as the river. Just as the science of chemistry shows how natural elements react to each other, repelling or attracting, the chemistry of human interactions plays out in curious ways. The power of the river experience has stirred much romance, uniting couples in a world filled with love.

Over the years, I have seen many river romances bloom for guests, river guides, and even myself. Maybe there is something magical in the water, for it has the power to make changes as astonishing as an illusionist's making a dove appear out of thin air. While magic creates the illusion that something is real that isn't, the river casts its spell over people to create real romances out of experiences that are so amazing they seem unreal. The fascination of not knowing how a trick is done inspires curiosity and appreciation for the fine art practiced by a great magician or a spellbinding river.

Other couples could tell tons of stories about how river experiences helped shape their relationships, much like the river sculpting the landscape by its power. This is my story of how Barb and I evolved into marriage and exchanged our vows on the river.

Unlike my first wedding, which was far too stuffy, this one was actually fun and far more meaningful. A major problem with marriage No. 1 was the wide difference in our religious beliefs (or lack thereof) and the lack of agreement on the ceremony itself.

My first wife came from a very religious family. I didn't. We compromised on having the wedding inside a church, and I had to wear a suit that made me feel extremely uncomfortable, as did the structured preacher/church vows that I mimically repeated although they didn't jibe with what I believed, or didn't believe. Heck, I had only worn a suit one other time in my entire life. That was when I graduated from college and went for a job interview. The second time was at that wedding, and to this day, it was the last time.

Things turned out a lot differently for my second marriage to Barb. After we met, through my newspaper ad, we ended up guiding and living together for five years until we wed. To me, marriage always seemed a mere formality made legal only by words on paper. I believe loving someone is more about how we relate to each other and is bounded by the rules of nature, not some manmade document. Real relationships are readily apparent in nature, free from the controlling hand of man.

It took a while for me to change my thinking. What won me over was realizing the importance of marriage and commitment to Barb, whose troubled childhood had included being abandoned by her biological parents. Such rejection and the resulting abandonment issues have great emotional impact.

I came to understand that getting married would help reassure to her that I would not abandon her. If legal papers added more legitimacy for her, I was ready to concede and make it happen. She also made a good point that if one spouse died, it would simplify legal entitlement of the survivor to anything left behind. In addition, it could make divorce proceedings fairer should things go south.

So it was in 2003, when we were invited to join an 18-day Grand Canyon trip. It was Barb's first and, as for most Grand first-timers, her experience was epically Grand. They call it "The Grand" for good reason. Once you go, you know.

Many stories could be told about that outrageous river journey, as many powerful events transpired there. However, it got off to a shaky start thanks to my 14-foot dory boat, which was more than 50 years old and had a leaky bottom that I had fixed before the trip. It turned into a bit of a problem when we launched it at Lee's Ferry the night before our trip embarked.

We had made a long two-day ride through hot and cold weather, which may have affected the sketchy patches that seemed to work fine the first time I tested the boat in the Salmon River. It was a different story on the Colorado, where overnight swelling of wood played havoc with our plans. Barb and I slept on the deck of the dory near the ramp, and when we awoke the next morning, the boat was half full of water.

To top that off, Barb looked out at the river and saw long strands of green moss in the emerald water, reminding her of a recurring nightmare she had while growing up. To her, it felt like a premonition of how she was going to die. That is not a good way to start a trip.

She was ready to abandon the dory and urged me to rent a larger 18-foot raft like those the rest of our party had. I had to do a lot of fancy dancing and smooth talking to convince her that the graceful dory would put smiles on her face and that there was no need to worry. Fortunately, she agreed.

Several days later, about half way through the trip, we made a side hike neither of us will ever forget. When we got to Deer Creek Falls, a spectacular 180-foot drop where the small creek pours over the lip of Tapeats Sandstone, we had to seek its power. There was a lovely pool below where we could wade out into the rainbow shrouded mist to drink in the glory of it all.

Then I told her about a unique hike above the falls that led to a magic world of enchantment with green moss-lined springs, small waterfalls, gnarly cottonwood trees guarding the emerald pools, and streambed sculpture of unreal beauty. Barb agreed to go and referred to it as Hobbitville once we got there.

It was a difficult climb through the steep, cliff-like sandstone, and not for the faint of heart. But she was up for it, though a bit apprehensive about negotiating such treacherous, nearly vertical terrain.

After gaining the top, we followed a trail on mostly large slab-like formations of bedrock to where Deer Creek comes out of the severely tapered canyon. Past the entry point along the narrow path overlooking the creek 20 feet below, the slot opens up into a grotto-like world of enchantment. We spent a lot of time exploring every nook and cranny before settling down to just relax and soak in such a paradise. We had it all to ourselves, and that in itself was a wonderful experience.

Eventually I began to get nervous about rendezvousing with the rest of our float party that was still upriver of us. So I told Barb that I would go back to the mouth of the canyon where the falls drops into the big river below because there is a good view upstream from there, and I could check to see whether the rafts were about to arrive, if not already waiting for us below.

However, that was a ruse. What I really did was scramble back down the cliffs as fast as I could, go to my boat, and row across the river to a large sandbar. Then I grabbed a big stick and proceeded to scrape out a large message in the white sand: "Will you marry me?" Then I hurried back across the river, up through the cliffs, and back to where Barb was still dabbling her feet in the pools.

On our way back to the boat, we stopped at the viewpoint. I thought she would see my message, but she was distracted by too many places of beauty. Somehow, I directed her attention to the sandbar far below and across the big river. It did not register at first, but when it did, she was nearly pulled over the lip of the falls by the weight of her jaw dropping. "Yes," she finally answered, and off we went, hand in hand, to return to our boat and wait for our friends.

Meanwhile, a big baloney boat with tons of commercial guests had parked below us, and several people were ascending to the place we had just came from, having been lucky enough to enjoy it in solitude all to ourselves.

Then a Park Service raft pulled in, and a ranger walked over to chat with us. Believe it or not, he reamed me out for marring the sandbar with my message, after I most happily revealed to him that I was indeed its creator. He was not as excited about it as I was. After scolding me for leaving behind what he thought was graffiti that would offend other people, he made me row across the river to rub out my sand proposal.

Later, we learned that people on the commercial trip had loved it and were as appalled as we were when they learned of the ranger's behavior. Many of them applauded and congratulated us. In a world inundated with the negative, people enjoy chancing upon positive events that help bring balance amid the turmoil we endure.

The river ranger's flimsy justification didn't hold water, because any sand message would soon be erased by the river's next rise, which occurs daily in the canyon due to dam releases. It's no wonder people get fed up with river bureaucrats. And making matters worse are recent revelations of sexist behavior by the Park Service's male river patrol rangers, whose scandalous antics apparently have been going on for several years.

A few days later, when we got to Lava Falls, the water level was not looking good. We scouted for three hours, hoping the water would change so we could run far left rather than down the ugly gauntlet of giant turmoil below the "Bubble Line" route. Recalling Barb's nightmare, I decided to lean on omen-clature to persuade her to walk around the rapid. I was not going to take a chance on testing whether her nightmare was a premonition.

I was almost as nervous as my day at the Devils Slide in 1978 on the Salmon River. I knew there was a very good chance of flipping the dinky dory, and its age and fragility would make it easy firewood material if battered on the big black rock at bottom right where much of the current went.

It eventually became apparent that the water level was not going to cooperate, so we decided to all run at the same time, with my boat in the middle of the pack to make rescue easier. My boat had the highest chance of flipping and having problems. Barb was to film our run, and I told her not to stop even if she saw the bottom of my boat. As it turned out, we all had fantastically exciting and hugely successful runs, which we celebrated that night with a party just as big.

Our entire April-May 2003 trip was wonderful. Our engagement was short, since we planned a wedding that fall on Sept 3. It, too, would be an experience revolving around the river world. Only this time it was the Salmon River and our home waters.

Our wedding was held on a small beach, which we now call "Wedding Beach," featuring a large overhanging boulder that we call "The Marriage Rock." It commands a wonderful view of a tight constriction in the canyon known locally as "The Crevice." It is my favorite place on the river, and now it is Barb's, too.

I had made special arrangements with a local professional jetboat pilot to shuttle some elderly people with physical challenges, including my folks, to the beach from the road across the river. However, he hit a rock soon after launching and was unable to get to the site where the guests were waiting. So they drove farther up the road to a place where many of our younger friends helped them down the steep rocky bank, then rowed them across the river to the wedding beach. I hadn't liked the idea of the jetboat in the first place, so it was poetic justice that oars prevailed over motors.

Meanwhile, Barb and I were upriver, out of sight from guests and each other, not knowing what all was transpiring below. We were waiting for a cue from our designated messenger to let us know when we could proceed downriver. We were in separate hard boats in different locations. Mike Kennedy was upriver from me in his dory with Barb and her son, Justin, in the bow. Hurricane Bob, a unique character extraordinaire who was our ceremonial drummer, sat in the stern.

I was in the bow of my driftboat, Itsiyiyi, with my niece Sena on the sticks. Mike's boat was out of their sight, so they had to wait for our signal before they would descend to the wedding beach.

The day was hot, in the low 90s, and my buckskin clothes and Barb's deerskin dress hugged our bodies so tightly that it was like being cocooned in a skin-tight personal sauna. We were nearly swimming in our own sweat.

It was a great relief when we finally got the signal that we could head downriver. Sena pushed out into the current as I stood in the bow and began drumming and singing. There had been no rehearsals for any of this wedding event; it was all a go-with-the-flow affair. I was so nervous that my drumming creeped into overdrive with a cadence faster than intended. To guests, it probably seemed I was on the warpath rather than coming down the liquid wedding isle. Barb said I sounded like a rock 'n' roll drummer. Nerves often play out in strange ways.

Once we parked on the upper end of the beach, I climbed up on top of the boulder overhang and continued drumming. When I stopped, it was the signal Mike was waiting for to begin floating the bride downriver. Hurricane Bob began his drumming as they drifted our way, unseen by us. It was like hearing the river's heartbeat being transmitted through him as the medium, getting closer and closer.

Mike let the three of them off on the lower end of the beach. Then Justin walked his mother up the makeshift feathered isle to where I was waiting with the lady who would be performing the official legal portion of our ceremony.

After Hurricane Bob did some more drumming and said a few words, Doug Dennis, another local guide whose many skills include being a genius songwriter and musician, played his guitar and sang Shania Twain's "Always and Forever" for us. Doug was a good friend with whom I had shared some exceptional river adventures.

The preacher was from New Zealand and had a cool accent. She read the script I had prepared, sprinkled with her remarks to make it all official. After Barb and I said the vows each of us had composed, all those attending threw touch stones and flower petals into the water as we shoved off in the Itsiyiyi, and Sena rowed us downriver into the sunset. Four golden eagles soared off the high cliffs above us, gracing our ceremony as they flew above and in sync with us.

Several friends in driftboats accompanied us downriver while the remaining rafts took guests back to the road, where other friends helped the elders back up the steep bank. Once our flotilla reached Spring Bar, we trailered our boats and headed back to the Wapiti Clan Boatland, where everyone gathered again for a gala reception.

For me and Barb it was really fun, meaningful, and how a wedding should be. And the good news is that we are still together sharing the magic of river life. Like sacred eddies, places like "Wedding Beach" and "The Marriage Rock" carry special significance, even if just for a couple of people.

Chapter 32

HYPNOTISM AND THE RIVER OF NO TURTLES

Several years ago Barb and I had the pleasure of guiding a very interesting hypnotist and his wife down the Salmon River for a few days. Being the son of a vaudeville escape artist and the grandson of a Cherokee "snake oil" salesman who had his own medicine show, he had showbiz in his blood. John-Ivan Palmer and his wife, Harue, who is of Japanese descent, were a lovely couple, and we had a great time. There were just the four of us on the kind of highly personalized trip that we like to run. Adventuring in such a small group allows more time to engage in informative conversations and to pursue a larger menu of experiences.

As we were floating along one day, the conversation naturally turned to John's profession of hypnotism. His showbiz claim is that he's "The World's Fastest Hypnotist." When asked who can be hypnotized, he said not everyone, but many who think they couldn't be hypnotized are vulnerable to suggestion. Perhaps including me.

John said the most fun subjects to hypnotize are big gnarly biker dudes who ooze toughness and project a mega-bad-boy image. Those who do fall under his spell during shows are great crowd pleasers, he explained. The mental image of them twirling about the stage like dainty ballerinas made me laugh.

Not long after I revealed to him that I didn't believe I could be hypnotized either, we floated past some rocks poking above the water. John looked near the shoreline and asked, "Is that a turtle over there?"

"No, it's just a stick that got washed up on that rock that looks like a turtle," I replied. In more than 30 years of running this river I have never seen one, nor heard of anyone else having seen one. "This is not turtle habitat, they don't live in this kind of environment," I explained.

But as we floated closer to the object, it did take on a resemblance to a turtle. In fact, it was looking more and more real the nearer we got. Holy cow! It was a turtle. And a big one at that, with about a 6-inch shell.

I knew no one would ever believe me, so I scrambled for my video camera. Just as I tried to turn it on, the turtle slid off the rock it was basking on and disappeared under water, leaving me with no proof of such a wild and rare claim. Could it have been merely my nebulous mind playing tricks?

To this day, everyone I tell about the turtle believes I was hypnotized. I continue to look for that turtle on every trip when I pass by that "basking rock," but so far, Mr. Turtle keeps hiding in the river, not my mind. The Salmon River is very hypnotic, but not that hypnotic.

After the trip, Barb and I went to Boise to watch John perform at the annual county fair. His show was very entertaining with many funny moments. One of the ladies John had hypnotized on stage carried on a most humorous conversation with another hypnotized guy, all in the "Martian" language. I chanced to bump into her later at the fair and just had to ask her about her experience. She said she did not remember any of it, but her husband had bought a video of the show so she could see how she acted.

It was a striking example of the curious power of suggestion and of how some people are more susceptible to it. On the river, John had told me the audiences he most enjoyed performing for were native folks, although they were the hardest to hypnotize. Finding subjects who were hypnotizable among them was a challenge.

Later, in an exchange of correspondence after the trip, I had to ask him if he had hypnotized me during our float trip. I wanted support for my turtle story when I told it to doubters. He assured me that, no, I had not been hypnotized.

Even more rewarding for Barb and me was another letter he wrote to us about his and Harue's experience on the river with us. It was quite revealing about the hypnotic power of the river. Here is his letter:

"Dear Gary and Barb,

"First we hope you like the photo. It is reproduced from a slide in our Idaho slide show. I think it's way cool, and captures in Gary that spirit of the lone adventurer which is so much a part of the Wild West + 100 years. The kind of spirit the aboriginals could respect. If Harue & I inspired a few names along the river (and we thank you very much for singing us into existence), then you guys have inspired a couple of names too. You are known, when I point to you with my toy called a "laser pointer," as "Medicine Man Garn" and his partner, "Shamanka Barb." And although I love the gasps of Minnesota wonder I go on to explain how apt the names really are.

"Glad you liked the show(s). Hypnosis is a very interesting phenomenon, and when I see, like you did, how fast people can be convinced of the most absurd realities, just think how certain people can be in their wrong headedness when they have a lifetime of suggestion working on them! Time to pull the plug! That's where your river medicine comes in & we're glad our excursion of the mind and your excursion of the soul met, like a confluence of two rivers.

"There's the question of the Sm (psych symbol for male subject) who ran off the stage. It's possible he could be lost forever in a hypnotic reality of someone else's making. There have been rare cases of bizarre sequelae from exhibitions of stage hypnotism, but the chances are about 99% that he simply got out while the getting was good. Adolescent Sm often act on impulse when it comes to leaving the stage. They like to jump, or leave by unconventional route as a way to get attention without playing the game.

"...and I have to tell you the big laugh we both have been having over that turtle incident, where everyone thinks you were hypnotized. What a hilarious situation. And frustrating too, I suppose. I asked around myself and no one said they'd ever seen a turtle on the Salmon River. Are the totems speaking?"

Our river trip with John and Harue was in July 2000. A lot of water has splurged down the canyon since that time. Surprisingly, on another trip in 2015, I talked to a fellow guide who said he had seen a turtle just like I had described in telling my story to a group of guests on the lower gorge. His experience happened in the same area and near the same time, so most likely it was the same turtle. I was shocked, but pleasantly so, because it added credibility to my story and to my efforts to convince people I was not hypnotized.

In the many years since that sighting, I still have never seen another turtle on the river, nor has the other guide, or anyone else that I know of. The old saying "If a turtle is on a fence post, it did not get there by accident" comes to mind as I continue to try to figure out the mystery.

The theory I believe makes the most sense is that it was a pet turtle that someone turned loose, or it got away and escaped into the river. The area where it was seen was only about 6 miles from a main highway, and several houses were near the river along that section.

In any case, thank you, Brother Turtle, for being a totem to the power of the river and the intriguing mysteries of nature, including human nature.

Chapter 33

AN UNBRIDLED WORLD AND NATURAL SELECTION

Riding a rowdy horse without a bridle is a sure-fire recipe for a wild ride and kissing dirt. The same can be said for giving industry free reign in extracting natural resources. Infinity may have no boundaries, but a circumscribed Earth does.

Like a metal mouth bit applied to a voracious extractionist, regulations are implemented to control the use of natural resources. Man is kinder to himself and the livelihoods of future generations by ensuring sustained yield on an annual basis rather than relying on the callous hand of natural selection.

However, it is not just the extraction industries that need checks and balances on a confined planet. The non-consumptive tourism industry, whose revenue is generated by a more benign pass-through system, is also subject to boundaries and ceilings. Even if humans are not extracting some tangible element from nature, they can still have a detrimental impact on the places they visit if free from restraints. Too many people can love a place to death.

Besides the tourism industry's physical footprint on the planet, it has the added dimension of a more subjective aesthetic perspective and impact to consider. While the size and number of campsites available to river runners are defined by geology, the amount of humans that can use them are determined by both physical restrictions and mental constructs. Only "x" amount of people can physically fit inside the same tent, but overcrowding can become a far more important limiting factor in determining appropriate comfort levels.

Just as having too many people crammed into one tent, where they cannot change positions without elbowing someone else, lessens physical comfort, so, too, can the values of solitude and tranquility be diminished by overcrowding on river trips.

You can't enjoy solitude in a filled football stadium or appreciate tranquility at an agitated pep rally. All animals have internally defined territories, and from a qualitative perspective, people are no different. When these natural boundaries are violated, conflicts inevitably arise. Having a sophisticated brain is no preventative for uncivilized behavior, including the extremes of barbarism. History is full of a vast array of atrocities of which man is capable.

In the public domain of rivers, be it for private or commercial use, all people can enjoy the natural world. Unlike private lands, which are often posted with "no trespassing" signs, and state lands that also often restrict or deny use to the general public, public lands are open to everyone.

All federal lands are under jurisdiction of the U.S. government under Article IV of the Constitution, which is the supreme law of the land. They are not, nor ever have been, owned by the state, despite many modern militia groups' allegations that federal over-reach has taken away their rights to full possession of such lands.

Even public lands are limited, and use must be restricted in some manner to control human numbers and their impact. Therefore, access for the public is dependent on how much of the federal domain is available and how it is managed.

From overgrazing livestock to the vast swaths of excessively clear-cut forests, man's blind lust for gaining every drop of profit is like a sightless bee slurping up every ounce of pollen from the very last flower and having no place left to put it. Extreme exhaustion calls for extreme measures.

Most public lands, including wildlife refuges, are managed by either the United States Forest Service (USFS), Bureau of Land Management (BLM), National Park Service (NPS), or United States Fish and Wildlife Service (USFWS), while state agencies manage fish and wildlife populations. Basically, the federal agencies manage habitat, while state agencies manage population numbers of fish and wildlife.

Additionally, in the state of Idaho, the Idaho Outfitters and Guides Licensing Board (IOGLB) is the agency that regulates the tourism industry and strives to balance proper levels of commercial use of public lands.

BLM and the Lower Salmon River (mid-1970s forward)

The Lower Salmon River between Whitebird and its confluence with the Snake River at the lower end of Hells Canyon flows through a mosaic of private property and BLM lands. Fortunately, due to do a series of exchanges, conservation easements, and buyouts by the BLM in the 1990s and near the turn of the millennium, most lands within a quarter mile of the river in the entire corridor are now public. It was the increase of recreational use of the river during the '80s and '90s that helped bring about these changes.

Before that time, there was not enough public use or human impact on this section of river to warrant much restraint from water's edge camping activities. Inevitably, growth and use patterns changed that dynamic, so more regulations were required to reduce the effects of trampling and overcrowding by too many humans. It was a necessary remedy to help conserve the basic thread and fabric of nature.

While there were a few outfitters that ran commercial trips on the Lower Salmon before 1975, use was quite low, and there was no immediate need for federal agencies to regulate the relatively small amount of touring activity. Old-time outfitters like Omar Drury, who helped pioneer early river use, did not amount to a significant enough human presence to necessitate many restrictions.

During my first three years rowing with Grand Canyon Dories, we rarely saw other groups, either commercial or private, on the lower gorge. However, by 1978, increased interest in commercial ventures did warrant extra federal attention to the ever expanding industry. The BLM in Cottonwood, Idaho, hired LuVerne Grussing as district river manager to address potential problems.

The year before he arrived, Bob Michaels and Winston Cheney had been hired as the first river rangers for the Lower Salmon. Besides doing river clean-up, they were tasked with disseminating information and educating both commercial and private user groups about how they could help preserve the river as a resource. They had no enforcement duties but were good emissaries to promote wise use of, and a healthy respect for, the river.

From 1978 onward, LuVerne hired a host of people who passed through the revolving doors of seasonal employment as river rangers. Some of those early patrollers were Tom Averett, Scott Faskin, Caroline Tan, Bob Ratcliff, Cindy Lots, Kristin Frish, Chris Hoffman, Heather Johnson, Mick and Kathy Riffie, Eva Worthington, and Jack Kappas.

Jack was an ex-GCD guide and personal friend of mine. In fact, he took his first apprentice trip with me on the Owyhee River in about 1977, during our early years of guiding together. We were already practicing most of the protective measures that the BLM's Johnny-come-lately (in our eyes) river rangers later began to promote. But it didn't matter, as we were all collectively interested in doing whatever was best for the river. Guides and rangers had a common goal because they all have the same teacher, the river.

Jack became a long-standing fixture and well respected river ranger stationed in the Riggins community. He lived in town but spent most of his time on or near the river. Integrity of the big and little river canyons was a serious concern to him, and he always promoted natural resource education whenever possible. One of his high priorities was raising river awareness among the local youth. He called on me to help at times when he gave educational presentations at our local schools, because he knew I valued the power of knowledge.

Often his mission was to emphasize the importance of our cultural heritage in respecting the canyon and river. It was a sophisticated ploy to remind kids to help keep our common "backyard" of sandy beaches and clean water free of beer-party litter, unsanitary toilet paper fields, and unsightly fire rings. His programs included education about the regional importance of migrating salmon and steelhead, the impacts of dams, hatcheries, and our responsibilities toward, and engagement with, the Nez Perce culture. These were values I strongly supported.

On one occasion, Jack invited Elmer Crow, a Nez Perce elder who still practiced traditional ways, to make a presentation at the grade school. Elmer demonstrated the use of many tools he had personally made for hunting and fishing, based on the great knowledge he had gained by his genetic ties to a long trail of ancestral wisdom. He was a big hit with the kids, as well as adults, and was an outstanding spokesman for his people's values. Unfortunately, he drowned at Buffalo Eddy on the Snake River after saving his little nephew who was swept into the current by a jetboat's wake while swimming there in 2013. It was a sad loss to all.

Kids are a product of their parents and environment, so in communities that sprang up with human values associated mostly with the extraction industries (minerals, grass, and timber), the parents' mindsets are ingrained in their offspring and become deeply embedded in the DNA of the culture. These genetic traits are not easily broken, even as time alters the environment, so strong is the relentless human resistance to any change in learned behavior. However, adaptations to new problems, which require different solutions, will eventually be required when humans want to be kinder to themselves. Otherwise, Mother Nature rules, plays no favorites, and dishes out harsh lessons for those who ignore her.

Historically, outfitter and guide services originated soon after the early settlement of the western frontier, when savvy outdoorsmen of the early 1900s began taking tourists from the cities into the wilds to experience a sanitized version of wilderness. Over time, as the human tide flooded westward and the last frontier was becoming more domesticated, all uses of nature's bounty escalated.

The Idaho Outfitters and Guides Licensing Board was set up in 1951 as an in-house means to self-govern big-game outfitters. However, it went through a major revision in 1961, as a broader range of tourism activities evolved.

The board is currently made up of five members, three of whom were outfitters appointed by the governor. It is charged with licensing all outfitters and guides, as well as addressing various problems, disputes, and violations of fish and game regulations or permit stipulations. Early on, a certified training program was developed for guides to help improve competence and provide more safety for people who hire professional guides for outdoor activities.

Guided activities throughout the state have been categorized into three broad types: hunting, boating, and general recreation. Not surprisingly, the boating segment is the most popular, fastest growing, and encompasses the highest number of commercial users.

Among boating outfitters there is a wide diversity of business interests, from small-scale mom-and-pop operations to much larger corporate enterprises, including some with national and international reach. But it was enough rate that there was no need to put a cap on the number of users. Special-use permits to run rivers were available for free until increasing demand for commercial use reached a level that forced the

IOGLB to draw a line in the sand, helping to set limits for the state's rivers.

It would seem like federal land management agencies would set use ceilings, but in Idaho, it was the IOGLB, looking out for the interests of its licensed outfitters, that helped define the limits and use restrictions. In some cases, it may have been more of a collaboration between the feds and the state in setting fixed maximums for special-use permits to control commercial ventures.

While the number of permits became fixed at different levels, based on the popularity of each river and/or section of river within the state, new businesses became available only by the dictates of supply and demand. Thus, they were only obtainable by those with the most financial resources. While permits could not be sold, business use could be, making it possible to transfer special-use permits as part of the transaction when an outfitter decided to sell out.

By 1985, a big bump in use by the tourism industry led to the licensing of a total of 315 outfitters and 1020 guides in Idaho. During the 1984-85 season's, more than 50,000 whitewater commercial guests were distributed among 149 river outfitters, 63 of which were from out of state. Those from outside Idaho accounted for 85 percent of public use. This does not count private use.

Remembering my days guiding on the Lower Salmon from 1975 to1979, I recall seeing very few other outfitters, even though each year saw incremental growth. Normally, while the human eye cannot discern the turning of green grass to brown on a daily basis, by seasons end the transformation is evident. So it was with river use, and by the early '80s, use was mushrooming like the effects of compound interest. More and more groups were floating the river and competing for limited campsites.

One of Idaho's great attributes is that it contains more than 63,000 miles of major waterways, which flow through a variety of geographic landscapes. Some of the more spectacular places became more popular than others, and consequently the numbers allowed there had to be much more highly regulated with access limits. Places like the Middle Fork of the Salmon and the Selway River gained so much fame that people flocked to the area.

Like yeast in a warm oven, the heat of demand made the dough grow until it could expand no more. The oven became a high-use, wait-in-line affair, with various methods tried in an attempt to create an equitable system for access to limited permits. A first-come, first-served distribution gave way to lottery systems with years of wait time, which escalated annually as interest rose exponentially. All were a result of increasing numbers of people starved to find sustenance on the limited amount of wilderness waterways.

Luckily, some of the less famous rivers and places did not require such stringent safeguards and can still be accessed simply by showing up without advance reservations. Such is the case for the Lower Salmon, as of this writing. How much longer this will continue depends on the whims of human nature, population growth, and the industrial economy.

While my gut tells me one thing, data provide more substantial evidence of river usage. For trips below Hammer Creek during the years I worked for GCD (1975-1979), the percentage of commercial users ranged between 60 and 77 percent, based on BLM statistics. By 1980, those figures began to drop. From 1980 to1990, it ranged downward from 60 to 46 percent; from 1990 to 2001, it dropped from 52 to 41 percent; and from 2000 to 2015, it fell from 36 to 25 percent. It was a fairly stable drop in all those ranges, despite a bump here or there, depending on outside factors like the national economy. This demonstrates the dynamic change from commercial to far greater private use as time progressed.

From another perspective for the same time frame, here is the average number of launches (commercial and private) per day:

Year

1975-79: 1.42
1980-85: 3.88
1986-90: 4.58
1991-95: 6.42
1996-2000: 7.77
2001-05: 7.78
2006-10: 9.09
2011-13: 8.43

Even more telling is the rise in use:

The average number of days with 10 or more launches per day:

1975-86: 0
1987-89: 4.3
1990-2000: 14.1
2001-10: 19.1
2011-15: 27

There was an unexplained spike of 30 days with 10 or more launches per day in 2012. It could have been caused by low water in other states causing river runners to turn their attention to Idaho, and since the Lower Salmon can still be run by just showing up, it became a mecca for private trips that are restricted in most other river systems.

Jetboat use mirrored the data history of the whitewater user groups. Rarely did we encounter them below Hammer Creek during my GCD days, but the ambience of a quiet and peaceful wilderness atmosphere was soon to change, too. Although jetboats averaged only around 5 percent of total use, their noise pollutes the air and their oily smells linger like smoke from cigarettes that is breathed in by everyone in a room.

In analysis of river use of the 1990s, the biggest rise in user groups has been private trips. While commercial outfitters still have the highest number of people per group, private groups have more boats per party, include more groups and more people, and are more widely scattered across available campsites. This has a huge impact on the availability of camps. As the total number of user groups goes up, the proportionate amount of available campsites goes down. This leads to overcrowding and the sharing of some campsites by more than one group at a time. It is ironic that people seeking remote river experiences to get away from crowds wind up amid congestion in the wilds.

The spread of guides and outfitters across the landscape resembles the way the West was won. Lands were first conquered by explorers, and then came the mountain men, trappers, miners, pioneers, and finally the settlers. Similarly, rivers were explored, pioneered, and finally filled with "settlers" as guides branched off the first generation of outfitters to form their own companies.

While the opportunity for outfitters to find their livelihood on the river increased, the resultant overcrowding begat more regulations, and secluded solitude became a rarity.

Natural Selection or Not

Two major forces impact the environment, man and nature, but only one remains in ultimate control. When it comes to the dynamics and demographics of river use, human experience will be sculpted by either man's wise choices or through natural selection by nature's hand. This is true for management of the Lower Salmon.

In the case of the more remote section of the lower gorge, from Hammer Creek near Whitebird, Idaho, to Heller Bar on the Snake River just below the Grande Ronde confluence, the number of commercial groups is limited, but private groups are not. Group size for both private and commercial trips is restricted to 30 people, including guides. However, the number of groups that can launch each day is not restricted for either commercial or private access. This is both good and bad.

This current freedom of entry is apparently because BLM does not consider carrying capacity to be at a high enough level to justify restricted use. The immensity of the canyon, long driving distances to access it, and incremental growth still allow for a reasonable amount of solitude and elbow room without further restrictions. But unless the use curve eventually flattens out, that will change.

Local people have appreciated being able to jump on the river any time they want, which is nice when it comes to having a backyard that is still unfenced. Early on, BLM river managers like LuVerne recognized this value and strived to keep the federal government's hand in restricting use to a minimum. This was very much appreciated by both local residents and outsiders.

Unfortunately, until the human population stabilizes or declines, there will be continually increasing numbers of people seeking to access limited natural resources.

Chapter 34

SOCIAL CONQUEST, EVOLUTION, AND SALMON RIVER SACRIFICE ZONES

Human behavior is a curious thing, though quite predictable through the lens of science. The same selective forces that gave rise to mankind continue to influence the evolution of river use patterns.

Many conservation biologists, including E.O. Wilson, credit multilevel (group and individual) natural selection as the mechanism of evolution for all organisms of the biosphere. Wilson claims that homo sapiens are eusocial, like ants, wasps, and termites. That is, they are members within a multiple-generation group who behave altruistically in terms of long-term survival. Old school "kin selection and the selfish gene" theory was used early on to explain evolution. But that vision of a process driven by individual-based natural selection has grown to focus more on groups made up of closely related alliances.

Fundamentally, two factors drive evolution of eusocial groups: nesting and division of labor. What matters is defending home territory and distribution of tasks to ensure effective protection for the group.

The importance of group dynamics can be seen everywhere, from people's allegiance to sports teams to their affiliation with a political party. All groups have in common members' loyalty to their own group and the belief that all other groups are inferior to their own. This same tribal phenomenon can be seen in the outfitter and guide world.

We are all someone else's "other," a viewpoint used to justify the importance of personal interests and the need to oppose that which is different because it is seen as a threat to one's status. Even if a threat is not real, the perception of there being one will have an impact. Conflict is often the result, mostly determined by which side of the telescope one is looking through, and which seems to generate more hate than love. The threat of losing something one loves will evoke hate. This dynamic love/hate relationship is always present when it comes to how our lands and waters are managed in the public interest.

The catch 22 for conservationists fighting for tomorrow's sanctuary is that while saving areas from over-development, we can eventually love them to death. This process occurs in the river world this way: Participants go home after a fun river trip, be it private or commercial, and tell friends and relatives, some of whom decide to go on their own trips, whether private or commercial, though commercial trips have a much farther reach. Some participants decide to get their own rafts or boats and become a part of the private crowd, then their kids also get the bug. Before long exponential growth turns a snowball into an avalanche.

When snow load reaches maximum capacity, gravity triggers collapse and launches the avalanche downhill, where it ends by burying everything at the bottom. This is when restrictions are imposed. "Use limitations" after the avalanche are put into place to prevent another one in the future. Be it the ski slope or the river, the same prescription is used for managing human behavior.

On a finite planet, there is a limit on natural resources, including set-aside refuges where people can go for solitude and to escape the everyday pressures of making a living. Rivers can take us to such venues of sanctuary, but even non-consumptive uses of them have boundaries. As human population rises, economic pressures and changing demographics influence use patterns on rivers.

Various methods have been used for several years to limit access to many of our rivers, with very few remaining that can be floated simply by showing up and self-registering on the spot. The Lower Salmon is one of those places that are still fairly unregulated. While the number of people per group is limited on the section below Hammer Creek, the number of groups to launch each day isn't at the time of this writing (2016). Above Hammer Creek on the Riggins Road section (Vinegar Creek to Hammer) there are no restrictions on group size. It is more or less a "crowd sacrifice zone" in terms of personal elbow room. "Walmart rafting" might be a more appropriate term during the busier months of July and August.

In 2016, there were 41 outfitters permitted to run river section SA8 (Hammer to Heller Creek) and 23 outfitters licensed on section SA7A (Vinegar to Hammer from March 15 to October 15). Nine nonprofit organizations also are permitted to run these sections.

Time will reveal how the river will be portioned out to the various river users, and what other values will be won or lost in the continuing confrontation with an industrial based society living with a dominionist worldview.

Natural Sacrifice Zones

Unlike the Lower Salmon gorge, which is more remote, the middle section between Whitebird and Vinegar Creek is paralleled by 40 miles of paved highway and 15 miles of gravel road. Therefore, a different river management policy applies to this more developed, un-wild section of river. It might better be called a "Sacrifice Zone." (see appendix 2 for stats)

Far fewer restrictions are imposed on this section of river. Not only is the number of groups unlimited, but there also is no ceiling on the number of people in each party. Unfortunately, a few of the bigger operators who are more interested in empire building and alpha status, often run trips more aptly described as cattle-company affairs. They cram people into

30 or more rafts, like sardines in a can. It is an extreme affront to river users who do not desire the Disneyland atmosphere of such riotous and raucous processions that these larger groups often morph into.

I've always questioned why the federal river managers have allowed this section to become a sacrificial area. Is it just because the river there is not as remote? If a sandbar on the lower gorge is restricted to 30 people per camp at any one time to help reduce negative human impact, why are sandbars along the highway section treated differently? Why are they sacrificed? All these sandbars contain outstanding beauty regardless of their proximity to roads.

It could be partly tied to the reactionary feedback given to BLM by those making the big bucks, akin to the influence that the titans of industry and lobbyists have on politicians in D.C.

Sure, the main highway parallels the lower half of this section, with a less obtrusive partly paved and gravel road along the upper half, but the canyon is still just as beautiful as anywhere else along the entire length of the river. Even though there is more private property and a moderate amount of development along this section of river, it is still possible to enjoy relative solitude and reasonable tranquility there. That is until the summer months, which is the busiest time of year when everyone wants to experience the canyon at the same time.

While many people are fed up with the divisiveness and partisan politics in Washington, D.C., the ripple effect trickles down and is eventually felt everywhere. There is no escape from the power of lobbyists and their unholy relationship with industry in this country. The theme of bio-politics is a common thread weaving through the life-web we all share.

Personal responsibility is the bottom line, be it by people managing a resource or those who are using it for pleasure or business. "Sacrifice Areas" entail giving up one thing to have something else. Sometimes that is good, sometimes bad. The critical issue is in the evaluation process when weighing out what to keep and what to eliminate.

In this case, the stakes are how much enjoyment humans gain in their relationship with the river and canyon in an overcrowded world. Integrity of the human experience is diminished when one's space is violated. Elbow room is not a nebulous concept. People have boundary areas in many aspects of their lives. "No trespassing" signs are a demonstration of this human trait, as is the distance people stay from each other when talking. Face-to-face engagement has a boundary that is unconsciously recognized.

How much space people need from others during their time on a river trip varies, but it is important to safeguard the benefits of solitude and sanctuary that people seek in temporarily escaping their fast-paced life and work world. Allowing more people on the river at a given time diminishes the integrity and efficacy of the river's soothing "medicine." Tolerance levels are challenged, and when a tipping point is exceeded, bad behavior results.

Natural selection never sleeps. It is always at work, has no feelings, and plays no favorites. People do have options in making decisions to shape their destiny. All decisions, or no decisions, matter. Only man cares what happens to fellow humans, so it is up to people to decide how nature's resources are distributed among themselves. Otherwise, natural selection will rule the tribe.

Chapter 35

CHIEF JOSEPH SAGA AND LOWER SALMON RIVER CROSSINGS

A quick study of the Nez Perce history of the past 200 years reveals an interesting relationship between them and the landscape that helped shape their culture. The Cooper Bar, Rock Creek Canyon, Tolo Lake, Camas Prairie, and Whitebird Canyon areas were of major importance to the Nimiipuu (Nez Perce for "we people") tribe. Of special interest was the war of 1877 and the epic saga of Chief Joseph and his people trying to escape a pursuing force of federal troops and find refuge in Canada. It is a sad story of around 750 men, women, kids, and thousand of horses and cattle who resisted being forced onto a smaller reservation because of a corrupt system of twisted and broken treaties, the nefarious instrument used to "win the West."

The tribe's initial treaty of 1855, which was signed by all the chiefs of the five Nez Perce bands, guaranteed that they could remain in a large part of their original homeland, although they agreed to relinquish more than a third of it. But greedy white people ignored laws and trespassed into these lands, drawn by the lure of gold and potential fortunes. Avarice led to governmental pressure for a new treaty reducing the size of the reservation and making access to the gold fields legal.

The new treaty of 1863 was called the Steal Treaty by the Nez Perce. It was signed by none of the chiefs except Chief Lawyer, who knew his word only represented his band, most of whom had become Christians, and not the entire nation, as claimed by the federal negotiators. The land reduction did not affect where Lawyer's band lived, but the total Nez Perce reservation was reduced by 90 percent. As had happened across the country, treaties were made with Indian people and then broken. For the record, none of the Indians ever went back on their word. It was always, and in every case, only whites who breached treaties. Native historians see it as the legal instrument that was the real weapon that drove them from their lands.

The Steal Treaty and the bitter repercussions it caused eventually led to the Nez Perce War of 1877, which was one of the last Indian wars in the nation, ending with the epic saga of Chief Joseph and the Nez Perce's engagements with General Howard and his troops. Five battles ensued, each won by the Nez Perce except for the last, which is the one that lost them the war.

Joseph had been given 30 days to move his Wallowa band from their summer home on the northern slopes of Oregon's Wallowa Mountains, now called the Eagle Cap Wilderness, to Lapwai, Idaho. This meant crossing the Snake River and Salmon River in high water. The Snake crossing was at Dug Bar, while the Salmon crossing was between Billy Bar and Cottonwood Creek. In the high water of June, it was a difficult feat for the men on horseback to pull bull boats fashioned out of willows and hides that were used to raft the women and children across the raging currents.

They eventually reached Tolo Lake, which was a popular area used for camping and gathering camas bulbs, to rest before the final leg to Lapwai. But not everyone was happy about the move, and soon a twist of human fate changed history. An embittered elder taunted a teenager named Wahlitits, or Shore Crossing, to avenge the death of his father, Eagle Robe, who had been killed by Larry Ott, a stubborn rancher who lived on the Salmon River near Horseshoe Bend and who had never been brought to justice for it.

On June 13, with whiskey courage, Shore Crossing gathered his cousin Sarpsisilpilp, or Red Moccasin Top, and a younger friend, Wetyemtmas Wahyakt, or Swan Necklace, and they headed for Ott's place. However, he got word of their coming and hid out, so the trio headed farther up the Salmon River to the mouth of Carver Creek (immediately upstream of Black Rock Rapids) where a retired sailor, Richard Divine, lived. He had a reputation for brutality and for having murdered a crippled Indian woman and receiving no punishment for it. To the young avengers, he was a worthy substitute for Ott.

Once they killed him, they began backtracking for Tolo, killing a few more white men and, in the process, sparking the Nez Perce War. It led to the first battle at White Bird Creek and the Indians' fighting retreat toward Canada via the old Nez Perce trail over the Lolo Pass (now Highway 12).

After the White Bird battle they crossed to the west side of the Salmon River near the shallow area upstream of Campbell Flat, then traveled downriver until they got to Cooper's Ferry before re-crossing the Salmon to the mouth of Rock Creek. They ascended Rocky Canyon back to Tepahlewam and Tolo Lake before crossing the Camas Prairie to gain the South Fork of the Clearwater River via Lawyer Creek/Suzie Creek to then follow the old trail toward Canada.

After a nearly 1,200-mile trek and a series of successful skirmishes and four major battles with the pursuing troops led by General Oliver Otis Howard, the severely outnumbered Nez Perce were defeated when Howard's troops were joined by a second force led by General Nelson A. Miles. The Nez Perce, unaware of Miles' approach, thought they had outdistanced Howard and paused to camp in the foothills of the Bears Paw Mountains of Montana, only 40 miles from safety in Canada. Miles struck with a surprise attack the morning of September 30. After a three-day standoff, Howard's force arrived and the Indians were defeated.

Chief Joseph then gave his famous surrender speech, saying, "From where the sun now stands, I will fight no more, forever."

Although Howard and Miles had promised that Joseph and 417 other Nez Perce who surrendered would be allowed to return to Idaho, the Indians were taken to Kansas and then Oklahoma, where they lived in wretched conditions until 269 survivors finally were returned to the Northwest in 1885. Joseph was never allowed to return to his homeland and died of a broken heart at the Colville Reservation in Washington on September 21, 1904, at age 64.

Despite Joseph's surrender, Chief White Bird and 232 members of his band did escape Howard's and Miles' forces at the final battle and reached sanctuary in Canada.

Chapter 36

SGT. ORDWAY, WAPSHILLA RANCH, AND JACKSON SUNDOWN STORY

After the end of the 1877 Nez Perce War, another interesting bit of history is that a separate group of Nez Perce escaped the final battle and somehow eventually made their way to a hide-out in Hells Canyon. Astonishingly, they were not found until 1933. I learned this on a float trip in the lower gorge (Salmon/Snake Rivers) in the spring of 2016 when meeting up again with one of my new friends, Morris Uebelacker. He is a professor of archeology and geography, as well as a part-time river guide for OARS (previously my parent company, Grand Canyon Dories). I first met him when he came to Riggins for the first annual Guides Rendezvous and also attended our annual Sacred Salmon Ceremony held the same weekend.

I found it interesting that he talked like many Indians do, slow and measured, and a sign of thinking before speaking. I suspected it was because he had grown up with many of them in his childhood. But the real cause was a bicycle accident he had had on campus. When he tried to avoid running into a child who suddenly jumped in front of him, he took a header and hit the sidewalk, causing a concussion and enough damage that it took him a long time to recover, including learning how to speak again.

Morris had walked the entire length of the Snake River in Hells Canyon, examining many archeological sites along the way, so he knew it well. He pointed out the site where that last group of Nez Perce had finally been found. It was near Cochran Island. The riverbed there once contained a drastic rapid, before the Army Corps cleaned out the stream channel in the early 1900s, and it was a popular Nez Perce fishing site.

Cougar Rapids Bar, slightly upstream of Cochran Island, is the large alluvial fan on the eastern shore that came out of Cougar Creek canyon long ago. We hiked part way up the narrow canyon draw, and Morris pointed out where a large longhouse stretching 30 or more feet once stood. It was located on a small flat knoll with surrounding geographic features that facilitated its use as a control point to keep horse herds contained in pasturage on the large grass-covered river bar. Before the Nez Perce War this bar held a small village of around 100 lodges. It was typical of the "winter village pattern" of use that took place over the 1,800 years before the Nez Perce were eventually removed.

Many interesting facts about this unusual place were discovered with the use of new technology that can look beneath the ground without digging, as well as sophisticated DNA signatures found in features that were unearthed.

With high-tech instruments, Morris was able to find a single tack that came from a small cargo box used during the Lewis and Clark Expedition of 1804-1806. He tracked down the actual box, which is now in a museum in St Louis. How did it get to that point?

It turns out this is along the route Sgt. John Ordway took when he left the Clearwater country on a fishing expedition to the Salmon River. It was on May 27, 1806, when he and a small group left the expedition's main camp on the Clearwater River near Kamiah to seek a supply of salmon for the remainder of their return trip over the Lolo Trail en route to the Missouri.

The Nez Perce told them that the cooing of doves indicated that salmon were on their way back upriver, and that is what prompted Lewis to send Ordway over to the Salmon River, where they thought they could get salmon quicker than waiting for them to come up the Clearwater.

But when Ordway's group reached the Salmon River on May 28, near the mouth of Deer Creek, the Indians living in a small village there told them they were too early and instructed them how to reach another village on the Snake River, where they might find fish. On May 29 they headed downriver on the north bank to the mouth of Wapshilla Creek.

They hiked up the creek bottom to the west branch, then followed it to the top of Wapshilla Ridge, where they gained access to Cottonwood Canyon and descended it for three miles to access a very ugly crossing route to a secondary ridge system of Cougar Canyon. They then descended down it to the mouth of Cougar Creek and a large Nez Perce village site.

The runs of salmon were just arriving, so Ordway's men got a few fish, but not as many as they had hoped. After a couple of days camping and trading with the Indians, they also learned of a better return route to rejoin their comrades waiting at Long Camp on the Clearwater River. After uniting with the main group, they all continued their eastern journey homeward.

The Wapshilla area is a unique location that has attracted additional characters who have enriched the landscape's historic fabric. At the bottom of the south side of Wapshilla Ridge is Wapshilla Creek. Not only was it used by early peoples described by the "winter village pattern," but also, several years after the Nez Perce War, people of a new culture immigrated to the area.

In 1910 a cowboy, Benjamin Reeves, and his wife discovered the area and a year later built a ranch a mile up the creek from its mouth. They raised horses and cattle and worked the ranch until the 1940s. The original house burned down in 1939, but all the other buildings still standing are the original ones.

Before migrating to Idaho, Reeves had briefly lived in the Cove, Oregon, area, where I lived before moving to Riggins and where a lot of my relatives still reside. Many of them are farmers and ranchers. My guess is that some of my older kin may have known Reeves' dad, Elijah, who raised horses in the Grande Ronde Valley, as he had done in his native Kentucky. That coincidental connection makes the history of the Wapshilla Ranch a bit synchronistic to me personally.

As a boy, Reeves worked as a trail boss for a Texan outfit herding thousands of cattle each year to Kansas. Later he rounded up wild horses in eastern Oregon, where he earned the nickname "Oregon Ben." By 1884 he had moved to the Craig Mountain area of Idaho and met Julia Nelson, whom he married in 1901. After they began ranching on Wapshilla Creek in 1911, they also had a ranch on Deer Creek, near Forest, and had several kids while in the canyon. They raised cattle that commanded high prices in eastern markets and eventually became one of the largest livestock operations in the west.

Among the many ranch hands they hired was Jackson Sundown, a nephew of Chief Joseph. He was a young kid during the 1877 war and escaped to Sitting Bull's camp in Canada by clinging to the side of his horse to make it appear riderless as he dashed away from the soldiers. As an adult, he won wide acclaim as what people today call a horse-whisperer, and he eventually made it back to his home country. He arrived back in Idaho in 1910 and married Cecelia Wapshela there in 1912. They lived on her ranch at Jacques Spur, 6 miles east of Lapwai.

His horsemanship became legendary and, at age 53, he became the World Champion Bronc Rider at the Pendleton Round-Up in Oregon in 1916. He was also known as Waaya-Tonah-Toesits-Kahn, or Blanket of the Sun, and as a rider was popular with the crowds because of his handsome looks, bright shirts, and long crow-black braids that were looped and tied together under his chin.

Artists made sculptures of him, and his exceptional physical appearance was once described by a British writer as a "sight for the gods."

From 1917 to 1921 he worked for Reeves on the Wapshilla Ranch, where he was valuable for herding horses and helping out with other important tasks. His way with horses continued to carry him with the winds of fortune.

Some of his time at the Wapshilla Ranch was recorded in a diary kept by Ben Reeves' daughter Margaret. She writes that Jackson always started his day with a bath in the river. Then he would build the kitchen fire, grind coffee, slice bacon, and get her mother up. He then fed horses, cleaned the stalls, and afterward tended to his main job of breaking green horses.

She remembered one day watching Jackson climb onto a bay horse that had never been ridden on the ranch. The ride was so wild and impressive that it became one of his more famous rides. It must have been quite spectacular considering how famous his rodeo rides had become. When he mounted the bay, she said, all hell broke loose, and never had she seen so many hoofs flying through the air at one time. He rode the horse to a standstill, dismounted, hunkered down, and put his head in his hands next to the horse, which was so tired it could only stand there with its head hanging close to the ground, too. That day the horse earned its name, Sundown.

When Jackson finally left the ranch, he cut his hair and gave his braids to Julia Reeves. Rumor has it the braids remain in an old family trunk, resting amid artifacts of a long forgotten past.

In the long march of time, all the ground truths tucked away in Mother Earth's hidden past are connected in a widely cast net of storied history. To me, layer by layer it all represents the complex threads of the Webmaster Spider cosmically weaving the strands together in elegant beauty beyond measure. The result is a magic blanket of great mystery, never fully understood but always inspiring. Part of that inspiration is that the more you learn, the more you know you don't know. Reaching out is the universal way to find meaning and make things matter while we make circles of fire with our given time.

Chapter 37

BLUE CANYON AND DEERHEAD RAPID

One of my more memorable river trips took place a few years after I had met Horace and Andrea Axtel at the Salmon Ceremony. One August we had extra space available on a five-day float in the lower gorge of the Salmon, so Barb and I decided to invite them. It was our way of thanking them for sharing their traditional Nez Perce ways and helping make our annual ceremony more meaningful.

My niece Sena and her boyfriend, Dieu, each rowed a raft, and I piloted my wooden dory boat. One of the guests, who was also an amateur astronomer, rowed his own catboat.

Barb came along to help in camp and to visit with the guests, many of whom were more like friends, having been on several trips with us previously. Most of our trips are small enough that normally they don't feel like a typical commercial venture. We treat everyone as friends, because they either already are or soon will be, and that is what makes each journey so enjoyable for us.

Our party also included one middle-age couple who had been on several trips with us and one young couple, quite in love, who were making their first river trip.

Horace was in his mid-70s while Andrea was a little younger, but both were reasonably capable of meeting the rigors of camping on those world class sand beaches for which the Salmon River is famous. We did, however, keep an eagle eye on them to be available should they need any help. Sena and Dieu thought we were showing them too much attention, over other guests, and that could be true. But we always pay more attention to our older guests as a precaution to avoid health problems or accidents.

Our first major stop was at the pictographs in Green Canyon, and I was excited over the possibility that Horace and Andrea, as Nez Perce people of today, might be able to offer insights about their ancestral people who created the rock art hundreds, if not thousands, of years ago. Unfortunately, any messages from the long ago have been stolen by time, leaving only a guessing game as to their meanings. There are lots of theories about what the rocks have to say. Some may have been used like calendars and maps to keep track of time and place. Some could be records of family clans and history. Others may depict hunts, battles, or communication with the spirit world.

I had visited the area many times, and it holds a special feeling of mystery for me, particularly one experience that I revealed to Horace. I wondered whether he thought it meant anything, or if it was just a fantasy of the mind. I knew that some Indian people consider the dream world to be an alternate reality that often can provide another layer of meaning to the life experiences of those who pay attention.

On a GCD commercial trip during my fledgling guide years, I had camped a quarter mile upstream of the rock art, on the north side of the river. The wall of red figures was on the south side, maybe 75 yards above a powerful eddy plowing into a rocky point guarding the entrance to Green Canyon. Sometimes it is possible to make it into the eddy and save guests a long walk to reach the rocks, but in high water, that option is too dangerous.

There is a possible access route requiring a longer hike across the river from where we were camped that night. After everyone went to bed, I sat beside the fire by myself and soon began to feel something calling me to those rocks. Along with that siren pull came the feeling that I had to show a proper respect in order to learn from whatever power was reaching out to me. It came to me that I must seek it out in a sacred manner, using a more naturalistic approach. Therefore, I did not use a flashlight, only starlight, and made the hike barefoot to feel a stronger connection to the earth.

As a guide, I always tell everyone never to walk at night, let alone barefoot without a light, because rattlesnakes come out in the dark to hunt. During sunny, hot summer days, the rocks and sand are too scorching for the snakes to crawl on them. Mice, on which the snakes prey, also come out at night for the same reason, to find food in more earth friendly conditions. Knowing all this, I was a bit nervous to set off on such a hare-brained mission, but the power drawing me was too strong a force for my innate spirit to resist.

Having arrived, I first stood facing the rock wall. On the right side of it is a major crack, which climbers call a chimney, that I had climbed a few times before. It is only about 3 feet wide from top to bottom and about 15 feet tall. With back against one side and feet against the other, one can ascend it by a slow process of shinnying.

On this night, I did not climb but instead moved in front of it and turned around to face the river. I heard a ringing, which seemed to be coming out of the crack but was probably made by river sounds reverberating off the amphitheater-like wall. The most spectacular thing was the trail of stars that soon captured my eye.

My position at that precise time made it appear that the Milky Way was emanating directly out of the crack and diffusely spilling stars out across the universe in a moonless sky. It was an astounding and awesomely beautiful sight that I will never forget.

After some contemplation under that cosmic spell, I decided to go around the crack to reach the top side by an easier route. Once there, I sat down and looked out at the river, where I could see the black silhouette of canyon walls merge with a sky full of orbs that seemed to wink at me, collectively transmitting messages from the far beyond.

I then had what I can only describe as a visitation. Some kind of entity began flying circles around me from about 4 feet away from my head. Its size seemed to be about that of a bat. My night vision had already kicked in (reduction of visual purple, otherwise known as rhodopsin), and I could see a few bats that also were flying around at the same time, but the entity was not a bat. Nor was it hallucinatory, despite not being visible to the naked eye. It was more like a mental telepathy from one entity to another, allowing me to feel a special kinship with the natural world beyond what I thought I already appreciated.

After contemplating the entire experience, I barefooted back to camp under the same starlight that had provided guidance for that exceptional mystical experience. When I awoke the next morning, I wondered if I had only dreamed it all, while knowing that I hadn't.

Horace said it was the ancients talking to me, and I believe he was right. It was the same answer he had for a similar, even more powerful experience I told him I'd had on the Grande Ronde River years earlier. But that story is best left for another time. Like in ancient Nez Perce ways, some stories can only be told at certain times and seasons.

Adhering to the more traditional values of native philosophies is sometimes referred to as "following the Red Road." However, I have no Indian blood that I know of, so I call it following the "Mother Earth Road." Like the sun that denies a shadow to no one, earth wisdom is available for everyone's digestion because all humans are native to the planet.

Once downriver of Green Canyon, we spent the next few days appreciating a common thread of good humor that flowed through everyone as we passed through the next series of micro-chasms within the larger gorge (Cougar, Snow Hole, and Blue).

One of my favorite campsites in that area is tiny but includes a special hike that I refer to as "Stairway to Heaven." I only share it with people if they agree to help keep it a secret and to hide while making the hike if any other groups float by as we are climbing toward Heaven. Basically, it is a huge cave with a secret passageway that leads to an amazing viewpoint. It is sometimes protected by a rattlesnake guard. Sorry, it's a secret, so its location won't be revealed unless you join me on the river.

It is a pretty difficult hike/climb and not for everyone, and only about half the members on this trip made it to Heaven. Horace wasn't one of them, but Andrea was in good enough shape to achieve this goal and was the eldest person to reach the top. She was immensely touched by the experience and by her personal achievement, which was also very inspirational for everyone else on the climb.

It was yet another example of people challenging themselves and discovering that they can accomplish much more than their fears have prevented them from doing in the past. We see this happen on many trips, and it is part of why we like to nudge people into being an active participant in the many opportunities for outdoor adventuring that are always available. The rewards can sometimes be life-changing events for many people, and witnessing such transformative experiences is awesome.

On our last evening, in Blue Canyon, which is Barb's favorite place, Horace graced us with a campfire ceremony. He rang bells, sang songs of old, and spoke words packed with wisdom gained from long ties with the land and his people. It was so impressive that the young couple on our trip, who were deeply in love, decided then and there to get engaged and seal their relationship with serious commitment. Then the other couple shared their story of getting engaged on the top of Mount Kilimanjaro.

It was a beautiful experience for all of us and yet another demonstration of power from the magic pill to be pulled from the Salmon River's medicine bag. However, the trip was still not over. The next day was our last on the water, but the spirit world was not done with us.

Coyote Trickster decided to put a final touch on our adventure when we got to Deerhead Rapid. In low water, it is the biggest rapid encountered, no matter which canyon (Hells or Salmon) one had come from, and that day it was at low water level. BIG, in simple terms. The metaphorical antlers of Deerhead were ready to butt heads with the bow of my dory that day as I chose to meet the challenge.

The rapid should not be that difficult, as it is a series of huge waves that can be simply run down the middle. A cheat run is available on either side for the weak and timid or, perhaps more aptly, those with more wisdom. But in the middle of the wave train is a mega-monster curl that crashes back on itself with significant glory.

When we met it head-on that day, it had Trickster power behind it as the huge curl engulfed our entire boat. I could barely see Horace and Andrea in the dory's bow until the wave cleared the stern and revealed them as thoroughly drenched river rats. It was quite a comical sight as they turned to look at me with deer-in-the-headlights shock, the wet hair hanging close to their heads with the life sucked out of it. Of course, that was only my take. Barb was too busy in the stern holding up her camera while trying to balance our trim as water emptied from the boat. My dory was filled gunwale to gunwale with water, almost enough for all of us to swim in. However, thanks to the drainage holes in the self-bailing dory, we only had to negotiate the bottom end of the rapid while the boat became more manageable as the excess weight swirled away.

The vision of that wave crashing over Horace and Andrea burned a memorable image in my brain that always brings a smile to my face whenever I am reminded of that day. What a cool and dynamic way to end a trip. It was a fitting practical joke and final stamp of approval from Trickster.

The Great Mystery prevailed on our human curiosity during the entire trip, like a poke in the eye with a stick, stimulating us to pay close attention to the Earth Mother. How we treat her is how she will treat us in turn. Proper respect is the fundamental requirement for understanding the true reciprocity of nature. Our trip came to an end, but it would not be the last. River trips, like all things in nature, are in a constant state of recycling.

Chapter 38

THE WAPITI MOMENT

In early summer of 2005, Kirk Barnum helped me on a three-day high-water run of the lower gorge. At that time of year, guides eyeball the Devils Slide rapid to determine whether a commercial trip is viable. Before our trip was to launch, flows were in excess of 25,000 cfs but on the back side of the peak and dropping, so it seemed like a reasonable trip for a group of guys seeking high-adrenalin adventure.

Those joining us were repeat guests who had been down Ruby in flows of 90,000 cfs plus. They also were of sound mind, in good physical shape, and had what my wife calls primordial testosterone poisoning. Knowing they would be good help, as well a fun bunch with whom to challenge the bigger water, I gave everyone the green light that our trip was on.

We launched June 18 from Hammer Creek with a flow of 22,000 cfs. It was dropping slowly, so Kirk and I knew the river would be beefy, throwing its weight around, and demanding rapt attention. Though most of the drops would be washed out, the rapids that weren't would be colossal rides, punchy with risks of high-siding and/or flipping a boat. It was just what these guys were looking for.

I had my 17-foot dory Eclipse, and Kirk rowed a 16-foot Air called Ruby Red. It was a good combination we often employ on longer trips to give guests the options of trying different styles of craft and levels of participation. Rafts are great for paddle assist, dories not so much.

I first met Kirk around 1994, soon after he came to the Riggins area and joined the guide community. He had gone to college, majoring in forestry, and eventually landed a job with the Forest Service out of New Meadows. After four years with them, he ended up as a caretaker at the Howard Ranch on Elkhorn Creek. It was there he met Roy Aiken, who was caretaking at Gail Ater's cabin on French Creek. Roy had seen Kirk peddling his bicycle along the road with steelhead sticking out of the front basket. It was a bike he had used in California when he had a job as a bike messenger. It worked for fish, too.

A year later, Gail acquired a permit and started a new river company called Canyon Cats. He hired Roy and Mike Hicks to run things for him. He also bought a place in town, across the street from my shop. Despite this seeming "in your face" competition, we became good friends and boated together.

They hired Kirk to help out for steelhead trips, as they did not have much fishing experience. Since Kirk didn't have much boating experience, it was a great trade-off all around. Kirk got his start on the river and that is how our paths first crossed. His first year was spent steelhead fishing in a driftboat, then the next year I teamed up with him and the cat boys on a lot of private boating trips during which we became good friends. I helped him gain whitewater experience and hired him to help me with some of my trips. Our friendship grew because we both had the same hearing problem: the call of the wild blowing in our ears.

After several more years of experience on the oars and in hard boats, Kirk was the perfect person to run with in high water. He had a good attitude, was a seeker of spirited outdoor engagements with "The Force" of nature, and, like an astronaut, had the "right stuff" for launching off into the abyss.

The following is taken from my (unedited) river journal:

Day 2 June 20 (Slide Day) 4 am 21,100, 8 am 20,900, noon 20,600, 2 pm 20,500, 4 pm 20,300.

Soon we were scouting the Slide. I bilged water out of my boat as the guys proceeded to climb the rocks. Finally I caught up and met them at "Fools Rock." Took some video and digital photos of the guys and the rapid, then tried to figure a good game plan. The river was at around 20,500 cfs, and it was not a pretty sight, knowing that we had about as good a chance of flipping as we did of making it right side up.

Two enormous waves at the crux of the V could be boat stoppers or flippers. Although the first wave looked doable down the middle, the second one wasn't near as friendly. It had too much pile building and falling and was more of a wall to punch. A bad hole on the left side prevented a far left sneak, but it did look possible to line a raft through, though not good. The steep drop hole and recycle action could tweak a raft and hold it there. Not a place for a wooden dory to go.

We decided the best plan was to hit the narrow slick of water on the left side of the first big wave, to hopefully hit just to the left side of the second wave, then survive the rest of the maelstrom and weirdness below that. The far side had a river of an eddy, all flowing hard back to the head of the rapid with a huge eddy fence and no place to be near.

Huge boils and whirlpools surged left and right at the bottom tail waves and was a mix master matrix of churning ugliness that sent shivers up my spine just thinking about a swim here.

So that was our route plan, and order of running was me first, followed closely by Kirk. It was more likely to flip a dory here than a raft, and I wanted him to be able to see me if I flipped, so he would be Johnny on the spot if we needed it. Of course, that is assuming that he had a good run himself. We both put our wetsuits on for this run, even though our guests had none. It was a hot day, and the water temp was perhaps 55-60 degrees, so not like snow melt, but not tropical either. But if we needed to help people, we needed all our energy possible.

I gave last minute instructions to everyone, put 3 people on my boat, and we were all primed and ready to roll. So off we went, headed for whatever the river was about to dish out to us. My plan was to enter very close to the bank rock, so as to hit the left side of the entry wave high above the vortex at the V of the tongue. It could slow a boat and cause loss of momentum and needed steam necessary to fight the current to get left of the vortex. Everything funnels to the V at lightning speed.

Then hopefully hit the right-side smooth part of the first wave, then be ready to high-side to the right as we were entering the 2nd and most menacing part of this rapid, if need be, and escape down the left side below.

Once rowing upstream as much as I could, and pulling out, it was too fast to get out far and build up any steam to go from right to left. So I just rode the current down and began pushing hard on my oars to the left, keeping my eye on the marker rock (the same one Clarence hit years ago when we ran together by chance meeting and I had Vietnam vet Neil on a solo run) so as to edge by it without hitting it.

This was actually fairly easy to do, and it did help keep me left of the big guard wave that I was worried could typewriter us to the V. Then I was able to keep pushing left and did hit the slick and smooth part of the big V wave. However, I was trying to turn my boat as I was going up this wave to hit the second one square. But I could not get it to turn.

Once on top of the first wave, I hollered at everyone to high side and we all went to the right side to slide down into the left side of the second wave just before it crashed on top of us. It almost stopped us but let us through right side up. We slid down into more chaos and bad swirls. I was trying to regain lost oars after high-siding, and a surge rocketed us toward the left wall.

I was afraid my boat was going to hit the wall and get badly crunched. But I was able to finally get the bow turned to the wall and was pulling away. Kevin and Colby in front of my boat (Chad in stern) were ready to fend off the wall. About that time Kirk came through right side up and the same surge was freight training him toward us. We both shipped our opposing oars just before the collision as his raft broadsided my dory.

Now we were both near the wall and fighting bad swirlage of the eddy monsters. But soon Kirk was able to get away from us, and we were able to get away from the wall unscathed. However, my gunwale was badly damaged from the hit, where my oar was slammed hard against it, in the collision.

We relived that run in many stories around our evening campfire, and that night is when Kirk invented the term "Wapiti Moment" to describe our wild collision below the vortex. It became indicative of many hairball runs and other unusual experiences of the Wapiti Clan when engaging the wilds of nature. I had not had a name for such events before then. For unknown reasons, strange happenings inevitably materialize from time to time, so now they became a named phenomenon.

That trip was history, but the "Wapiti Moment" lived on, thanks to Captain Kirk. A year or two later he was helping me on a Grande Ronde trip when we experienced a Wapiti Moment as we had to rescue another party that had flipped a canoe. Captain Kirk had to abandon his two elderly fly fishing guests to chase canoe carnage, and then we had to figure out how to rescue our own guests afterward.

Another Wapiti Moment was repeated often in Alaska thanks to Captain Kirk, who at that time was living with his girlfriend, Kim, in a yurt with 16 Siberian Huskies near French Creek. The dogs were kept in a pen near the river but out of sight, so it was a perfect setup for me to fool fishing guests when we got near them. There is a good steelhead tailout there at the bottom of what I call the Wolf Hole, and I would tell guests that I could call wolves there. Of course, everyone wanted to hear that, so I would do my best howl, and sure enough, I always got an answer. Kirk's pack of dogs sounded just like wolves and made me a hero. That is until he moved and my wolf calling prowess left with him.

Kirk was training his dogs to fulfill his dream of running Alaska's famed Iditarod Sled Dog Race. He quit guiding for a while, moved to Montana where dog training conditions were much better, and eventually followed his dream north to mush under the magic spell of the aurora borealis. It finally became a reality with his first Iditarod in 2008, followed by three more later. Because of various dog problems, he was only able to finish two of the races, placing 67th in one and 48th in the other. However, listening to his stories about the race makes me believe he should write his own book.

One story he told me was about a Wapiti Moment that occurred at one of the most challenging obstacles on the Iditarod course. Just past Partridge Flat, he had to climb over Rainy Pass and drop down the throat of the Dalzell Gorge. It was a steep, frozen river course that reminded him of entering the V of a big whitewater rapid with me. He had an audible vision of hearing and seeing me coyote howling and drumming, which I often do at the head of a big rapid just before dropping into it. It was a habit I formed long ago when leading trips, mostly to unleash my own exuberance sparked by the river's electricity, but also to warn/remind anyone following to get their own ducks in proper alignment with the extreme powers ahead that demand much respect.

To experience the beauty of a Wapiti Moment, one must embrace it and not panic. Kirk got his ducks in V formation at the top of the race course V with the dogs poised to take flight down into the gauntlet of a frenzied frozen rock garden. But before his dogs jerked him forward into the hellish hall of the Dalzell Gorge, he reached out and grabbed a small rock for Wapiti, to give me later when he returned to Idaho. He knew I would appreciate the significance of the gift, and I did.

The rock was a great token of our kinship and a wonderful memento giving testimony to his survival-of-the-fittest endurance in answering the true call of the wild. He had successfully run the gorge and captained his way through thick and thin, from 50-below temps to blinding blizzards, and had handled all the many other unworldly surprises nature is never shy to dish out. I like to think the Wapiti Moment may have helped him out just a little.

The Iditarod is not for sissies. It is seriously harsh and anyone who finishes it is a super winner in my book. Only those who seriously hear the call of the wild and desire to explore the depth of their soul need apply.

Like my own solo wilderness river experiences in Alaska, and in the outback anywhere, I have learned that there will always be a Wapiti Moment somewhere, sometime, but also a Wapiti Way Out. The trick is not to panic but rather to embrace the experience and calmly shapeshift into a river magician. The seemingly impossible can be achieved by way of reason and keeping one's wits under pressure, buoyed by the knowledge that there is always a "way" to solve the problem.

Chapter 39

TUMBLEWEED SWEDE
FOLLOWING RIVER AND WIND

One day in Riggins, the wind blew in a big semi-truck cab pulling a double-deck trailer with two dory boats, obviously looking for a river. A few kayaks were sticking out of the back of the tow-truck, making it look like a porcupine, and on the front bumper's bug screen a sticker read, "Widowmaker."

For a dory man like me, nothing draws the eye more than a dory boat, especially when surrounded by kayaks and that word. I immediately thought of the "widowmaker" on the Owyhee River, which has the power to be just that to any man daring to run it. I was soon to learn that tempting bulls could have the same result.

The entire mobile affair was something I just had to check out. Anyone dragging behind such an attention grabbing menagerie is bound to have a story to tell. Especially for me, seeing the elegant curves of the dory design is like looking at a beautiful glove worn by nature. Among the other virtues of nature possessed by a dory boat is its ability to provide wild rides that are sure to spawn fascinating stories, so I had to track down the oarsman to discover what tales his boats had brought him.

I soon made my way to the crazed looking guy hauling those dory boats destined for a put-in somewhere. Having seen the wooden dory boat in front of my shop, he had found a large parking spot across the street to get a better view. He, too, was inflicted with the same curiosity and had to check out a fellow dory lover. Like all rivers seeking the sea, dory people are naturally attracted to one another, probably due to something in the water.

His name was Swede Peterson, and he had a contagious smile, a moderate build, tight muscles, and the look of a well-tuned athlete. I soon learned that he used to pack horses and herd sheep in the high country, was a rodeo clown for many years, and had grown up kayaking during his teenage years in Washington state.

Swede's account of our first meeting, at the Rodeo Club in Riggins where local guides often gathered to drink and tell tall ones, differs from mine. Fortunately, I write things down, and I never had my memory bank stepped on by a rodeo bull. Much smoke, many drinks, and tons of river passage time later, memories have a way of morphing into tangled webs and shades of gray.

His stories are more adventurous than mine, because he is more courageous and willing to go into places I am more timid about chancing. I hate to admit to being called a conservative, but when it comes to risky endeavors, that is at least my initial approach.

Jumping into holes and off waterfalls isn't on my bucket list, because they might be cause for kicking the bucket prematurely and eliminating a lot of other things my wish list's bucket is intended to hold. My modus operandi for boating is trying to run a rapid and be right side up at the bottom end. Not upside down, swimming, or ending up dead.

Swede? Well, not so much. He is much more cavalier and willing to take on harder obstacles and challenges. Of course, this may be an erroneous assumption on my part, because all things are relative. A person with greater skill is better matched for higher-risk events, so when the risk/skill fraction is divided out, two over four renders the same result as four over eight, only the numbers are different.

In 1993, Swede ran the White Mile of Canada's Chilko River solo in a dory boat in flood stage. That is like running Lava Rapid north on the Colorado back-to-back. It was a section of the Chilko/Chilcotin/Fraser River that I shuttled around in the mid-1970s when running my dory, the Ne Parle Pas, on a trip Martin Litton had booked for Grand Canyon Dories.

Having flown over the canyon and determined that the White Mile would not be good for commercial trips, especially with dory boats, Martin arranged for our "drive around" passage of that section. Even so, the declivity and rapids on many other severe sections of that waterway were a top-of-the-totem-pole challenge. I remember getting sucked into a giant whirlpool, seeing only the tops of heads in another dory boat slide by us as I battled my way out and told my guests to be ready to high-side and to never lose contact with the boat if it flipped. Another time, a gargantuan boil in the middle of the river surged my dory 4 feet higher than the shoreline cliff, momentarily froze us in time as it gathered more strength, and then shot us toward the ugly headwall while I pulled my kidneys free trying to keep off it.

Wave trains were like running Ruby back-to-back on the Salmon, and in a few places, I surfed some of the smoother giants like being in a kayak. It was all extreme enough for me. But unlike Martin, who never returned for more commercial trips, Swede did. He formed his own company called Wild Horse Dories and ran trips on the entire system, including the White Mile that we had bypassed. He purchased two dory boats from Curt Chang, who was Martin's river manager at Boatland in Lewiston.

Amazingly, I had rowed both boats that Swede acquired. I had flipped the Redwood Creek at the epic Devils Slide high-water fiasco of 1978 and had run the Ne Parle Pas on the Chilko/Chilcotin minus the White Mile.

Swede has survived many more amazing challenges, some of which have never been duplicated, that would be worthy of inclusion in a great adventure book. However, he is not interested in fame and glory, or one-upmanship. His true love is adventure for adventure's sake. Like many a guide, he, too, has the "hearing problem" that responds to the "call of the wild."

Being willing to jump in front of, or over, a sharp-horned Brahman bull to save a rodeo cowboy speaks volumes about bravery and exemplifies serious athleticism. There was a time when I thought I wanted to try riding a tornado on four legs, just once, to see what it was like. But I outgrew that urge before putting the plan into action. Ironically, all my cowboy friends, who had one or more broken bones, thought kayaking was dangerous. I had zero broken bones, as water provides a much softer landing when getting bucked off during a wild ride, and there is no intimidation from a brutish animal trying to stomp you deeper into the dirt. It was all proof enough to me that they were the crazy ones.

Besides dodging bulls and clowning around, Swede had developed his own style of approaching a big rapid in his dory boat. Just before entering the tongue, he would lie down on his back, put his legs in the air, and go through the motion of riding a bicycle upside down. Then he would jump back to the oars and do his run. I'm not sure where this came from or why, but I suspect it was more of an iconic behavior to represent his craziness. Like a rodeo clown in a barrel, he would drop over and into bullish water in what seemed like a most appropriate symbolic manner.

I remember a time in the lower gorge, around the turn of the century, when Swede was rowing his dory as a baggage boat for a company called Osprey. When our separate commercial trip passed him at one of his stops in Blue Canyon, he had a surprise for us. Having known we were on the river, he had hurried ahead, put on his horned helmet and Viking outfit, and climbed some cliffs high above the water to await our passage. It was like a comedy skit that included a Viking rite of passage granting permission to enter the sacred canyon. Blue Canyon is, indeed, a special place, bathed in the primordial light of ancient wisdom for those open to such "learnings."

In 1999, Swede began running for Mark Kennedy, whom he had met shortly before when both had been engaged in the horse world. Mark had migrated from Texas and was guiding big-game hunters for Boulder Creek Outfitters in the Whitebird area. Because both spoke the same horse and river language, they hit it off. That is also when Swede met Doug Dennis, who spoke the same tongue and had the same "call of the wild" hearing problem.

Doug was also a Texan transplant, living only 100 miles from Mark, though they did not meet until 1996, when both were working for Jeff Peavey of NWV. That is the same year I met Doug. We ran the Little Salmon together in extreme flows. When Doug got pitched out of the raft he was rowing, a guy in the bow named Ani Paum, who was from India, suddenly faced a dilemma of his own and had to scramble for the oars a few holes downstream of Rapid River confluence. Luke Brubaker, who was rowing a 10-foot raft solo, reached Doug first to rescue him. I was having my own problems pirouetting in a hole I was trying to avoid. I thought I had tipped over in it but soon discovered I was swimming inside my own raft and luckily managed a self-recovery.

Doug and Luke were both with the group that planned to run the 100-year flood of the little river on New Year's Eve of 1996-97, when it rearranged the local geology. Like a bad omen, a huge tree sprang up and hit the bridge from which we were scouting, causing us to abandon that mission. However, the next day, I still wanted to make the run, and only Luke was available and willing to join me. I knew he had the right stuff, because Doug had told me how he had seen Luke flip his 10-footer the day we ran the river at the highest any of us had ever tackled before the big flood. He saw Luke get gobbled up in a hole and disappear, boat and all, only to appear downstream back inside and on the oars.

As described in an earlier chapter, Luke and I finally managed to do two runs on the lower mile the next day, after the river peaked during flood stage.

Doug had been drawn to the dory boat world when he saw my wooden beauty. After taking some measurements and noting the self-bailing ideas I had implemented for my Eclipse, he built his own dory from scratch out of aluminum. He was a master welder and built a boat with a deck big enough to square dance on.

He also ran the Devil's Slide in very high flows and ended up with carnage stories of his own. Like Swede's right-side solo run of the White Mile, Doug had run the Slide at 32,500 cfs solo. And just as I had done on my run in 1978 at 35,000 cfs, he, too, tipped over. His self-rescue was epic. On another occasion, he ran the Slide solo in moonlit water at 15,000 cfs. All I can say is, Holy crap.

In case you haven't figured it out yet, there are a lot of river guides who have the "call of the wild" hearing problem, are slow learners, and enjoy hanging out together like a pride of lions. All our seemingly strange connections are just more proof for the theory of six degrees of separation and more evidence of the wonderful ways all things are connected in nature. Boats, people, and rivers are bonded together by some shared thread.

However, I think Swede may have broken the mold for crazy. He always wanted me to go run the White Mile with him, which I really wanted to do, but the timing was never good. Unfortunately, it always conflicted with my summer season on the Salmon and my fall bow-hunting season for elk, so I never got around to making the run. It became one of my biggest regrets as the age of wisdom kicked in, overpowering my undaunted desires and immortal beliefs based on the fallacies of youth.

Swede lives a nomadic life to the fullest and is seldom far from a boat of some kind and a body of water. He has built kayaks, dory boats, and sailboats, and he became a master of them all in their respective realms. However, sailboats represent him best. Whenever he phones me from out of the blue and I ask him where he is heading, he always answers: Whichever way the wind is blowing. And that is a true answer, as a free spirit can say that and mean it. After all, adventure awaits everywhere, like a spider needing only a victim to enter its web. Then the strands will be woven by the cat-and-mouse play between the two as they connect the dot-to-dot dance of living life fully and creating a beautiful picture of nature's ebb and flow.

Like a tumbleweed no longer tied down to the land, wherever the wind goes, there goes my good friend Swede, tumbling down a river, waterfall, or ocean wave somewhere. The place doesn't matter. Adventure does.

Chapter 40

SURVIVAL OF THE FITTEST

In April 1995, Riggins became a vortex that sucked in world class athletes from throughout the nation. ESPN scouts looking for a place to film an extreme racing competition called "Survival of the Fittest" found our little town to be the perfect location. Like the first astronauts, Riggins had the "right stuff," and soon the local buzz centered around the attention our piece of paradise would be gaining in the public's eye.

Race organizers did not have to travel far from town to find every aspect of river and land that would provide challenging terrain for each event. Cliffs for climbing and rappelling, opposing cliff walls for a Tyrolean traverse, rough roads for mountain biking, and the river for kayaking, swimming, and platform jousting.

What the filming and rigging crews liked most was that Riggins was unmatched in serving as a central location that was not too far from any of the event venues.

When I learned of the type of events they were planning, I wanted to participate, even though I was a bit older than most of the entrants. However, the $12,000 purse for each division drew topnotch sponsored athletes, which precluded just anyone from entering. I was disappointed but followed all the activities anyway because I appreciate an opportunity to observe highly skilled competitors in any sport.

I also sneaked in late in the evening, after everyone had gone back to town, to test my own abilities on some of the obstacle courses they had set up. It gave me a real appreciation for the difficult challenges the events presented. Wow.

From 1979 to 1989, NBC had filmed the survival race series, so this was an attempt by ESPN to resurrect it. It reminded me of the "Wide World of Sports" I used to watch, including kayakers running mega waters of the Yampa, Devils Gorge of the Susitna, and the magnum rapids of the Niagara River. The photography was outstanding, and the deeds were indeed heroic.

These types of scenes were playing in my head as I sat in an eddy of the Salmon River as a safety kayaker for one of the events. The race started with a Tyrolean traverse across the river at the Crevice near the Manning Bridge. The walls are vertical on both sides of the river and are around 200 yards apart.

Four lines were stretched tight from one side to the other, slightly downstream of the bridge. The racers started from the south side of the bridge. The route and multi-faceted challenge from there involved running across the bridge; climbing a steep trail about 200 feet above to the cables; using a basket body sling for a hand-over-hand race to the opposite cliff; detaching and running down the hill to the bridge again; crossing it and running a quarter mile upstream to inflatable kayaks on the beach above the island; paddling downriver to the overhang on the south side of the bridge; grabbing a knotted rope dangling from the overhang and climbing up it about 30 feet; descending to a zip line near the bridge support and rolling across the river but releasing grip before reaching the other side, dropping into the frigid water, and swimming to shore; climbing the rocks half way to the road and running through them for about 100 yards; returning to the river to swim a 10-foot span of an underwater gate, then back to shore; climbing boulders, crossing the road, and continuing up another steep 300-foot pitch to grab ropes and rappel down a sheer cliff wall to the road again; crossing it and running back down to the river to grab a log and swim it all the way across to the other side; climbing that bank up to another zip line 30 feet above the shore and zipping back toward the other side but dropping into the middle of the river and swimming to shore; climbing through rocks to the road and sprinting 100 yards to the finish line. It is tiring just trying to write about the course, let alone traversing it all.

I watched one Navy SEAL, who was a super athlete, doing gymnastic moves on the Manning Bridge supports to warm up before the race began. He nearly completed the course and was on the last zip line when tragedy struck. He slipped and fell into the rocks before getting to the water and broke his ankle or lower leg. Race over. Time for a rescue.

Earlier one of the super fit women had also suffered a broken limb while running down the mountainside in a footrace from School Marm Peak to the section of road directly above the Mill Wave. It was treacherous terrain to even walk down, and these racers were running down it at break-neck speed. So perhaps she was lucky it was not her neck that she fractured.

Beyond those two events, there was a mountain bike race down the Partridge Creek Road and another extreme obstacle course at the Allison Creek campsite. That course included a combination of giant cargo nets and zip lines, but it was not as severe as the major tyranny of the Tyrolean traverse event at the river. However, it was still a challenge, as I found out by trying it when no one was around. Again, wow.

The concluding race was a jousting battle. It was reminiscent of the "Gladiators" television series that was popular at the time. However, these Salmon River gladiators faced off out in the middle of the river 15 feet above water level.

Two large cables stretched tight across the river supported a wooden platform about 8 by 8 feet wide. Contestants would paddle out to the structure and climb up a rope ladder to the platform. Then they would grab a padded jousting pole, wait for a starting whistle, and try to knock each other off the platform and into the river. The last one to remain on the platform, or hit the water last, was the winner. It was great entertainment that I watched as a safety kayaker from river level.

Although I unfortunately never saw the series when it came out on TV, I got to see the real thing in the raw and get my own pictures. Recordings never trump reality, no matter how sophisticated the special effects or outrageous the filming angles and close-ups. A picture of an ice cream cone is never as good as eating it.

Chapter 41

SWALLOWED WHOLE BY THE SALMON RIVER ILT-SWI-TSICHS

Ilt-swi-tsichs? Yes, this is the name given to a great monster that roamed the very heartland of Nez Perce Indian country before the Nez Perce came into being. According to the tribe's creation legend, before people, the monster with a mega appetite dominated the landscape of west-central Idaho and eastern Oregon. It had a voracious appetite and devoured every animal it could find. Desperately, the few remaining animals called upon their hero "Coyote - the Trickster" to work a magic trick on the monster to save them. So Coyote hatched a cunning plan.

He tied himself down with wild grape vines, then taunted the giant Ilt-swi-tsichs to suck him into its cavernous body. The monster huffed and puffed, and finally sucked Coyote into its giant stomach. All the other animals were there to greet Coyote after his ride down the slippery esophagus and passage into the big digestive room. But Coyote was smart; he had a knife tied to his shin. He took it out and stabbed the monster in the heart from the inside. Then he cut a passageway out and freed all the animals.

What to do next? Fox suggested, "Why not make people out of all the monster's body parts?" So Coyote did. He cut off the head and made the

Flathead tribe. The feet became the Blackfoot tribe, and all the various body parts became separate Indian tribes. Lastly, when Coyote held up the heart, trying to figure out what tribe to make next, a drop of blood dripped to the ground. Up sprang another people. People of the Heart, now called the Nimiipuu or Nez Perce.

In the Kamiah Valley you can see a stone that is said to be the result of the Great Mystery that turned the heart into a rock form to remind the people of where they came from. This geologic wonder is along the Clearwater River, but I found another place in Blue Canyon that has a similar stone form that may have served the same purpose for the Nez Perce who, along with leaders like Chief White Bird and Toolhoolhoolzote, occupied the heartland of the Salmon River Country. Thoughts of the legend always come to my mind when passing this unique riverine landscape.

When I float on the Salmon River's waters, I feel like I, too, have been swallowed up by the Ilt-swi-tsichs. Descending the river is like sliding into the giant monster's stomach, which encompasses a vast wilderness. I sense a timeless emptiness but also the full essence of everything. That fullness carries all the powers of an infinite origin and expansion - a bigness that highlights smallness. It is incomprehensible and utterly humbling in all its mystery. And I am thankful for that.

River - As Best Metaphor for Life

The more time you spend on the river, the more time it spends on you. Absorbing it, as it absorbs you, brings a closeness to source and an appreciation for the essence of nature. Everything we do, experience, and become is aptly represented by a river working through all its powers.

Rapids represent all the barriers we experience in life. Figuring out how to avoid such obstacles and negotiate safe passage through troubled waters applies both on the river and in our time living on this planet.

Topophilia - When You Become the River

"Topophilia" is a word from the Greeks meaning "love of place." Often I find that the more I run a river, the more it becomes a part of me, and I it. I find that as I engage more with the same environment, my learning improves and my understanding of the place increases. It is as if by some kind of osmosis my body is entered by unseen but ambient spiritual entities that enrich the land and water through which I travel. My identity is absorbed by the place, which makes me a part of the geography itself.

When our time on Earth ends and our personal histories are remembered by the next generation, perhaps our spiritual vapor trail will help keep the ancestral ties connected to the living. From time immemorial, humans have developed bonds with the places where they live and interact with nature. Succeeding generations that do not forget those who came before them assimilate this primal connectivity. The longer a people stays within an area rather than moving about, the stronger is their love of place and sense of connection to it.

The original native people who first inhabit a region have the greatest common history tied to the place. They are closer to the roots of the tree that gave them life than emigrant groups that grew from colonizing "seeds" that were wind blown to other places and took root as new trees. The evolving seedlings are like the parent tree but vary because they grow in differing environments.

A culture evolves over time as a people builds its history through collective experiences and engagement with the place they inhabit. Groups become defined by their common pursuits, such as mountain people who travel the high country or river people who run rapids in the canyon country. Each becomes a kind of tribe or clan with specialized abilities and skills that facilitate survival amid the innate dangers of their territory.

As a river person, I appreciate many of the names of rapids that are born of bad experiences others have had there. It is a curious aspect of human nature that we name things after personal disasters and include the person's name, such as Scottie's Drop or Wendy's Rock. And often it is the trouble itself that inspires a name, like Hell to Pay or Widow Maker. Or it might reflect a rapid's threatening nature, such as Demon's Drop or Room of Doom.

The reputations of these rapids continue to grow as river runners continue to challenge them and new stories are created that add to the power of the place. Their experiences build the character of the people and the place, driving more meaning deep into the planet where we make our home. Seeing Earth from space as a blue dot confirms its watery nature. The rivers and oceans are the life blood without which neither man nor any other life form could exist.

Chapter 42

A MAN AND HIS BOAT

Love affairs happen. While the most basic of love affairs is between a man and a woman, humans often have meaningful relationships with inanimate objects, too.

One such example of animate-inanimate entanglements is that found in the river world between a man and his boat, or, with so many fine women at the oars running rivers these days, between a woman and her boat. The entry of women into the "boatman's" world was met with skepticism in the early days, but they have proved to be as skilled and adept as any man in all aspects of the river scene and guide world. Feminine finesse often outshines masculine muscularity.

Reflecting back over my years of rowing, I am reminded of my many love affairs with the different boats with which I have danced on a multitude of rivers. Boats I rowed in Litton's dory fleet included the Tenaya, Clearwater, Hetch Hetchy, Redwood Creek, and Ne Parles Pas. Like sensuous women, each had a different beauty and a unique feel. There was a most pleasurable high from being wedded together which each craft and a sad low when being separated. Anthropomorphism is a strange and curious trait of human nature.

When off the river, time spent on boat maintenance was merely another opportunity to polish the bond between oarsman and dory. Tending to minute details and painting them for the next trip was like applying makeup to accentuate their natural beauty.

Most boatmen feel that a pretty boat is a happy boat and try to keep them that way on the water. They politely share with guests that a clean boat is a happy boat. At least they hope guests appreciate reminders to keep sandy feet to a minimum in the boat.

Dory boats in my own fleet are the Itsiyiyi, an aluminum Koffler driftboat; the Inua, a double ender Woodie Hindman dory; and the Eclipse, a modified, totally self-bailing Briggs Dory.

Naturally, my wooden dory, Eclipse, became my long-term love affair that has passed the test of time. The love has grown during all the years we have spent together. In my fantasy world, I imagine my muscles on the oars like eagle's wings that empower the boat to move and soar through the rapids. My intentions align with the wood grain of boat and oar as one, with the essence of my soul to propel us onward. The idea is always to impregnate an intimate part of myself into the graceful lines of the inanimate architecture born of such elegance to help leave behind a beautiful run through the whitewater. Just getting through the chaos of churning water is one thing, but making it an act of polished symmetry is quite another.

The more time a person spends with their boat, gaining experiences that shape a course and outcome, the greater is the bond that results. The innate character of wood, no longer nourished by its connection to soil and water, soon takes on a life in communion with the person transferring their energy into the wood. The boat expresses through movement the essence of the oarsman's navigational prowess.

The intent within the human spirit that goes into each stroke passes like an expressive shock wave, rippling through the water. Each dip of the oar imparts some form of primordial respect that is transferred into the water and radiates downriver as a meaningful water-borne message: love for all natural beauty.

Painting art on my boat also symbolizes my love affair with it and helps give meaning to our mutual dance upon the waters. My spirit rubs off into the fabric of the boat's essence. My soul merges with its soul. The two become one, and inseparable. Life's organic energy elevates the inanimate object into a higher form of being. It is enlivened by my soul to produce a special kind of mutual movement that neither can make alone. Both contribute to whatever form our river dance will take.

To be one with the boat is to be one with the river, and everything that is. The human experience mirrors nature and is why it is called "human nature."

Fundamentally, nature is always about process, movement, and transition. Thus, the river becomes the conduit for the recycling of those elements we humans confront within ourselves and with everything else we encounter in life. It is how we shape meaning for our place in the scheme of the universe, whatever that ultimately is, and radiate it forward with invisible flow into the matrix of everything that ever was, or is.

Nirvana is reached by various people in a multiplicity of ways. Be it by intuitiveness, faith, or reason, reaching final paradise is more like trying to find an end to infinity. Nirvana is not a place that can ever be reached, only strived for. For me, riding the river is my chosen course of action as I pursue my ephemeral time on planet earth.

I often feel like I am the river. Not arrogantly, but respectfully, and in appreciation for the feeling that it is as much a part of me as I am a part of it. When two things collide, they may explode, be repelled, or merge and become one. Luckily, I have merged with rivers and my world has been filled with appreciation for water and its ways. I am merely a voice for what the rivers have taught me.

A river also reminds me how the perpetual patterns of nature often contain much primal wisdom. Its recycled flow is like the essence of a circle. There is no beginning or end, and no matter where you go, you are always in the middle of it, just as the center of the cosmos is everywhere. Humans are a moving dot, each at the center of everything, coming from wherever and going to wherever.

We perpetually rise and fall, ebb and flow, to the tune of a circadian rhythm dictated by an unseen regulator of natural energy. In the process we are what we make of it all as we round the sacred hoop of life. Long live the force.

Chapter 43

RIVER MEDICINE

While the naked eye is quite limited in what it can see both at a distance and up close, the use of specialized instruments can reveal much more on the micro or macro level. These tools stretch our understanding of our respective place adrift in the cosmos.

Peering through a telescope, we can see celestial bodies too far away for the unaided eye to see, while looking through a microscope, we can see tiny things undetectable to the unaided eye. Both prove that so much exists beyond the range of our normal comprehension. Absence of evidence is not the same as evidence of absence. Pushing over new horizon lines leads to the discovery of things never before imagined. It just requires new ways to see and measure.

As one who has always held science in high regard as one of the best ways to discover truth, I often replay in my mind a scene from an old movie about scientists who were searching for the Loch Ness Monster.

In the film, a consortium of the world's best scientists gather hoping to locate the monster by using state of the art technology. But despite having all the best scientific tools available, they never find the monster.

In the last scene on the shore of Loch Ness, all the scientists are toasting each other with champagne for having proved that the monster does not exist, while behind them in the background out of their view, the monster serpentines out of the water, arching like a rainbow as it slides back into the lake and disappears.

Science is always evolving, revealing new discoveries and potentialities. It does not claim to reveal the ultimate truth, unlike those with unwavering faith who claim access to a realm where they absolutely know that God exists and rules over all things.

Who could have foreseen 40 years ago all the fancy smart phones, computers, and other amazing feats of high technology that enable humans to do and know things unimaginable in the past. New discoveries and creations are constantly opening new possibilities.

Perhaps in the near future someone will invent a "spiritscope" that will enable humans to see the spirit world of the soul, if one does indeed exist. What if there are spirits and what if they can influence what happens in the physical world? What if we can learn to communicate or align with such spirits and their actions?

If living things have spirit, as many believe they do, it seems reasonable that they have some purpose or can join together to create one. Perhaps all entities are kincentric and connected by spirit threads.

What if there really is a world of mysticism where the science of cold hard facts can unite with spirits that flit about in other realms? Science is not absolute. The rule of nature is change.

As I reflect on my life's history in the mirror of time, the rivers of wrinkles on my face grow ever deeper. They furrow into my flesh like eroded riverbeds exposed by the years and rivers that have coursed through my life, like Mother Earth continuously revealing geologic change. Nature leaves a mark on all things.

Long before the "Star Wars" movies came out, I began referring to the power that creates movement in all things as the "force." It seemed like a good word to describe the unseen world of creation, ultimately unexplainable but understood at various levels through degrees of intuitive knowledge and evidentiary science.

Indian people living close to the earth, not yet circumscribed by sophisticated technology that separates people from nature, gained a worldview based on intuitive perspectives that contain much wisdom.

Science can be used arrogantly to claim superiority in knowing truth, but intuitive knowledge is not necessarily misaligned with fact. One does not have to know why the sun comes up and goes down every day, only that it indeed does. A simple fact.

More importantly, it is how facts are used that has the biggest impact on what happens to our environment. Compared to the dominant man-centered worldview, where technology is left unchecked or erodes through deregulation, the nature-centered (interconnected) worldview seems less disruptive and better suited to living more harmoniously within the ecological systems energizing all life communities.

Indians learned long ago to adapt when new technologies came along, as they continue to do today, yet they have not lost their humble respect for, and reciprocal relationships with, all life entities.

They also recognized the "force" empowering all things and often refer to it as the Great Mystery. Like wind and current, the human soul, or spirit, is a flow of energy that cannot be seen but whose presence is revealed by movement through physical forms.

For me, rivers have been the best metaphor for living more in tune to nature, with the most potential for being in harmony with all other life forms.

Difficult rapids are like all life obstacles, which help strengthen our confidence when we overcome challenges; peaceful pools are similar to a mirror that inspires reflective introspection when we examine ourselves from a deeper perspective. Like all rivers born of the ocean and returning to the ocean, we are absorbed into the ebb and flow to be recycled back into the matrix of elemental "force."

To feel the utter essence of the power that surges through all things, one must go to the Source for such medicine, and that, my friends, is the River.

Simply following the river will lead you to a place where you can intimately appreciate the true efficacy of its medicine and the magical spell of all nature's wonderful mystery.

BIBLIOGRAPHY

Books:

Lewis and Clark Among the Nez Perce: Strangers in the Land of the Nimiipuu **August 12, 2013** by Allen V. Pinkham **(Author),** Steven R. Evans **(Author),** Frederick E. Hoxie **(Foreword)**

Nez Perce Coyote Tales – The Myth Cycle by Deward E. Walker, Jr. in collaboration with Daniel N. Matthews. 1994

The Nez Perce Indians and the Opening of the Northwest **(American Heritage Library) Paperback – Abridged, April 30, 1997** by Alvin M. Josephy Jr. **(Author)**

Yellow Wolf: His Own Story by McWhorter, Lucullus Virgil (Jan1, 1940) 1983

Ordway's Salmon River Fishing Expedition – Research Results for Summer 2002

HTR Technical Report No. 01A03 - July 1, 2003 Steve F. Russell, PhD. P.E. Associate Professor Iowa State Univ.

Links:

www.blog.pendleton-usa.com/2012/09/13/jackson-sundown-and-the-pendleton-round-up/

Celebrating America's Treasures - Jackson Sundown and the Pendleton Round –Up. www.fs.usda.gov/detail/npnht/learningcenter/history-culture/?cid=fseprd539250

USFS : Jackson Sundown
www.nezperce.org/History/Jacksonsundown.htm

Nez Perce History - Jackson Sundown
www.historynet.com/nez-perce-war.html

Nez Perce War   6/12/2006 • **American History**
www.everyculture.com/multi/Le-Pa/Nez-Perc.html

Nez Perce – Overview by Laurie Collier Hillstrom and Richard C. Hanes
www.youtube.com/watch?v=OQwbOYx0ojM

Patty Clayton~Performing Songwriter, Published on Oct 18, 2012
Follow filmmaker Patty Clayton in her quest to find an 1884 homestead in the remote Idaho hills, and experience the journey of her family through the years, in this Deep West Video that premiered during the 2008 National Cowboy Poetry Gathering. Length: **12:23**.

Her great grandfather and grandmother were Ben and Julia Reeves who homesteaded the Wapshilla Ranch.

Ranchhand Jackson Sundown by Margaret Reeves Heartburg via personal email communications with Patty Clayton

Agencies:

www.oglb.idaho.gov/
Archived Board Meeting Minutes (IOGLB) : 1961-2012

APPENDIX 1

Original BLM River Stats: from Ryan Turner email: March 23, 2015 (with my interpolations)

On the lower gorge below Hammer Creek, between 1975 and 1984 commercial rafting use dominated river trips. It averaged 63% commercial with a range of 55% to 80%. From 1985 to 1990 commercial use averaged 54% with a range of 48%-59%. By 1991 use patterns did a flip-flop, as private use became dominate. Between 1991 and 2001 commercial use averaged 44% and ranged from 40% to 48%. Then from 2002 – 2014 commercial use dropped even more. It averaged 30% and a ranged from 25% to 36%. Also, by 2002 several organizations applied and were granted permits to run trips. These figures were included in the private use column.

Float Traffic below Hammer Creek:

Year	Total users	Comm	% comm	% priv	Grand total users		
1975	326	188	63%	37%	514	*1975-1984*	*average: 66%*
1976	625	326	66%	34%	951		*range: 55%-80%*
1977	890	347	72%	28%	1237		
1978	1184	290	80%	20%	1474		
1979	1518	803	65%	35%	2321		
1980	1786	961	65%	35%	2747		
1981	2023	1232	62%	38%	3255		
1982	2333	1127	67%	33%	3460		
1983	2594	1730	60%	40%	4324		
1984	3028	2460	55%	45%	5488		
1985	2817	3041	48%	52%	5858	*1985-1990*	*average: 54%*
1986	3233	2986	52%	48%	6219		*range: 48%-59%*
1987	3728	2795	57%	43%	6523		
1988	3635	2538	59%	41%	6173		
1989	3674	2874	56%	44%	6548		
1990	3591	3277	52%	48%	6868		
1991	2972	3164	48%	52%	6136	*1991 - 2001*	*average 44%*
1992	3532	4121	46%	54%	7653		*range: 40%-48%*
1993	3165	3647	46%	54%	6812		
1994	3054	3972	47%	57%	7026		
1995	2591	3811	40%	60%	6402		
1996	2806	3915	42%	58%	6721		
1997	3070	4033	43%	57%	7103		
1998	3216	4218	43%	57%	7434		
1999	3068	4253	42%	58%	7321		

	Comm	Priv	Org Grp	Total	%comm	% priv (include org grp) (Prv + org)	(% org)	
2000 -	3181	4531	16	7728	41%	59%	4547	1%
2001 -	2709	3482	185	6376	42%	58%	3667	5%
2002 -	2427	4497	241	7165	34%	66%	4738	5%
2003 -	2238	3842	177	6257	36%	64%	4019	4%
2004 -	1452	3914	400	5766	25%	75%	4314	9%
2005 -	1735	3883	334	5952	29%	71%	4217	8%
2006 -	1658	3740	527	5925	28%	72%	4267	12%
2007 -	2233	4096	199	6528	34%	66%	4295	5%
2008 -	1641	3639	348	5628	29%	71%	3987	9%
2009 -	1647	4328	342	6317	26%	74%	4670	7%
2010 -	1675	4046	164	5885	28%	72%	4210	4%
2011 -	1250	3502	20	4772	26%	74%	3522	1%
2012 -	1486	4201	181	5868	25%	75%	4382	4%
2013 -	1943	3324	204	5471	36%	64%	3528	6%
2014 -	1844	3374	229	5447	34%	66%	3603	6%

2002-2014
avg: 30%
rge: 25%‑36%

The dynamics of group launches also changed dramatically over the years. From 1975 – 1986 there was never a time when there was 10 or more launches per day. That changed in 1987 and never slowed down:
1987 - 1991: avg number of days with over 10 launches per day – 6
1992 - 2002: avg number of days with over 10 launches per day - 15
2003 - 2013: avg number of days with over 10 launches per day – 21
The year 2012 had the very most at 30 days with more than 10 launches per day.

Average Launches per Day
75-79: 1.42
80-85: 3.88
86-90: 4.58
91-95: 6.42
96-20: 7.77
01-05: 7.78
06-10: 9.09
11-13: 8.43

The section of river above Hammer Creek and the Riggins area is managed (or not), as a different kind of animal. It is more like an Eastern or California and Colorado river, where conveyor belt-like systems seem to rule use patterns. Also, there is more jetboat use in this area, too. Following are some stats for this section:

Commercial Users Only

Vinegar Ck – Riggins (users/%)					Riggins – Hammer Ck (users/%)				
Year	float	%	jet	% total	float	%	jet	%	total
2000	16449	99%	231	1% 16680	595	99%	5	1%	600
2001	17008	96%	764	4% 17772	822	99%	5	1%	827
2002	16437	96%	765	4% 17202	685	96%	30	4%	715
2003	14961	96%	651	4% 15612	1171	98%	20	2%	1191
2004	12103	95%	597	5% 12700	445	97%	12	3%	457
2005	13696	97%	464	3% 14160	497	97%	13	3%	510
2006	11998	93%	873	7% 12871	326	99%	2	1%	328
2007	12602	97%	437	3% 13039	430	99%	4	1%	434
2008	10939	92%	955	8% 11894	428	94%	28	6%	456
2009	10147	93%	786	7% 10933	387	96%	16	4%	403
2010	8908	94%	530	6% 9438	515	95%	28	5%	543
2011	6260	97%	206	3% 6466	197	96%	8	4%	205
2012	9379	94%	577	6% 9956	385	92%	33	8%	418
2013	7846	96%	318	4% 8164	262	99%	3	1%	265
2014	13211	95%	675	5% 13886	427	92%	35	8%	462

Here are some additional figures describing both float and jetboat use for the section below hammer Creek.

Total Number of Commercial Users
(floaters plus jetboaters)
from Vinegar Cr – Heller Bar

1975 - 326   1975 – 1980 (less than 1500 users per year)
1976 – 625
1977 – 890
1978 – 951
1979 – 1185
1980 – 1419
1981 – 2887   1981 – 1988 (more than 2500 but less than 10000 users per year)
1982 – 3644
1983 – 6112
1984 – 7087
1985 – 7573
1986 – 9463
1987 – 8800
1988 – 9605
1989 – 10699   1989 - 1994 (more than 10000 but less than 15000)
1990 – 11987

1991 – 13641
1992 – 13871
1993 - 13120
1994 – 14877
1995 – 15822   1995 – 2003 (more than 15000)
1996 - 16537
1997 - 16537
1998 – 17325
1999 – 18813
2000 - 17673
2001 – 18002
2002 – 17916
2003 – 16234
2004 – 13632   2004 – 2014 (ranging from approx 8000 -16000)
2005 - 14759
2006 – 13897
2007 – 15002
2008 – 13046
2009 – 12080
2010 – 10849
2011 - 8049
2012 – 11111
2013 – 10293
2014 - 15623

Total Private Boater Trips (power and float) below Hammer:

2005 - 514
2006 -528
2007 – 669
2008 – 568
2009 – 689
2010 – 637
2011 - 610
2012 – 673
2013 – 532
2014 - 584

One of the interesting demographics these figures illustrate is that ever since 1991 there were far more private groups launching trips than commercial. Yet the commercial trips had more people on them. Thus private groups were smaller, but also had more boats on the water than commercial. This demonstrates evolution of more people rowing their own boat/raft and the need for more elbow room.

Day trips   Above Hammer (com only)

	(above Riggins)		(below Riggins, but above Hammer)	
2000	trips	users	trips	users
Float:	1453	16449	967	595
Jet	33	231	28	5
Total	1486	16680	995	600
2001	trips	users	trips	users
Float:	1763	17008	1027	822
Jet	115	764	34	5
Total	1878	17772	1061	827
2002	trips	users	trips	users
Float:	1602	16437	998	685
Jet	107	765	72	30
Total	1709	17202	1070	715
2003	trips	users	trips	users
Float:	1426	14961	233	1171
Jet	95	651	51	20
Total	1521	15612	284	1191
2004	trips	users	trips	users
Float:	1061	12103	670	445
Jet	76	597	64	12
Total	1137	12700	734	457
2005	trips	users	trips	users
Float:	1182	13696	751	497
Jet	63	464	50	13
Total	1245	14160	801	510
2006	trips	users	trips	users
Float:	938	11998	664	326
Jet	89	873	87	2
Total	1027	12871	751	328
2007	trips	users	trips	users
Float:	1033	12602	678	430
Jet	54	437	51	4
Total	1087	13039	729	434
2008	trips	users	trips	users
Float:	1126	10939	772	428
Jet	127	955	100	28
Total	1253	11894	872	456

2009	trips	users	trips	users
Float:	1037	10147	712	387
Jet	81	786	66	16
Total	1118	10933	778	403

2010	trips	users	trips	users
Float:	976	8908	506	515
Jet	71	530	49	28
Total	1047	9438	555	543

2011	trips	users	trips	users
Float:	519	6260	364	197
Jet	28	206	20	8
Total	547	6466	384	205

2012	trips	users	trips	users
Float:	879	9379	584	385
Jet	85	577	52	33
Total	964	9956	636	418

2013	trips	users	trips	users
Float:	667	7846	482	262
Jet	45	318	44	3
Total	712	8164	526	265

2014	trips	users	trips	users
Float:	1208	13211	898	427
Jet	95	675	60	35
Total	1303	13886	958	462

APPENDIX 2

Appendix 2

Original BLM River Stats:
from Ryan Turner email: March 23, 2015
(with my interpolations)

Commercial Use Above Hammer Creek by Float and Power Boats
Note: Private Use Stats are Not Available for any User Group
Commercial Use Only - Above Hammer Creek - By Number of Users

YEAR	Percentage Float Trips				Percentage Power Trips				GRAND TOTAL USERS
	DAY	OVERNIGHT	TOTAL USERS	% FLOAT	DAY	OVERNIGHT	TOTAL USERS	% JET	
2004	12103	767	12870	95%	614	0	614	5%	13484
Percentage	94%	6%	100%		100%		100%		
2005	13696	838	14534	97%	472	0	472	3%	15006
Percentage	94%	6%	100%		100%		100%		
2006	11998	699	12697	94%	847	0	847	6%	13544
Percentage	94%	6%	100%		100%		100%		
2007	12602	944	13546	97%	437	5	442	3%	13988
Percentage	93%	7%	100%		99%	1%	100%		
2008	10939	1018	11957	93%	933	1	934	7%	12891
Percentage	91%	9%	100%		99%	1%	100%		
2009	10147	831	10978	93%	786	5	791	7%	11769
Percentage	92%	8%	100%		95%	5%	100%		
2010	8908	649	9957	96%	396	35	431	4%	9988
Percentage	93%	7%	100%		92%	8%	100%		
2011	6260	611	6871	97%	206		206	3%	7077
Percentage	91%	9%	100%		100%		100%		
2012	9379	854	10233	95%	577	0	577	5%	10810
Percentage	92%	8%	100%		100%		100%		
2013	7846	644	8490	96%	318	10	328	4%	8818
Percentage	92%	8%	100%		97%	3%	100%		
2014	13221	1091	14312	96%	675	0	100	4%	14987
Percentage	92%	8%	100%		100%		100%		
2015	11034	1013	12047	93%	694	0	694	7%	12741
Percentage	92%	8%	100%		100%		100%		

Note: while there are no stats available for private users along the road section, it is reasonable to assume that patterns of change in the lower gorge should reflect a parallel history. Thus, it is most likely that private use has significantly risen each year, in this area, too.

ABOUT THE AUTHOR

Outfitter and owner of Wapiti River Guides, Gary Lane might best be described as a professional wildlife biologist turned river guide. He has over 40 years river experience, yet continues to find his river adventures a never-ending source of enthusiasm, discovery and satisfactions.

Generation One. How Riggins gained status as the Whitewater Capital of Idaho.

The transformation from Mill town to Play town began in the early 1980's and is a significant example of how the changing face of economics can have high impact to rural communities dependent on natural resources as a base to their livelihoods.

Gary's stories come from the land and river that helped create them and is testimony to the power of place in shaping not only personal character, but the cultural shift in community development.

For comments about this book or information relating to potential river trips offered by Gary for whitewater, fishing, and chukar hunting, contact:

For trip information: www.doryfun.com
For comments: www.facebook.com/Riverdoryfun/

Made in the USA
San Bernardino, CA
16 July 2018